Best of the Best
from

MINNESOTA

Selected Recipes from Minnesota's
FAVORITE COOKBOOKS

BEST of the BEST
from
MINNESOTA
Selected Recipes from Minnesota's
FAVORITE COOKBOOKS

EDITED BY
Gwen McKee
AND
Barbara Moseley

Illustrated by Tupper England

QUAIL RIDGE PRESS

Library of Congress Cataloging-in-Publication Data

Best of the best from Minnesota: selected recipes from Minnesota's favorite cookbooks / edited by Gwen McKee and Barbara Moseley; illustrated by Tupper England.
    p. cm.
Includes bibliographical references and index.
ISBN 0-937552-81-X
    1. Cookery, American. 2. Cookery--Minnesota. I. McKee, Gwen.
II. Moseley, Barbara.
TX715.B4856394   1997
641.59776--dc21   97-23253
                                         CIP

QUAIL RIDGE PRESS
P. O. Box 123 • Brandon MS 39043
1-800-343-1583

CONTENTS

Headwaters of the Mississippi River in Itasca State Park.

PREFACE

The Land of Sky Blue Waters . . . the Land of 10,000 Lakes . . . the Gopher State . . . the North Star State . . . Minnesota has many nicknames. But no matter how you refer to it, Minnesota is a *beautiful* state. In a land rich with more than a million acres of forest and over ten thousand sparkling lakes, it offers opportunities for wildlife adventure, outdoor sports, and tranquil retreats. It is indeed a four-season wonderland where spring is vibrant, summer is spectacular, fall is fabulous, and the winter is absolutely wondrous.

Indeed Minnesota has been blessed with a natural setting that is nothing short of incredible. And it's a healthy environment, too. But what makes it extra special is its people. This is the land where Judy Garland was born, where Fran Tarkenton introduced "the scramble," where Paul Bunyun was fabricated, where Garrison Keillor brings entertainment and laughter to the world each week on the radio, and where lots of other delightful Minnesotans care about their state and have a strong connection to their land, their history, their culture . . . *and* their food.

To know Minnesota cooking is to know its people. And whether they are from the great North Woods, the Prairie Land, the Twin Cities, or the Iron Range, Minnesota people take great pride in the food they put on their tables. Naturally, what is produced there dictates the fare. Throughout the state, milk products dominate, but beef cattle and hog marketing are also important. Major crops are corn, soybeans, hay, wheat, sugar beets, oats and barley. Minnesota produces 85% of the world's wild rice supply. Other staples grown within the boundaries are potatoes, apples, green peas, turkeys and chicken eggs. And of course, hunting and fishing provide many a main course for their meals. With all this at their fingertips, it is no wonder that such outstanding recipes abound from Minnesota.

Many of the recipes have been handed down from generation to generation, and have roots in the old country, particularly the Scandinavian countries. As would be expected, kringles, lefse, lutefisk, flat bread, and streusel recipes are included. There are also pasties from the miners' lunch pails, fish dishes from the lakes' bounties, bread recipes from their many mills, and plenty of wild rice dishes from the abundant rice stands. So many unexpected taste temptations are included: Stuffed Mushroom Italiano, Cranberry Glazed Brie, Pumpkin Bowl Stew, Byerly's Butterscotch-Nut Bars, Honey Glazed Pineapple Carrots, Walla Walla Onion Pie, Rice Porridge with Raspberry Sauce, Perfectly Marvelous Mishmash...the list goes on and on.

The recipes that appear in this book come from 64 of the leading cookbooks in Minnesota. Each of these cookbooks submitted a few of their favorites, thereby giving you a sample of their own special cookbook. The contributing cookbooks are compiled by junior leagues, symphony guilds, charitable societies, churches, schools, art museums, garden clubs, bed & breakfasts, as well as individual authors and families.

Compiling a cookbook such as *Best of the Best from Minnesota* takes a tremendous amount of teamwork and cooperation from a lot of people. Minnesota people could not have been more helpful, courteous, and enjoyable to work with. We wish to thank all the cookbook contributors for their assistance, enthusiasm, and cooperation—they were all absolutely delightful to talk to and work with. Each of these cookbooks has its own unique features and flavors, and we have tried to retain this by reproducing the recipes as they appear in each book, changing only the typeset style for uniformity. A complete catalog listing of the contributing cookbooks begins on page 253. We do beg forgiveness for any books that might have been included but were inadvertently overlooked.

We are grateful to the many food editors of newspapers across the state who recommended books for inclusion, as well as book and gift store managers, tourist department and chamber of commerce personnel for their factual information. We wanted this book to be as accurate and "Minnesota-true" as we could possibly get it, and that would not have been possible without the tenacious "digging" that Sheila Williams and Annette Goode did here in our office to locate and contact potential contributors. Our faithful artist, Tupper England, has added delightful illustrations that reflect the flavor of the state.

It is with great pleasure that we present this tasteful collection of favorite Minnesota recipes. We invite you to partake of this prized fare. Yah, it's the Best!

Gwen McKee and Barbara Moseley

St. Croix River Valley at Interstate State Park.

Contributing Cookbooks

Anoka County 4H Cook Book
Bake Yourself Happy
Bears in My Kitchen
Bethany Lutheran Church Celebrating 110 Years
Bethany Lutheran Church Celebrating 125 Years
Braham's Pie Cookbook
Centennial Cookbook
The Centennial Society Cookbook
Chickadee Cottage Cookbook
Chickadee Cottage Cookbook 2
Clinton's 110th Cookbook
The Clovia Recipe Collection
A Dish to Pass
Dorthy Rickers Cookbook: Mixing & Musing
Duluth Woman's Club 70th Anniversary Cookbook
Favorite Recipes of Lester Park & Rockridge Schools
Feeding the Flock
Finn Creek Museum Cookbook
First United Methodist Church Cookbook
From Minnesota: More Than A Cookbook
From the Recipe File of Agnes Gaffaney
Great Cooks of Zion Church
Herbs in a Minnesota Kitchen
Kitchen Keepsakes
Kompelien Family Cookbook
License to Cook Minnesota Style
Lutheran Church Basement Women
Maple Hill Cookbook
Martha Chapter #132 OES Cookbook
Minnesota Heritage Cookbook I
Minnesota Heritage Cookbook II
The Oke Family Cookbook

Contributing Cookbooks

Old Westbrook Evangelical Lutheran Church Cookbook
One Hundred Years of Sharing
Our Beloved Sweden: Food, Faith, Flowers & Festivals
Our Family's Favorites
Our Favorite Recipes
Our Favorite Recipes/Aurdal Lutheran Church
Our Heritage Cookbook
People Pleasers
Potluck Volume II
Queen of Angels Anniversary Cookbook
Recipes and Memories
Recipes from Minnesota with Love
Recipes from St. Michael's
Recipes from the Flock
Recipes of Note for Entertaining
Red Oak Grove Lutheran Church Family Cookbook
Salem Cook Book II
Sears Through the Years Cookbook
Sharing our Best to Help the Rest
Sharing our Best/Bergen Lutheran Church
Sharing our Best/Home of the Good Shepherd
A Taste of Faith
A Taste of Kennedy Cook Book
A Thyme For All Seasons
Treasured Recipes from Treasured Friends
Treasured Recipes of Chippewa County
Ultimate Potato Cookbook, The
Vaer saa god Cookbook
Wannaska Centennial
When Friends Cook
Winniehaha's Favorite Recipes
Winning Recipes from Minnesota with Love

Appetizers

A night time view of the Minneapolis skyline.

Artichoke Dip

Assemble ahead; put in oven just before guests arrive.

2 (8¹/2-ounce) cans artichoke
  hearts
1 cup fresh grated Parmesan
  cheese

1 cup mayonnaise
8 ounces shredded Mozzarella
  cheese
Pinch of garlic

Mix. Put in casserole dish. Bake at 350° for 25-30 minutes.
Serve with crackers.

Variation: Omit Mozzarella cheese and garlic. Or substitute 2
tablespoons no-fat sour cream and ³/4 cup no-fat yogurt (room
temperature) for mayonnaise and add 4 drops hot sauce.

Sharing our Best to Help the Rest

Hot Spinach Artichoke Dip

A hit with everyone.

1 (15-ounce) can artichoke
  hearts (not marinated)
1 (10-ounce) package chopped
  spinach, thawed and drained
1 small jar pimento, drained
  and chopped or ¹/2 cup red
  pepper, diced
4 ounces Mozzarella cheese,
  shredded

¹/4 teaspoon garlic salt
1 cup mayonnaise
1 cup Parmesan cheese,
  grated
¹/2 cup ripe pitted olives,
  chopped

Drain artichoke hearts and cut into small pieces. Add remaining ingredients and mix. Spoon into sprayed 1-quart glass casserole. Bake at 350° for 30 minutes. Serve warm with tortilla
chips. Serves 12-20, depending on what else is served.

Chickadee Cottage Cookbook 2

Claes Oldenburg's "Spoonbridge and Cherry," a colossal fountain-
sculpture, is located in the Minneapolis Sculpture Garden.

Hot Pecan Dip

1/2 cup pecans, chopped
1 tablespoon butter
1/4 cup green pepper, minced
1 (8-ounce) package cream
  cheese

2 tablespoons milk
1/2 cup sour cream
4 ounces dried beef, chopped
2 tablespoons onion, minced
1 teaspoon garlic powder

Sauté pecans in butter until lightly browned. Mix other ingredients together and add pecans. Bake at 325° for 25 minutes or until bubbly. Serve with triscuits. Keep warm. Serves 10.

A Thyme For All Seasons

Hamburger Dip

1 pound hamburger
1/2 package spaghetti sauce
  (dry mix)
1 (15-ounce) can tomato
  sauce
1/2 cup chianti wine (add
  more!)

1 tablespoons cornstarch
12 ounces Cheddar cheese,
  shredded
4 ounces Mozzarella cheese,
  shredded

Brown hamburger. Add spaghetti sauce, tomato sauce, wine and cornstarch. Add cheeses slowly allowing to melt. Simmer. Serve over low flame to keep warm. Dip with large Frito chips and sliced French bread.

From the Recipe File of Agnes Gaffaney

Layered Oriental Dip

3/4 cup cooked chicken or
  turkey, finely chopped
1/2 cup shredded fresh carrot
1/4 cup unsalted peanuts,
  chopped
3 tablespoons sliced green
  onions
1 tablespoon chopped fresh
  parsley

2 tablespoon soy sauce
1/4 teaspoon ground ginger
1 clove garlic, minced
1/2 cup Sweet and Sour
  Sauce
1 (8-ounce) package cream
  cheese, softened
1 tablespoon milk

Combine first 8 ingredients, mix well. Cover and refrigerate several hours to blend the flavors.

SWEET AND SOUR SAUCE:

1/4 cup brown sugar, firmly
  packed
2 tablespoons cornstarch
1 cup water
1/4 cup ketchup

2 tablespoons vinegar
1 tablespoon Worcestershire
  sauce
3 drops hot pepper sauce

In a small saucepan, combine sugar and cornstarch. Gradually stir in the remaining ingredients. Cook, stirring constantly, over medium heat about 5 minutes or until slightly thickened. Cool. Cover and refrigerate.

To serve, combine cream cheese and milk. Beat until smooth and fluffy. Spread over the bottom of a 12-inch diameter serving platter. Spoon chicken mixture evenly over the cream cheese. Drizzle with sauce. Serve with Wheat Thins or other crackers.

The Clovia Recipe Collection

Tortilla Chip Dip

1 pound ground beef
1 (12-ounce) package Jimmy
Dean Hot Sausage
1 (8-ounce) can tomato sauce
1 (6-ounce) can tomato paste

1/2 small can green chiles
1/2 small can chopped jalapeño
peppers
1 pound Velveeta cheese,
cubed

Brown beef and sausage. Add remaining ingredients. Heat altogether in microwave till cheese melts. Serve warm with chips.

Maple Hill Cookbook

Salsa

5 quarts tomatoes, peeled and
chopped
2 cups onions, chopped
2 cups vinegar
2-3 green peppers, chopped
2-3 jalapeño peppers
2-3 red peppers

4-5 (3-ounce) cans tomato
paste
1/2 cup sugar
2 tablespoons canning salt
1 tablespoon cayenne pepper
2 tablespoons cumin

Cook 2 hours, adding more cayenne for more heat. Pour into pint or quart jars, seal and process. Makes 5-7 quarts.

A Taste of Kennedy Cook Book

Vidalia Onion Spread

2 Vadalia onions, thinly
sliced
1 cup water
1/4 cup white vinegar

1/4 cup sugar
Mayonnaise
Ritz crackers

Marinate onions in water, vinegar, and sugar for 3-4 hours. Drain and pat dry. Finely chop onions and mix with mayonnaise. Serve on Ritz crackers.

When Friends Cook

Cranberry Glazed Brie

3 cups cranberries
3/4 cup brown sugar
1/3 cup dried currants
1/3 cup water
1/8 teaspoon dry mustard
1/8 teaspoon ground allspice

1/8 teaspoon cardamom
1/8 teaspoon cloves
1/8 teaspoon ginger
1 (2.2-pound) brie cheese
  wheel

In a saucepan, combine cranberries, brown sugar, currants, water, and spices. Cook over high heat for 5 minutes. Remove from heat to cool. Cover and refrigerate. (This may be made up to 3 days in advance.) Set brie on a heat-proof platter. Using a sharp knife, cut a circular top off rind, leaving 1/2-inch border. Spread cranberry marmalade over brie and refrigerate for 6 hours. Remove from refrigerator 2 hours before serving and bring to room temperature. Bake at 300° for 12 minutes. Serve with fresh fruit slices such as apples or pears, and/or crackers. Serves 12.

Recipes of Note for Entertaining

Red Pepper Mascarpone

For a really unusual treat, serve on top of hot pasta!

1 (8-ounce) jar roasted red
  peppers, drained
1 garlic clove
8 ounces unsalted butter,
  softened

8 ounces cream cheese,
  softened
Crackers

Process peppers and garlic in food processor or blender until smooth. Add butter and cream cheese, a little bit at a time, to food processor or blender until well mixed. Allow to stand in refrigerator for about one hour. Serve with crackers. Yields 30.

When Friends Cook

Herbed Pita Bites

3/4 cup butter or margarine,
  softened
2 tablespoons minced
  fresh parsley
12 tablespoon snipped chives

1 large clove garlic, minced
1 tablespoon lemon juice
Salt and pepper to taste
4 pita breads, halved into
  rounds

Cream butter, parsley, chives, garlic, lemon juice, salt and pepper. Spread on pita bread halves and broil just before serving. Cut each into 8 wedges. Makes 32 pieces. Fat 4.5 grams per serving.

Minnesota Heritage Cookbook II

Hot Cheese Cubes

1 (3-ounce) package cream
  cheese
1/4 pound Cheddar cheese,
  cubed

1/2 pound butter
2 egg whites, stiffly beaten
1 pound bread, unsliced

In a double boiler, add the cream cheese, Cheddar cheese, and butter. Cook, stirring, until melted and fully blended. Let stand a few minutes. Fold in the stiffly beaten egg whites. Trim the crust from the bread and cut into 1-inch cubes. Dip each cube in the cheese mixture and place on a greased cookie sheet. Bake at 375° for 12-15 minutes. These can be made the night before and refrigerated and reheated in the oven or microwave. Makes 36 cubes.

Recipes from Minnesota with Love

Mystery Cave in Preston is the longest cave in Minnesota with over 12 miles of natural passages. It is an example of a maze cave with many interconnecting passages. The cave is used by all four species of hibernating bats found in Minnesota. Niagara Cave in Harmony differs from other caves, having canyons and gorges with ceilings more than 100 feet high. It features a 60-foot waterfall in a rock-vaulted dome more than 120 feet high.

Pepperoni Appetizer

3 cups milk
3 eggs, beaten
3 cups all-purpose flour
1½ cups shredded muenster
   cheese

1 teaspoon salt
Dash pepper and oregano
1 large stick pepperoni, sliced
   thin (1½ cups)

Combine milk and eggs. Mix in flour with mixer until smooth (blender works well). Add remaining ingredients and stir to incorporate well. Bake in greased 9x13-inch pan at 425° for about 40 minutes. Serve warm.

Feeding the Flock

Miniature Reubens

8 ounces pastrami or corned
   beef, sliced
1 (8-ounce) can sauerkraut,
   drained
¾ cup Thousand Island
   dressing

1 tablespoon onion, finely
   chopped
30 slices party rye or 8 ounces
   rye bread, thinly sliced
8 ounces Swiss cheese

To make with food processor: Place first 4 ingredients into bowl and use metal blade. Turn on and off until shredded enough to spread easily, but not a paste. Make one recipe at a time.

To make with blender: Do half recipe at a time. Cut across meat a few times and through sauerkraut as well. Add next two ingredients and blend until of spreading consistency.

Spread mixture on bread. Top with slices of Swiss cheese to fit. Broil until cheese has melted. May be cut in half for 60 bite-size servings. Freezes beautifully. Yields 30 pieces.

When Friends Cook

Pickled Fish

Fresh fish fillets
Salt
White vinegar to cover fish
1 cup white vinegar, for
  syrup

1 tablespoon mixed pickling
  spices
1¼ cups white sugar
4 ounces white port wine
Onion, thinly sliced

Place fish fillets in jar or crock in salt brine (one cup salt to one quart water) for 24 hours. Drain, and cover with white vinegar for 24 hours. Drain; cut in pieces.

    Make a syrup from vinegar, mixed pickling spices, and white sugar. Boil for 5 minutes. Cool; add wine. Pack fish in layers with onion. Pour syrup over fish. May be eaten in 24 hours.

A Taste of Faith

Polynesian Chicken Wings

3-4 pounds wings, cut at
  joints
1 cup water
1 cup soy sauce
1 cup sugar

¼ cup pineapple juice (drained
  off pineapple)
¼ cup oil
1 teaspoon ginger
1 teaspoon garlic powder

Marinate chicken wings in mixture of remaining ingredients for 24 hours. Bake in same marinade for 1½ - 2 hours at 350° for 30 minutes, then turn down to 325° for remainder of baking time. Place wings in one layer only.

Treasured Recipes from Treasured Friends

Dressed-up Brussels Sprouts

2 (10-ounce) packages frozen baby Brussels sprouts
2 cups your favorite oil-free Italian or vinaigrette dressing
2 tablespoons lemon juice
1 (3½-ounce) jar diced pimento, drained
Chopped fresh parsley

Cook Brussels sprouts as directed on package. Marinate overnight in dressing and lemon juice. Garnish with pimento and parsley; serve with toothpicks. Makes 6-8 servings. Fat 0 grams per serving/Vit C/Fiber/Cruciferous.

Minnesota Heritage Cookbook II

Baked Caramel Corn

2 sticks margarine
2 cups brown sugar
½ cup white syrup
1 teaspoon salt
1 teaspoon vanilla
½ teaspoon soda
8 quarts popcorn, popped

Mix margarine, sugar, syrup, salt, and vanilla. Boil 5 minutes over low heat (careful or it will burn). Remove from heat and add soda. Pour over popcorn. Use a large container for mixing it up.

Heat oven to 250°; put popcorn in cake pans or cookie sheets. Bake for one hour, stirring every 15 minutes. Spread on wax paper to cool.

Bethany Lutheran Church Celebrating 110 Years

Popcorn Cake

20 cups popped corn
1 pound peanuts
1 pound small gumdrops
1 pound marshmallows
½ cup butter or oleo
½ cup corn oil

Mix popcorn, peanuts, gumdrops together. Microwave marshmallows, butter or oleo and oil. When melted and smooth, pour over corn mixture and pack into greased angel food pan.

Clinton's 110th Cookbook

Oven Baked Potato Wedges

6 tablespoons butter
4 large Idaho potatoes
1 medium onion, minced
1 teaspoon pepper

About 40 minutes before serving, heat oven to 425°. Spray cooky sheet or 17½ x 11½-inch pan with vegetable spray. Melt the butter in pan in the oven. Remove pan from oven. Cut each unpeeled potato into 8 wedges; add to the butter in pan. Sprinkle minced onion over wedges. Bake 30 minutes and evenly brown them by turning occasionally. Salt and pepper to taste. Yield: 4 servings; 345 calories each serving.

The Ultimate Potato Cookbook

Stuffed Mushrooms Italiano

12 large fresh mushrooms (5 ounces)
1 tablespoon butter
¼ cup onion, finely chopped
¼ cup (1 ounce) diced pepperoni
2 tablespoons green pepper, finely chopped
½ clove garlic, minced
¼ cup Ritz crackers, finely crushed
4 teaspoons grated Parmesan cheese
2 teaspoons parsley
¼ teaspoon seasoned salt
⅛ teaspoon oregano
Dash pepper

Remove mushroom stems and chop. Drain mushroom caps on paper towels. Combine butter, mushroom stems, onion, pepperoni, green pepper, and garlic. Microwave for 2 minutes until tender. Stir in cracker crumbs, Parmesan cheese, parsley, seasoned salt, oregano, and pepper; mix well. Mound into caps. Microwave for 4 minutes until hot. Yield: 12 servings.

Anoka County 4H Cook Book

 The world famous health center, the Mayo Clinic, is in Rochester. William W. Mayo and his two sons founded it and attracted an exceptional medical staff. It is believed people are healthier in Minnesota, mainly because they have to be tough to live here to begin with!

Witches Brew

1 gallon apple cider
12 ounces orange juice
 concentrate, thawed

1 gallon cranberry juice
1 pound dry ice

Mix juices in large container; add dry ice broken in pieces for steam effect. Drink with halloween spirit.

Anoka County 4H Cook Book

Hot Chocolate Mix

1 (8-quart) box powdered
 milk
1 (2-pound) box Quik

1 (8-10-ounce) jar
 Coffee-mate
1/2 - 1 cup powdered sugar

Combine all ingredients in very large bowl. Store in 5-quart ice cream bucket or other sealed container. To use add 1/4 cup mix for each mug of boiling water.

Feeding the Flock

Breads and Breakfast

Bales of hay dot the landscape of an Minnesota farm. Somewhere in
southeastern Minnesota.

Knicke Brod
(Flat Bread)

1 cup buttermilk
1 cup cream
4 tablespoons melted
   shortening
1 teaspoon salt
1/4 cup sugar

2 teaspoons baking powder
1 teaspoon baking soda
1/2 cup crushed cornflakes
3/4 cup whole wheat flour
White flour

Mix buttermilk, cream, shortening, salt, sugar, baking powder, and baking soda. Add cornflakes, whole wheat flour, and enough white flour to make a stiff dough. Roll thin and bake in hot (400°) oven.

Wannaska Centennial

Norwegian Flat Bread

1 small-size package corn
   muffin mix
3/4 cup whole wheat flour

3/4 cup white flour
1 teaspoon baking powder
1 cup buttermilk

Mix in order given. Form dough into pieces the size of a bun. Roll out thin on floured pastry cloth or board. Cut with pastry wheel or knife into halves or thirds. Put on cookie sheet. Bake 8-10 minutes at 350° until golden brown. Store in an airtight container.

Duluth Woman's Club 70th Anniversary Cookbook

Grandma's Flat Bread

3 cups white flour
1 cup whole wheat flour
1/2 cup cornmeal
2 teaspoons salt

1 teaspoon sugar
11 tablespoons shortening
3 cups boiling water (maybe a
   little more)

Mix flours, cornmeal, salt, and sugar well. Put shortening into boiling water and boil a little; pour over flour mixture and stir and cool. Make into about 15 balls. Roll paper thin. Use lefse rolling pin. Bake at 350° until crisp, about 5-6 minutes.

Vaer saa god Cookbook

Lefse

Won first prize.

5 cups riced or mashed
  potatoes
1/2 cup cream

3 tablespoons melted butter
2 1/2 cups flour
Salt to taste

Mix potatoes and cream. Mix well. Add melted butter, flour, and salt; mix well. Roll out a small piece at a time into a circle as thin as possible. Fry until lightly browned; turn and brown other side.

The Ultimate Potato Cookbook

Sand Hill Church Lefse

This is a delicious lefse and quite easy to roll out.

2 cups flour
1/4 pound butter
1/2 teaspoon salt

1 tablespoon sugar
7 cups riced potatoes (cold)
1/2 cup cream

Mix flour, butter, salt and sugar like pastry. Add potatoes. Knead. Add cream. Knead. Roll out and bake on hot lefse grill.

Our Favorite Recipes / Aurdal Lutheran Church

 Traditionally lefse was eaten wrapped around a piece of meat or fish. Now it is more common to butter a pie-shaped wedge and sprinkle it with cinnamon sugar and eat it rolled or folded.

Focaccia

Serve with any Italian meal.

1 package dry yeast	3 cups flour
1 cup warm water (105-115°)	Olive oil
3 tablespoons rosemary	Freshly grated Parmesan
3 tablespoons olive oil	cheese
2 teaspoons salt	

Dissolve yeast in warm water in large bowl. Stir in rosemary, oil, salt, and 2½ cups flour. Knead dough on lightly floured surface, adding flour as needed. When smooth and elastic, place in greased bowl. Brush with oil and cover. Let rise until double (about one hour). Punch down and press in oiled 12-inch pizza pan. Brush with olive oil and sprinkle with cheese. Let rise another 30 minutes. Bake in preheated 400° oven for 20-25 minutes.

Herbs in a Minnesota Kitchen

Swedish Rusks

3 eggs, beaten	1½ teaspoons baking
¾ cup oil	powder
2 teaspoons almond extract	3½ cups flour
1 cup sugar, add gradually	

Mix in order given. Shape into 2 rolls, length of jellyroll pan, lightly greased. Bake at 350° for 30 minutes. Remove from oven. Slice immediately into 1-inch slices. Turn on sides. Bake for 45 minutes at 250°.

Finn Creek Museum Cookbook

Swedish Cardamom Rusks

This is a dry, crisp rusk, faintly sweet, delicious with coffee.

1 cup margarine or butter
1 1/3 cups sugar
2 eggs
1 cup milk or sour cream
4 cups flour

3 teaspoons baking powder
2 teaspoons ground
cardamom
1/2 teaspoon salt

Cream margarine and sugar. Add eggs and mix. Stir in dry ingredients, which have been sifted together, alternating milk and dry ingredients. Mix well. Batter is very thick. Place batter in greased 9x13-inch pan. Sprinkle 1 or 2 teaspoons sugar on top of batter. Bake at 350° about 35 minutes. Test to see if center is done. Remove pan from oven and reduce temperature to 275°. Let cake cool 15-20 minutes, or until cool enough to handle. Cut cake into strips, four across and 16-18 lengthwise, or about 1/2-inch slices. Lift pieces gently from pan and place on 2 ungreased cookie sheets, cut-side-down, close together, but not touching. Return to 275° oven and bake 45 minutes. Turn pieces over and bake 45 minutes longer. Store in tight container.

Our Heritage Cookbook

Herb Bread Sticks

1/3 cup margarine
2 tablespoons grated Parmesan
cheese
2 1/4 cups flour
1 tablespoon sugar
3 1/2 teaspoons baking
powder

1 teaspoon basil (substitute
other herbs to taste)
1 tablespoon fresh parsley,
minced
2/3 cup skim milk
1/2 cup light sour cream

Preheat oven to 400°. Melt margarine in 13x9-inch baking pan. Combine all ingredients except milk and sour cream. Stir milk and sour cream into dry ingredients until moist. Knead dough on floured surface 10 times. Roll dough to 12x6 inches. Cut strips. Dip into melted margarine; twist and return to bake pan. Bake 20-25 minutes.

Feeding the Flock

Swedish Rye Bread

1/2 cup warm water
2 packages yeast
2 tablespoons shortening
1 1/2 cups warm water
1/4 cup brown sugar

2 1/2 cups rye flour
2 teaspoons salt
1/4 cup molasses
1/2 cup dark corn syrup
5 cups white flour

Mix 1/2 cup water and yeast in small bowl until dissolved. Mix remaining ingredients well; let rise until double. Form loaves and let rise again. Bake at 350° for 45-60 minutes.

Our Family's Favorites

Zucchini Bread

3 cups flour, sifted
1 teaspoon salt
1 teaspoon soda
1/4 teaspoon baking powder
2 cups sugar
3 large eggs

3 teaspoons vanilla
1 cup oil
3 cups zucchini, grated
Chopped nuts, as desired
Chopped dates, as desired

Combine flour, salt, soda, baking powder, sugar. Mix with spoon. Add eggs, vanilla, oil, and beat with beater. (Batter will be very stiff.) Add zucchini; this will liquidize the batter. (However, if frozen zucchini is used, after it has thawed an drained, save some of the liquid, as you may have to add some to the batter.) Beat with beater till smooth (5-6 minutes). Fold in nuts, dates, etc. with a spoon. Grease or Pam 2 bread pans, line each pan with waxed paper, and Pam again. Divide batter into the pans and bake at 350°, middle shelf, for about one hour. Freezes well.

Sharing Our Best / Home of the Good Shepherd

The Chanhassen Dinner Theatre is the largest dinner theater complex in the nation.

Tavern Bread

1³/4 cups beer (or water)
¹/2 cup cornmeal
¹/2 cup molasses
2 tablespoons shortening
1 package dry yeast
¹/2 cup warm water
2 teaspoons salt

4-5 cups flour (part whole wheat)
1 pound Cheddar cheese, cut in ¹/2-inch cubes
¹/2 pound summer sausage, cut in ¹/2-inch cubes (optional)
Cornmeal to sprinkle

Combine beer and ¹/2 cup cornmeal in a heavy 2-quart saucepan. Bring to a boil, stirring frequently; cook until thickened. Remove from heat and stir in molasses and shortening. Cool to lukewarm. Soften yeast in warm water; add to cornmeal mixture and mix well. Add salt and enough flour to make a stiff dough. Knead on well-floured surface until smooth, about 5 minutes. Place in greased bowl and cover. Let rise until doubled, about one hour.

While dough is rising, prepare a jellyroll pan by lining with aluminum foil, dull-side-up. Sprinkle with cornmeal in the areas where the loaves will be. Divide dough in half. Roll or press each half into 12 x 8-inch rectangle. Press half of cheese and sausage cubes into each piece of dough. Beginning with the long side, roll up tightly, and place on prepared pan. Let rise until doubled, about one hour. Heat oven to 350°. Bake until loaves are rich golden brown and feel firm, 40-45 minutes. Cool loaves on wire racks. If desired, brush loaves with butter before cooling. Makes 2 loaves.

The Clovia Recipe Collection

Lemon Poppy Seed Bread

1 package lemon cake mix
1 (3-ounce) package instant
  vanilla pudding
1/2 cup (scant) salad oil

1 cup water
4 eggs
1/4 cup (1 ounce) poppy
  seeds

Mix the above ingredients with an electric mixer. Pour into 2 greased and floured 9x5-inch bread pans. Bake at 350° for 40 minutes, or until toothpick comes out clean. Or you may make 4 small loaves, and bake them for 35 minutes. Drizzle with icing while bread is still warm.

ICING:

1 cup powdered sugar

2 tablespoons lemon juice

Centennial Cookbook

Rhubarb Bread

2/3 cup salad oil
1 1/2 cups brown sugar
1 cup sour milk or (1 teaspoon
  vinegar and 1 cup milk)
1 egg
1 teaspoon salt

1 teaspoon vanilla
1 teaspoon baking soda
2 1/2 cups flour
1 1/2 cups rhubarb, chopped
1/2 cup chopped nuts

TOPPING:

1/2 cup granulated sugar

1 teaspoon melted butter

Combine salad oil and brown sugar. Add milk and egg. Beat well. Add in salt, vanilla, baking soda, and flour. Mix until smooth. Add in rhubarb and nuts. Pour into greased loaf pans. Mix topping ingredients. Sprinkle onto batter. Yield: 2 medium loaves.

Anoka County 4H Cook Book

Some of the famous people from Minnesota: Walter Mondale, Judy Garland, Prince, Sinclair Lewis, Bob Dylan, Jessica Lange, The Andrews Sisters, Robert Preston, Charlton Heston, Charles Schultz, Jane Russell, Loni Anderson, Pinky Lee, Guindon, and Jean Paul Getty.

Soft-A-Cake

Makes a great breakfast treat!

2 loaves white bread dough	**1 cup sugar**
½ pint cream	**1 tablespoon cinnamon**

Place 2 loaves of frozen white bread dough in greased cake pan. Cover with greased waxed paper and let rise overnight or 9 hours. In the morning, flatten slightly and punch holes with handle of wooden spoon. Pour cream over the top and sprinkle the sugar and cinnamon mixture over the cream. Bake at 350° for 35-45 minutes.

Old Westbrook Evangelical Lutheran Church Cookbook

Painless Potica

Traditional nut-filled holiday bread.

1 cup butter or margarine	**¼ cup warm water**
½ cup low-fat milk	**(105-115°)**
2 tablespoons sugar	**3 eggs, separated**
¼ teaspoon salt	**2½ cups all-purpose flour**
2 packages active dry yeast	

In saucepan, heat butter, milk, sugar, and salt; cool to 105-115°. Dissolve yeast in warm water. Add to butter and milk mixture. Stir in egg yolks and flour; mix well. Cover bowl and refrigerate 8 hours or overnight. Dough will be soft.

FILLING:

2 cups ground nuts	**¼ cup low-fat milk**
1 teaspoon cinnamon	**1 tablespoon honey**
3 tablespoons sugar	**1 cup sugar**

Combine nuts, cinnamon, 3 tablespoons sugar, milk, and honey; heat until well blended; cool. Beat egg whites until stiff, gradually adding one cup sugar and beating until sugar is dissolved. Fold into nut mixture. Divide dough in half and roll each half to a 10x11-inch rectangle. Spread each with half of filling and roll like jellyroll. Place in greased 10-inch tube pan, one roll on top of the other; prick top. Do not let rise! Heat oven to 350°. Bake for about 65 minutes. Cool before removing from pan. Yield 1 coffeecake (16 servings). Fat 22.8 grams per serving.

Minnesota Heritage Cookbook II

Microwave Rommegrot

Enjoy!

2 cups milk
1/2 cup margarine, butter or
   corn oil

1/2 cup flour
1/4 cup sugar
Pinch of salt

Heat milk in kettle on stove (scald). In a casserole, melt margarine in microwave. Stir in flour with a whisk until smooth. Cook until it bubbles—approximately one minute (in microwave). Stir in milk. Stir until smooth and cook for 3 minutes. Take out each minute and stir until it reaches desired consistency. Add sugar and salt and cook 3-5 seconds. Top with melted margarine or butter and cinnamon.

Our Favorite Recipes / Aurdal Lutheran Church

Corn Spoonbread

1/2 cup butter, melted
2 eggs, lightly beaten
1 (8-ounce) can cream-style
   corn
1 (8-ounce) can whole kernel
   corn, drained

1 cup sour cream
1 (8-ounce) box corn muffin
   mix
4 ounces Swiss cheese,
   grated

Preheat oven to 350°. Combine all ingredients except Swiss cheese. Pour into a pan or casserole. Bake in 350° oven for 45 minutes. Sprinkle cheese over top and bake 10-15 minutes longer.

Sharing Our Best / Home of the Good Shepherd

Angel Biscuits

1 cup warm water
2 packages yeast
4 tablespoons sugar
3/4 cup oil

2 cups buttermilk
1 teaspoon soda
5 cups self-rising flour

Sprinkle yeast over water; add sugar when yeast starts to bubble. Add oil and buttermilk and soda; mix well. Add flour and mix well. Put in oiled covered container for a few hours, or overnight in refrigerator. When ready to use, stir slightly. Dip out with a spoon onto a floured board. Roll out, or pat out with hand, and cut with biscuit cutter.

Bake for 12 minutes at 450°. Remaining dough can be kept covered in refrigerator for a week or 10 days. You can make doughnuts by adding sugar and cinnamon before rolling out.

People Pleasers

Sweet Cream Scones

2 cups flour
1 tablespoon baking powder
2 tablespoons sugar
3/4 teaspoon salt
6 tablespoons (3/4 stick)
   unsalted chilled butter

1/2 cup currants
1 egg
1/2 cup cream
1/2 cup milk

Combine flour, baking powder, sugar, and salt in a bowl. Cut chilled butter in small pieces. Cut in butter with pastry blender until mixture resembles coarse crumbs. Add currants. Set aside.

In small bowl beat egg with fork; add cream and milk. Stir egg mixture into flour mixture until just blended. Turn out onto floured board; put some flour on top. This is soft dough.

Pat out to 3/4-inch high. Cut with biscuit cutter. Place about 1-inch apart on sprayed cookie sheet. Bake at 375° for 12 minutes or until golden brown. Serve hot or reheat in the microwave a few seconds or your regular oven a few minutes at 250°. They freeze well, too. Makes 12 scones.

Chickadee Cottage Cookbook

Scuffles

1 package yeast	1 cup butter
1/4 cup lukewarm water	1/2 cup milk
1 teaspoon sugar	2 eggs
3 cups flour	1 cup sugar
3 tablespoons sugar	2 tablespoons cinnamon
1/2 teaspoon salt	

Soak yeast in lukewarm water and one teaspoon sugar for 15 minutes. Mix flour, sugar, salt, and butter as pie crust. Add milk, eggs, and yeast. Knead dough until soft. Let stand in refrigerator overnight. Divide dough into 5 parts—roll as pie crust. Then, sprinkle a mixture of sugar and cinnamon over it on both sides of dough. Cut into wedges and roll wide end to narrow end. Bake at 350° for 15 minutes.

Our Family's Favorites

Hot Cross Buns

2 packages active dry yeast, or	1/2 cup sugar
2 cakes compressed yeast	3/4 teaspoon salt
1/2 cup warm water	31/2 - 4 cups sifted flour
1/4 cup milk, scalded	1 teaspoon cinnamon
1/2 cup oil or melted	3 beaten eggs
shortening	2/3 cup raisins

Soften active dry yeast in warm water. Combine milk, oil, sugar, and salt. Cool to lukewarm. Sift together one cup of the flour and cinnamon. Stir into milk mixture. Add eggs and beat well. Then add yeast and raisins. Add remaining flour to make a soft dough. Beat well.

Cover and let rise in warm place for about 1 1/2 hours. Punch down and turn out on a floured surface. Roll out 1/2 inch thick. Cut rounds with a 21/2-inch biscuit cutter. Place buns on a greased baking sheet. Cover and let rise one hour.

Cut a cross on each bun with a sharp knife or scissor. Brush tops with slightly beaten egg white. Bake in 375° oven for 15 minutes or until lightly browned. Frost a cross on each bun while hot. Makes about 2 dozen buns.

Our Favorite Recipes / Aurdal Lutheran Church

Buns

These are wonderful buns, always requested at family dinners and usually all gone before the day is over.

1/2 cup yeast	1/2 cup lard
2 cups lukewarm water	2 teaspoons salt
1 cup sugar	7 - 7 1/2 cups flour

ORIGINAL RECIPE:

At noon soak yeast in one cup water. When soft add 2 cups lukewarm water, sugar, lard (melted), salt, and flour to make dough softer than a bread dough. Put in a covered bowl and knead down 4-5 times during the afternoon as it rises. Late at night (around 10 P.M.) make into buns and put into pans, bake right away in the morning. Bake at 350° for 15 minutes or until golden brown. Makes 3 dozen.

FOR BREAD MACHINE:

Use 1/2 recipe except for yeast. Use the 1/2 package yeast as recipe calls for. Put in machine on dough mode. When it buzzes, empty dough out on counter and let rest 15 minutes. Set into 20 buns and let rise double in size before baking. It takes longer to rise (not much yeast).

Sears Through the Years Cookbook

Danish Puff

CRUST:

1 cup flour
1/2 cup butter

2 tablespoons water

Mix like a pie crust. Pat on a cookie sheet in 2 (12x3-inch) strips.

PUFF TOP:

1/2 cup butter
1 cup water
1 teaspoon almond flavoring

1 cup flour
3 eggs

Mix butter and water. Bring to a boil. Remove from heat; add flavoring. Beat in flour quickly. When smooth, add eggs one at a time beating well after each. Divide in half and spread evenly over crusts. Bake at 350° for about one hour. It will shrink. Frost with confectioners' sugar frosting. Sprinkle with nuts.

The Queen of Angels Anniversary Cookbook

Danish Coffee Cake

4 cups flour
1 cup margarine
3 tablespoons butter
1/2 cup sugar
1 teaspoon salt

1 package yeast
1/2 cup warm water
1 cup scalded milk
3 beaten egg yolks

Mix flour, margarine, butter, sugar, and salt like a pie crust. Dissolve yeast in water. Add to the milk and egg yolks. Add crust ingredients to flour mixture and mix yeast enough so flour disappears. Refrigerate overnight.

Divide dough into four parts and roll in a strip about 8 inches wide and the length of a cookie sheet. Let rise about 5 minutes. Use apricot jam or cooked chopped prunes for center. Put filling down the center of strip. Fold each edge to the center until edges meet. Brush with milk and sprinkle with sugar mixed with chopped nuts. Bake at 350° for about 25 minutes or until brown. Makes 4 strips of coffee cake. This can be made without filling or topping, and frost with almond-powdered sugar frosting after baking.

Treasured Recipes of Chippewa County

Versatile, Variable, Dependable Commendable Coffee Cake

1 cup sugar
4 eggs
1 cup oil
2 cups flour
1/4 teaspoon salt
1 teaspoon baking powder

1 teaspoon vanilla
1 can apricot (or other) pie
  filling
Sugar and cinnamon
Powdered sugar frosting

Mix sugar, eggs, oil, flour, salt, baking powder, and vanilla. Spread half of mixture in 9x13-inch pan. Spread can of pie filling over this evenly. Spread remaining batter over pie filling. Sprinkle with sugar and cinnamon. Bake 30-40 minutes at 350°. Drizzle powdered sugar frosting (powdered sugar and water) over top.

Dorthy Rickers Cookbook: Mixing & Musing

Raspberry Cream Cheese Coffeecake

2 1/2 cups flour
3/4 cup sugar
1 cup margarine
1/2 teaspoon baking powder
1/2 teaspoon baking soda
1/4 teaspoon salt
3/4 cup sour cream
1 egg

1 teaspoon almond extract
1 (8-ounce) package cream
  cheese
1 egg
1/2 - 3/4 cup raspberry
  preserves
1/2 cup sliced almonds

Heat oven to 350°. Grease and flour bottom and sides of a 9- or 10-inch springform pan. In large bowl, combine flour and 3/4 cup sugar. Using pastry blender, cut in margarine until mixture resembles crumbs. Reserve one cup. To remaining crumb mixture, add baking powder, baking soda, salt, sour cream, egg, and almond extract. Blend well. Spread batter over bottom and 2 inches up sides. In small bowl, combine cream cheese, 1/4 cup sugar, and egg; blend well. Pour over batter in pan. Carefully spoon on preserves. Sprinkle reserved crumbs and almonds over top. Bake 45-55 minutes, or longer. Cool 15 minutes. Remove sides. Refrigerate.

Great Cooks of Zion Church

Heath Brunch Coffeecake

2 cups flour
1/4 pound softened butter
1 cup brown sugar
1/2 cup white sugar
1 cup buttermilk, or sour
   regular milk with 1 teaspoon
   vinegar

1 teaspoon baking soda
1 egg
1 teaspoon vanilla
1/2 package Heath miniatures,
   approximately 16 bars
1/4 cup chopped pecans or
   almonds

Blend flour, butter, and sugars. Remove 1/2 cup of mixture. To rest, add buttermilk, baking soda, egg, and vanilla. Blend well. Pour into greased and floured 9x13-inch pan. Crush finely the Heath bars; mix with nuts and 1/2 cup of mixture. Sprinkle over top of batter; bake at 350° for 30 minutes.

Note: It's easier to crush the Heath bars if they are refrigerated first.

The Centennial Society Cookbook

Rich Cranberry Coffeecake

1 (8-ounce) package cream
   cheese, softened
1 cup butter or margarine
1 1/2 cups sugar
1 1/2 teaspoons vanilla
   extract
4 eggs
2 1/4 cups all-purpose flour,
   divided

1 1/2 teaspoons baking
   powder
1/2 teaspoon salt
2 cups fresh or frozen
   cranberries, patted dry
1/2 cup chopped pecans or
   walnuts
Confectioners' sugar

In a mixing bowl, beat cream cheese, butter, sugar, and vanilla until smooth. Add eggs, one at a time, mixing well after each addition. Combine 2 cups flour, baking powder, and salt. Gradually add to butter mixture. Mix remaining flour with cranberries and nuts; fold into batter. Batter will be very thick. Spoon into a greased 10-inch fluted tube pan. Bake at 350° for 65-70 minutes. Let stand 5 minutes before removing from the pan. Before serving, dust with confectioners' sugar.

Old Westbrook Evangelical Lutheran Church Cookbook

Rhubarb-Strawberry Coffee Cake

FILLING:

3 cups rhubarb, chopped
1 (16-ounce) package frozen
  strawberries

1 cup sugar
1/3 cup cornstarch
2 tablespoons lemon juice

Combine and cook fruit for 5 minutes. Mix sugar and cornstarch and stir in the lemon juice. Cook and stir until thick; cool.

BATTER:

3 cups flour
1 cup sugar
1 teaspoon soda
1 teaspoon salt
1 teaspoon baking powder

1 cup butter
1 cup buttermilk
2 eggs
1 teaspoon vanilla

Sift dry ingredients in bowl and cut in butter. Quickly stir in buttermilk, eggs, and vanilla until moist. Spread half of batter in a 9x13-inch pan; add filling. Dot with remaining batter.

TOPPING:

1/2 cup flour
3/4 cup sugar

1/4 cup butter
1/2 teaspoon cinnamon

Mix ingredients; sprinkle on top of batter. Bake at 350° for 40 minutes.

Potluck Volume II

Danish Kringle
(Pronounced Kreeng' - leh)

3/4 cup firm butter
3 1/4 cups flour, divided
1 packet active dry yeast
1/4 cup warm water
3 tablespoons
1 egg, slightly beaten

3/4 cup cold milk
1 teaspoon salt
1 cup raisins
1/4 cup sugar
1/4 cup almond slices

Cut or blend together butter and 1/4 cup flour just until flour disappears. (Do not cream.) Wrap and chill. In mixing bowl, soften yeast in water. Combine 3 tablespoons sugar and egg, reserving 1 tablespoon for topping. Add milk and salt. Stir in approximately 3 cups flour until dough is stiff enough to roll.

Roll out on floured surface to a 12-inch square. Roll out butter-flour mixture on heavily floured surface (or between waxed paper) to a 10x4-inch rectangle. Place in center of dough. Fold over ends to overlap. Turn one-quarter way around, roll out again to 12-inch square. Repeat the folding and rolling 2 more times. Wrap in plastic wrap. Chill at least one hour or overnight.

Cover raisins with boiling water. Let stand 5 minutes; drain well. Prepare Filling. Roll out dough on floured surface to 24x12-inch rectangle. Cut lengthwise into 2 (24x6-inch) rectangles. Spread each with 1/2 of filling to within 1/2-inch of outside edge. Sprinkle with raisins. Moisten outside edge and ends with water. Roll each strip as for jellyroll, starting with inside 24-inch edge. Seal and stretch to a generous 30 inches. Place on foil-lined and well-greased cookie sheet in pretzel shape. Flatten to 1/2 inch. Brush with reserved sugar-egg mixture. Sprinkle with a mixture of 1/4 cup sugar and 1/4 cup almonds. Cover; let stand at room temperature 30 minutes. Bake at 375° for 25-30 minutes, or until rich golden brown. Makes 2 coffeecakes.

FILLING:

1/4 cup butter
1/2 - 1 teaspoon ground
  cardamom

1 - 1 1/2 cups powdered
  sugar
Few drops of milk

Soften butter. Add cardamom. Add powdered sugar; mix well. Blend in a few drops milk until of spreading consistency.

The Clovia Recipe Collection

Kringles
(Sweet Rolls)

2 cups milk
1 cup cream
1 cup sugar
2 cakes yeast
1 teaspoon salt

1/4 teaspoon anise oil
2 heaping tablespoons
   shortening
5-6 cups flour

Bring to boil milk, cream, and sugar; cool to lukewarm. Then add yeast, salt, anise oil, shortening and flour; add the flour gradually. Can use electric mixer until 3 or 4 cups of flour have been used. Knead in the rest of flour on greased and floured board. Place in greased bowl and cover with a cloth. Let rise in a warm place until double in bulk. Take small amount of dough and roll into long strips 15 inches or so (the thickness of your small finger).

Form into figure 8 and place in greased pan; let rise again. Bake in preheated oven at 400° for 15 minutes or so. Brush the tops with Sugar Water. These freeze well, too.

SUGAR WATER:
1 cup sugar
1/2 cup water

2 drops anise oil

Bring sugar and water to a boil. Add anise oil.

Bethany Lutheran Church Celebrating 110 Years

Easy Cinnamon Rolls

2 1/2 cups warm water
2 packages yeast
2 eggs

1 yellow cake mix (dry)
6 - 6 1/2 cups flour
Butter, sugar, cinnamon

Mix first 5 ingredients in order given. Knead well. Let rise until double in size. Roll out and spread with butter, sugar, and cinnamon. Roll up and cut in slices. Bake at 350° until golden brown.

First United Methodist Church Cookbook

Caramel Rolls

2 loaves frozen bread
1/2 cup butter
1 cup brown sugar
1 (3-ounce) package vanilla
  pudding (not instant)

1 (3-ounce) package
  butterscotch pudding (not
  instant)
2 tablespoons milk

Partially thaw bread. Grease 9x13-inch pan. Cut pieces of dough and arrange in pan. Heat rest of ingredients and simmer a few seconds. Pour over dough. Refrigerate overnight. Bake at 350° for 30-40 minutes in morning.

Martha Chapter #132 OES Cookbook

Nutty Cinnamon Ring

1/3 cup chopped pecans
3/4 cup sugar
1 1/2 teaspoons cinnamon

2 (8-ounces) cans refrigerated
  buttermilk biscuits
1/3 cup butter, melted

Heat oven to 350°. Sprinkle half the nuts into a 9-inch ring mold. Combine sugar and cinnamon. Dip each biscuit in melted buter, then in sugar mixture. Place biscuits in ring mold. Sprinkle with the reamining nuts. Top with remaining coated biscuits. Bake for 25-30 minutes; turn onto serving plate, and let pan remain there for a few minutes to allow syrup to run over biscuits.

Kitchen Keepsakes

Dough Balls

*Called New Year's Eve Balls, these were served with pots of hot choco-
late on New Year's Eve.*

3 tablespoons dry yeast
1/3 cup warm water
1 1/2 cups powdered milk
3 cups lukewarm water
1 cup sugar
1 tablespoon orange peel

3 eggs
2 tablespoons soft butter
Salt to taste
5 flour
2 cups raisins

Mix yeast and water; set aside. In mixer bowl put powdered
milk, lukewarm water, sugar, orange peel, and eggs. Mix on
low speed. Add soft butter and some salt. Mix in about 3 cups
flour. Beat hard about 3 minutes. Remove into large bowl. Stir
in another 2-3 cups flour and raisins that have been soaked and
squeezed dry. Mix and let rise until double. Stir down and rise
again.

   Have a kettle of hot fat ready to fry, 375°. Dough will be
soft. Spoon into fat by tablespoonful; must not be too hot, so
will cook until medium brown and done in middle.

Scars Through the Years Cookbook

Doughnuts

3 eggs, beaten
1/4 teaspoon salt
2 tablespoons melted butter
1 cup sugar
1/2 teaspoon vanilla

1 teaspoon soda
1 cup buttermilk
3 cups flour
1/2 teaspoon nutmeg

Mix eggs, salt, butter, sugar and vanilla. Mix soda in buttermilk; add flour alternately with the buttermilk. Drop with a
doughnut maker. Fry in hot fat at 375°. Turn often.

Sharing our Best / Bergen Lutheran Church

Potato Doughnuts

1 cup sieved, cooked potatoes
  (warm or cold)
1 cup liquid (reserved from
  cooking potatoes)
3/4 cup vegetable shortening
1/2 cup sugar
1 tablespoon salt

1 package active dry yeast
3/4 cup warm water
  (105-115°)
2 eggs, beaten
5-6 cups flour
Shortening

Mix potatoes, potato cooking liquid, shortening, sugar, and salt. Dissolve yeast in warm water; stir into potato mixture. Stir in eggs and enough flour to make dough easy to handle. Turn dough onto lightly floured surface; knead until smooth and elastic, 5-8 minutes. Place in greased bowl; turn greased side up. (Don't punch down.) Cover; let rise until double, 1 - 1 1/2 hours.

Pat dough on lightly floured surface to 3/4-inch thickness. Cut doughnuts with floured, 2 1/2-inch cutter. Let rise until double, about an hour. Heat 3-4 inches of shortening to 375° in heavy pan. Fry doughnuts 2-3 minutes on each side or until golden. Drain on paper towel. If desired, glaze or roll in sugar. Makes about 3 dozen.

The Ultimate Potato Cookbook

Potato Pancakes

3 cups grated raw potatoes
1 small, chopped onion
2 eggs, beaten
4 tablespoons milk

3 tablespoons flour
1/4 teaspoon baking powder
3/4 teaspoon salt

Mix all together well. Cook pancakes on a well greased hot griddle.

The Ultimate Potato Cookbook

Mingle with the munchkins in Emerald City. Judy Garland's birthplace and museum is in Grand Rapids on the banks of the Mississippi River.

Finnish Oven Pancake

4 eggs
3/4 teaspoon salt
1/4 cup honey
2 1/2 cups milk

1 cup unsifted flour
4 tablespoons butter or oleo,
  softened

Preheat oven to 400°. Put 9x10-glass baking dish in oven for 10 minutes. Beat eggs, salt, honey, and milk; add flour and mix. Add butter to glass baking dish. When butter is melted, pour batter in slowly. Bake for 30-35 minutes or until set. Makes 4-6 servings.

Finn Creek Museum Cookbook

German Oven Pancake
with Prune-Raisin Sauce

3 eggs
1/2 cup flour
1/2 teaspoon salt

1/2 cup milk
2 tablespoons vegetable oil
4 strips bacon

Heat oven to 450°. Beat eggs thoroughly. Gradually add flour and salt, beating well. Blend in milk; batter should be smooth. Stir in oil. Pour into buttered 10-inch skillet or 9x9x2-inch baking dish. Arrange bacon on top. Bake 20 minutes; reduce oven temperature to 350° and bake 10 minutes longer. Serve immediately with syrup or Prune-Raisin Sauce. Serves 3-4.

PRUNE-RAISIN SAUCE:
2 cups water
10-15 prunes
1/3 cup raisins
1/2 - 1 teaspoon cornstarch

1 teaspoon cinnamon
1/2 teaspoon nutmeg
1/2 teaspoon sugar
Dash of salt

Heat water to boiling; add prunes and raisins. Reduce heat and simmer about 25 minutes. Thicken, starting with 1/4 teaspoon cornstarch, keeping liquid not too thick. Add spices, sugar, and salt. Add more boiling water if sauce is too thick. Serve over pancakes. Makes about 2 1/2 cups.

From Minnesota: More Than A Cookbook

Oven-Baked Apple Pancakes

3 cups apple slices
1/4 cup butter
3/4 cup Bisquick

1/2 cup water
3 eggs
1 teaspoon sugar

Sauté apple slices in butter until tender. Pour in a greased pie plate or 8x8-inch pan. Mix remaining ingredients. Pour batter over apples. Sprinkle with sugar and chopped nuts. Bake 15 minutes at 375°.

Kompelien Family Cookbook

Overnight Caramel French Toast

1 cup brown sugar
1/2 cup butter
2 tablespoons light corn
  syrup
12 slices sandwich bread

6 eggs, beaten
1 1/2 cups milk
1 teaspoon vanilla
1/2 teaspoon salt

Combine firmly packed brown sugar, butter, and corn syrup in a small saucepan. Cook over medium heat until thickened, stirring constantly. Pour syrup mixture into a 13x9x2-inch baking dish. Place 6 slices of bread on top of syrup mixture. Top with remaining 6 slices of bread. Combine eggs, milk, vanilla, and salt, stirring until blended. Pour egg mixture evenly over bread slices. Cover and chill 8 hours. Bake, uncovered, at 350° for 40-50 minutes or until lightly browned. Serve immediately. Yield: 6 servings.

Recipes and Memories

One-third of Minnesota is covered by forest. The Chippewa National Forest is the oldest natural forest in the US.

Raspberry Streusel Muffins

¼ cup plain nonfat yogurt
1⅓ cups sugar
1 egg
2⅓ cups flour
1 tablespoons plus 1 teaspoon
  baking powder
½ teaspoon salt

1 cup skim milk
1½ teaspoons vanilla
1½ cups red raspberries
¼ cup sugar
2 teaspoons cinnamon
¼ cup flour
1 tablespoon margarine

Cream yogurt and 1⅓ cups sugar; beat at medium speed until light and fluffy. Add egg, beating well. Combine the flour, baking powder, and salt. Add to creamed mixture alternately with milk; stir well after each addition. Stir in vanilla and fold in raspberries. Spoon batter into greased muffin pan, filling ⅔ full. Combine remaining ingredients until crumbly. Sprinkle on top of muffin batter. Bake at 375° for 25-30 minutes or until golden brown. Remove from pans immediately; cool on wire rack. Makes 6 large muffins.

Potluck Volume II

Yummy Strawberry Yogurt Muffins

2 cups unbleached flour
3 teaspoons baking powder
1/2 teaspoon salt
1 1/2 cups fresh sliced
  strawberries
2 large egg whites
1/3 cup canola oil

3/4 cup dark brown sugar,
  firmly packed
1 cup lowfat vanilla yogurt
1/4 cup skim milk
2 teaspoons pure vanilla
  extract
Raw sugar

Preheat oven to 400°. In a mixing bowl, using large fork, combine flour, baking powder, and salt. Add strawberries and stir lightly to mix. In a large mixing bowl, using a large fork, vigorously mix together egg whites and oil. Mix in brown sugar. Stir in yogurt, skim milk, and vanilla. Add flour mixture to egg-oil-sugar mixture, mixing only until dry ingredients are moistened. Batter should be lumpy. Divide batter equally into 12 paper-lined muffin cups, filling generously. These will be large muffins! Sprinkle each muffin with 1/4 teaspoon raw sugar. Bake.

Bake muffins 18-20 minutes, until lightly browned. Remove from muffin tin, and serve warm. Store leftover muffins covered in refrigerator. Makes 12 muffins.

Bake Yourself Happy

Peaches and Cream Muffins

1/2 cup butter
1/2 cup white sugar
1/2 cup brown sugar
1 teaspoon vanilla
1/2 cup sour cream
1 egg, room temperature
1 1/2 cups flour

1 1/2 teaspoons baking
  powder
1 cup chopped peaches (fresh,
  frozen, or canned, drained
  well)
1 cup chopped pecans
  (optional)

Cream butter and sugars. Beat vanilla and sour cream into creamed mixture. Add egg. Combine flour and baking powder; add to creamed mixture. Chop peaches and fold into muffin batter. Add pecans if desired; mix to blend only. Grease muffin tins. Spoon batter, filling 2/3 full. Bake at 350° for 30 minutes.

Recipes from the Flock

Banana Muffins

1 cup sugar
1 stick butter
1 egg
1/2 cup sour cream
1 cup ripe bananas, mashed

2 cups flour
1 teaspoon vanilla
1 teaspoon soda
1/2 cup nuts, finely chopped

Mix in order given. Fill greased muffin tins 3/4 full. Bake at 350° for about 20 minutes.

Sharing our Best / Bergen Lutheran Church

Breakfast Dish

6-8 slices of bread, crust removed
3 tablespoons butter or margarine
1 (4-ounce) can mushrooms, drained
1 bunch green onions, chopped (1/2 cup)

1 cup bacon or ham, crumbled or diced
2 cups grated cheese (Cheddar, Swiss, Mozzarella)
1 1/2 cups milk
4-10 eggs, beaten
1/2 teaspoon salt

Butter bread and place buttered-side-down in 9x13-inch buttered pan. Layer mushrooms, onions, meat, and cheese. Beat milk and eggs together with salt; pour over cheese. Refrigerate overnight. Bake at 350° for one hour.

Variation: Add one teaspoon dry mustard, 1/8 teaspoon pepper; chopped green pepper may also be added in layer.

Sharing our Best to Help the Rest

Bernie Good Morning Brunch

2½ cups seasoned croutons
2 cups shredded cheese
2 pounds sausage
4 eggs
2½ cups milk

¾ teaspoon dry mustard
1 can cream of mushroom
  soup
½ cup milk

Place croutons in a 9x13-inch greased pan. Put cheese on top of croutons. Fry sausage and drain. Arrange over cheese. Beat eggs, mustard, soup and milk. Pour over top. Cover and refrigerate overnight. Bake at 300° for 1½ hours.

Red Oak Grove Lutheran Church Family Cookbook

Overnight Brunch Casserole

1 (6-ounce) box hash brown
  potatoes, with onion
4 cups hot water
5 eggs
½ cup cottage cheese
1 cup shredded Cheddar
  cheese

2-3 tablespoons minced onion
1 teaspoon salt
Dash of pepper
6 slices cooked bacon,
  crumbled

Pour hot water over hash browns; let stand 10 minutes, and drain well. Beat eggs; add potatoes and all other ingredients. Pour in greased 10-inch pie pan. Cover, and refrigerate overnight. In morning, place, uncovered, in cold oven. Bake at 350° for 35 minutes, or until potatoes are tender and eggs are set. Makes 6 servings.

Note: Croutons mixed with melted margarine can be put on top just before baking, if desired.

The Centennial Society Cookbook

A few years ago, Saint Paul was named the "most livable city" in the US for its array of free and low-cost attractions and events; safe, clean streets and parks; accessibility to other metro locations; down-to-earth ways, and cultural sophistication.

Breakfast Pizza

1 package crescent rolls (8)
1 pound ground pork
  sausage
1 cup frozen hash browns,
  thawed
1 cup Cheddar cheese and
  Mozzarella

5 eggs
1/4 cup milk
1/2 teaspoon salt
1/8 teaspoon pepper
2 tablespoons Parmesan
  cheese

Press crescent rolls into pizza pan to form crust. Spoon sausage and potatoes on top. Add cheese. Beat eggs, milk, salt and pepper together and pour over crust. Sprinkle Parmesan cheese over. Bake 375° for 25 minutes. May use jellyroll pan.

First United Methodist Church Cookbook

Meatless Summer Sandwiches

3 cups shredded Swiss
  cheese
2/3 cup chopped tomato (best
  when homegrown)

1/2 cup chopped green onion
2/3 cup mayonnaise
1 loaf pumpernickel or rye
  bread

Mix cheese, tomato, green onion, and mayonnaise. Spread on bread, making sandwiches. Wrap individually in foil. Bake at 350° for 25 minutes. Serve hot. Yield 6-8 sandwiches.

Duluth Woman's Club 70th Anniversary Cookbook

Pizza Wiches

2 pounds hamburger
1/4 cup diced onion
1 (4-ounce) package shredded
  Mozzarella cheese
1 (4-ounce) package sharp
  Cheddar cheese

2 cans tomato soup
1/4 teaspoon garlic
1/4 teaspoon oregano

Brown hamburger and onion and cool. Mix together cheeses, soup, garlic, and oregano. Mix with hamburger and onion; chill. When ready to serve, spread mixture on 1/2 bun. Broil until bubbly.

Clinton's 110th Cookbook

Cheese Sandwich Filling

1 tablespoon sugar
1 tablespoon butter
1 tablespoon flour
1/2 cup half-and-half
1 egg, slightly beaten
2 eggs, hard-boiled

1/2 pound American cheese
1 tablespoon or less chopped
  onion
1 small jar pimento
Salt and pepper to taste

Make white sauce of sugar, butter, flour and half-and-half. When thick, stir in one slightly beaten egg and salt to taste. Stir thoroughly; do not boil. Set aside to cool. Grate the boiled eggs; grate cheese; add eggs to cheese along with chopped onion, pimento, and white sauce mixture. Salt and pepper to taste.

Bethany Lutheran Church Celebrating 125 Years

Soups

Big Island Rendezvous Festival in Albert Lea.

Norsk-Svensk Suppe
(Fruit Soup)

1 cup prunes	1-2 sticks cinnamon
1/2 cup tapioca (sago)	1/2 cup raisins
1/2 cup sugar	1/2 orange, peeled and cut
2 quarts water	3 large apples, diced
Juice of 1/2 lemon	

Cook prunes for 1/2 hour; add sago or tapioca, and remaining ingredients. Cook for 1/2 hour more. Remove cinnamon sticks. If more thickness is needed, use one tablespoon cornstarch and simmer some more. Good served warm or cold.

Variation: Grape juice may be added; also other dried fruit may be added as preferred.

Note: Sago is preferred, but tapioca is fine, too. If using sago, soak the prunes and sago several hours, or overnight. Then add water to cover all.

Wannaska Centennial

Pumpkin Bowl Stew

Served in its own shell, pumpkin stew is a festive main course for Halloween or Thanksgiving.

1 medium pie pumpkin (pie pumpkins have thick, meaty sides)	1 (10½-ounce) can chicken broth
1 cup sliced carrots	1/4 teaspoon allspice
1 cup diced potatoes	1/4 teaspoon cinnamon
1 cup sliced parsnips	2 tablespoons chopped basil
1 cup chopped onion	3 tablespoons chopped Italian parsley
1 cup chopped celery	1 tablespoon chopped thyme

Clean the pumpkin, remove the seeds, and scrape the inside. Reserve the "hat." Put the ingredients (uncooked) into the pumpkin. Place the pumpkin on a cookie sheet. Bake in a preheated 300° oven for 3-4 hours. The pumpkin and root vegetables will combine to make their own thickening. Replace "hat."

Herbs in a Minnesota Kitchen

5-Hour Stew

2 pounds stew meat
Flour
1 cup chopped celery
1 pinch salt
Pepper
Basil
Parsley

1 tablespoon sugar
4-5 carrots, sliced
3-4 potatoes, cubed
1 quart stewed tomatoes
1 medium onion, chopped
1/4 cup minute tapioca

Dredge meat in flour. Mix all together in a large covered casserole. Bake 5 hours at 250°. I have baked 6-8 hours at 200°, and it was great.

A Taste of Kennedy Cook Book

Burning Bush Soup

2 quarts nettles
2 cups water
1 1/2 tablespoons flour
1 1/4 quarts pork stock and
   water from nettles

1 tablespoon butter
Salt
White pepper

Wash the nettles well and drain. Cook in slightly salted water for 10 minutes or until tender. Strain, reserving the water. Chop the nettles finely or pass through a sieve. Melt the butter. Add the flour and stir until well-blended. Add the stock while stirring, and simmer for 10 minutes. Add the nettle purée and season.

Serve with poached eggs or with hard-boiled eggs cut into halves or sections.

Our Beloved Sweden: Food, Faith, Flowers & Festivals

Paul Bunyan is a character of legend and lore, born of the imagination of lumberjacks in Akeley. To honor him and his legendary ox, Babe, 18-foot statues were erected along the shore of Lake Bemidji in 1937. World famous, these statues rank among the Midwest's most photographed attractions.

Wedding Soup

Don't wait for a wedding to try this one.

2 eggs
1/4 cup bread crumbs
1/4 cup grated Romano
  cheese

Lemon rind to taste
Pinch of nutmeg
3 cups chicken broth
Parsley

Mix first 5 ingredients. Let stand a few minutes. Drop by tea-spoonfuls into boiling chicken broth and simmer until done. Garnish with parsley. This recipe makes 2 servings; just multiply as needed.

Variation: Make your own favorite meatball recipe. Form into balls about the size of marbles. When egg drop is done, add meatballs to broth and cook a few minutes. Makes 2 servings.

Our Favorite Recipes

Paul Bunyan's Split Pea Soup

Paul Bunyan sent one of his cooks to a nearby town to get a wagonful of split peas. On the journey home, the wagon broke and spilled the full load of peas into a lake. To make the best of the situation, Paul threw 300 hams into the lake and then built a big fire around it. Dozens of cooks paddled around in rowboats to keep things from scorching. After a few hours it was ready—a lake full of split pea soup! Everyone said it was the best soup they had ever eaten.

1 pound dried split peas
1/2 cup chopped celery
1/2 cup chopped onion
1/2 cup chopped carrot
1 clove garlic, minced
2 tablespoons butter or
  margarine

1 or 2 smoked ham hocks
  (about 1/2 pound each)
1/4 teaspoon pepper
1 1/2 teaspoons salt

Cover peas with water and soak overnight. The next day, sauté celery, onion, carrot, and garlic in butter until tender. Drain beans and reserve liquid. Add enough water to soaking liquid to make 10 cups. Put in a pot and add the rest of the ingredients. Heat to boiling and then reduce to low heat. Cover and simmer 3 hours. Remove meat from ham hock and return meat to soup. Serves 8.

Winning Recipes from Minnesota with Love

Lentil Soup

1/4 cup salad oil
3 cups diced, cooked ham
1/2 pound Polish sausage, cut in
  1/2-inch slices
2 large onions, chopped
1 clove garlic, crushed
2 cups celery with leaves,
  chopped

1 large omato, peeled and cut in
  wedges
1 pound lentils, washed
3 quarts water
1/2 teaspoon Tabasco
1 1/2 teaspons salt
1 (10-ounce) package frozen
  leaf spinach, thawed, cut

In large kettle, heat oil; add ham, sausage, onions, and garlic; cook 5 minutes. Add celery, tomato, lentils and water, Tabasco, and salt. Cover and cook over low heat for 2 hours. Add spinach and cook 10 minutes. Yield: 4 quarts.

A Thyme For All Seasons

Black Bean Soup

16 ounces dried black beans
8 cups water
1 tablespoon vegetable oil
2 medium onions, chopped
1 carrot, shredded
4 cloves garlic, minced
1 green pepper, chopped
1/2 teaspoon cumin seed, crushed
1 teaspoon whole dried oregano
1 teaspoon salt
1/2 teaspoon pepper
2 tablespoons lemon juice
2 cups hot cooked brown rice
1 cup plain low-fat yogurt
Chopped green onions

Rinse beans and place with water in large kettle. Cover; let stand overnight. Or heat to boiling and boil for 2 minutes; cover and let stand for one hour. In skillet, heat oil. Add onions, carrot, garlic, green pepper, cumin, and oregano; sauté until soft. Stir into beans with salt and pepper. Heat to boiling; reduce heat to low and simmer, covered, for 1 1/2 - 2 hours or until beans are very tender, stirring occasionally. Stir in lemon juice. Serve in soup bowls over rice, topped with yogurt and onions. Makes 8 servings. Fat 1.5 grams per serving/Fiber.

Minnesota Heritage Cookbook II

Mushroom Barley Soup

2 large yellow onions, chopped
3 medium carrots, sliced
2 stalks celery
1/2 pound mushrooms, sliced thin
4 cups beef broth
1/4 cup chopped parsley
1/2 cup medium-size barley
1/4 teaspoon pepper
Salt to taste

Place all ingredients in pan and boil for 4 minutes. Simmer partly covered for 40 minutes or until the barley is tender. Serves 4.

The Oke Family Cookbook

Ely is the jumping-off place, nearly in Canada, known for its wilderness, fishing and wild rice. It is the "Canoe Capitol of the World."

Cream of Asparagus Soup

Early Spring and buying just-picked asparagus at a Farmer's Market. . . what fun! This is a basic cream soup. Other puréed vegetables such as carrots, cauliflower, or spinach can be substituted with equally satisfactory results. Try your favorite herb for additional flavor interest.

2 cups fresh asparagus	**2 cups coffee cream, evaporated**
1/2 cup butter	**milk or evaporated skim milk**
3/4 cup flour	**Salt and white pepper to**
4 cups fresh or canned chicken	**taste**
broth	

Wash and cut asparagus in 1-inch pieces; cook in 1/2 cup water until tender, and purée in blender. Melt the butter in soup kettle. Whisk in the flour. Add the chicken broth, which preferably has been heated. Whisk vigorously. When the mixture is thickened and smooth, continue cooking over low heat for 10 minutes.

To puréed asparagus, add enough water to make 2 cups. Add it and the cream to the thickened broth and heat another 5 minutes. Season the soup to taste and remove from heat. Serve topped with a few crisp-cooked asparagus tips and croutons. Makes 6 main dish or 10-first course servings.

Note: Use the top 4 inches of the fresh asparagus as a special vegetable course and the less tender bottoms to make a wonderful soup.

Chickadee Cottage Cookbook

Broccoli-Cauliflower Soup

3 chicken bouillon cubes
3 cups water
3-4 carrots, diced
3-4 stalks celery, diced
1 green pepper, diced
1 head cauliflower florets

1 bunch broccoli florets
3 cups milk
1/3 cup butter, melted
1/3 cup flour
2-3 cups Velveeta cheese,
    cubed

Dissolve bouillon cubes in water. Cook all vegetables in this broth until tender. Add milk. Cream butter and flour until smooth. Add to mixture, stirring to keep smooth. Turn heat to low. Add Velveeta cheese; heat until cheese melts, stirring to prevent sticking.

Kitchen Keepsakes

Irish Leek Soup

4 leeks
1 medium onion
4 medium potatoes
1 1/2 tablespoons butter

4 cups chicken broth
1 cup sour cream
Pepper, to taste

Cut leeks into 1/2-inch slices; dice onion; peel and dice potatoes. In large pot melt butter; add leeks and onions. Cook, covered, until tender, stirring occasionally. Add potatoes and broth; simmer, covered, 40 minutes. Add sour cream and heat to serve. Do not boil. Season with pepper.

Feeding the Flock

Cheese Soup

1/2 cup butter
1/2 cup flour
4 cups milk
1/2 cup carrots, grated
1/4 cup onions, finely
  chopped

1 stalk celery, chopped
1/4 cup green pepper, finely
  diced
1 pint chicken broth
1/2 pound Cheddar cheese
Sherry (optional)

Melt the butter and blend in flour and then the milk. Cook until thickened while stirring constantly. Parboil the vegetables in the chicken broth. Melt the cheese in a double boiler or in the milk mixture. Combine all the ingredients and bring to boil. Add one tablespoon sherry to each bowl of soup when serving. Top each bowl of soup with a design cut from a slice of cheese and sprinkle parsley if desired. Garnish with popcorn. Makes 6-8 servings.

A Thyme For All Seasons

Minestrone Soup

1 pound Italian sausage
  (cased)
1 tablespoon oil
1 cup onion, diced
1 clove garlic, minced
1 teaspoon basil
1 cup carrots, sliced
2 small zucchini, sliced

1 (16-ounce) can Italian
  tomatoes
7 cups beef broth
3 cups finely chopped
  cabbage
1 can Great Northern beans
Pepper to taste

Brown sliced sausage in oil. Add onion and garlic; cook 10 minutes. Add basil the last 5 minutes. Add carrots and zucchini. Chop tomatoes—do not drain—mix with the broth and add to soup with the cabbage. Simmer for 2 hours or longer. Add the undrained beans and pepper; simmer for 30-45 minutes.

Treasured Recipes from Treasured Friends

Italian Sausage Soup

1 pound Italian sausage
1 cup coarsely chopped onion
2 garlic cloves, sliced
5 cups beef broth
1/2 cup water
1/2 cup red (burgundy) wine
2 cups stewed tomatoes
1 cup sliced carrots (or grated)

1/2 teaspoon basil leaves
3 tablespoons parsley
1/2 teaspoon oregano leaves
1 medium green pepper, chopped
Parmesan cheese

Cook sausage and drain. Add onion and garlic. When fully cooked, add rest of ingredients. Simmer 35-45 minutes. You can add cut-up regular or cheese tortellinis to soup. Sprinkle Parmesan cheese on each serving.

Maple Hill Cookbook

Duck-Wild Rice Soup

1/4 cup wild rice
4 cups chicken broth
1/2 cup diced celery
1/4 cup diced onions
1/2 cup diced carrots
2 tablespoons fresh mushrooms, sliced
1/2 cup diced green pepper
1/4 cup butter
1/3 cup flour
1/2 teaspoon salt

1/4 teaspoon pepper
1/2 teaspoon garlic
1/2 teaspoon basil leaves, optional
2 tablespoons almonds, optional
1 tablespoon pimiento, optional
Chopped cooked duck
1 cup half-and-half or cream

Cook rice in chicken broth until tender. In a separate pan, saut° celery, onions, carrots, mushrooms, and green pepper in butter. Add flour, and stir. Add chicken broth and rice slowly, stirring constantly. Add salt, pepper, garlic, basil leaves, almonds, and pimiento. Add duck; stir well. Add half-and-half; heat thoroughly.

A Taste of Faith

Wild Rice Soup

3 cups water
1 can chicken broth
8 ounces wild rice
6 pieces bacon
1/2 cup onion, diced
1 cup celery, diced

1 can mushroom soup
2 cans cream of potato soup
2 cups light cream
6 slices American cheese
Salt and pepper

Combine water, broth, and wild rice. Bring to boil and simmer for 45 minutes. Sauté bacon, onion, and celery until done. Heat slowly, do not boil, mushroom and potato soups. Add cream and cheese. Stir in drained bacon mixture and rice. Salt and pepper to taste. Makes 12 cups.

Recipes from St. Michael's

Creamy Wild Rice Soup

6 tablespoons butter
4 tablespoons flour
2 cups half-and-half
3 cups chicken broth
1 cup chicken or turkey, diced
1/2 cup onion, chopped

1/2 cup thinly sliced celery
1/2 cup thinly sliced mushrooms
1 1/2 cups cooked wild rice
1/2 cup white wine
Rosemary to taste
Thyme to taste

Melt butter and add flour. Cook 2 minutes, but do not brown. Add half-and-half and one cup of broth slowly; whisk constantly. Let come to a boil and cook 2 minutes. Add rest of ingredients. Simmer 30 minutes. Garnish with shredded blanched carrot.

Sharing Our Best / Home of the Good Shepherd

Turkey Soup

1 (12 - 16-pound) turkey
  carcass
1-2 bay leaves
5-6 whole cloves
Salt and pepper to taste
2 tablespoons butter
3 tablespoons flour
2 tablespoons chicken base
1/2 cup uncooked rice
1/4 cup chopped onion

1 cup chopped celery
1 cup leftover gravy and
  turkey dressing
1/4 teaspoon curry powder
  (Optional)
1 hard cooked egg, minced
1/2 cup orange juice
1/2 cup Port wine
6-8 orange slices

Cut meat from bones, and cover carcass with water. Add bay
leaves, cloves, salt and pepper. Simmer for 3-4 hours. Remove
bones and drain stock through a colander. Make a roux by melt-
ing the butter and adding flour and chicken base. Add this to
the drained liquid a little at a time. Bring to a boil, using a wire
whisk to blend throughly. Add rice, onion, celery, and season
to taste. Cook about 25 minutes until rice is done. Add diced
turkey and about one cup of the leftover gravy and turkey dressing. If using curry, mix it with a little broth and add to the
soup. Simmer until serving. Add minced egg, orange juice and
wine just before serving, and top bowls with orange slices.
Makes 6-8 servings.

Minnesota Heritage Cookbook I

Beef Vegetable Soup

2 pounds beef, diced
2 medium onions, diced
2 cups diced potatoes
2 cups sliced carrots
2 cups green beans
2 cups chopped celery

2 cups tomatoes and juice
2 quarts water
1/3 cup ketchup
1/2 cup rice
1 tablespoon salt

Fry beef with onions until slightly browned. Add remaining
ingredients. Simmer until vegetables are tender. Serves 18.

First United Methodist Church Cookbook

Salads

The Pines Golf Course at Brainerd.

Cauliflower Salad

1 head cauliflower
1 (10-ounce) package frozen
   peas
1 cup chopped celery
2 tablespoons green onion
   tops

1 cup Miracle Whip
1½ tablespoons Hidden Valley
   Ranch dry dressing mix
¼ cup milk
3 or 4 slices bacon

Clean cauliflower. Pour boiling water over peas and let stand 5 minutes; drain. Mix ingredients (except bacon) together and let salad stand overnight in refrigerator. Fry bacon and crumble into salad before serving.

Maple Hill Cookbook

Broccoli Supreme Salad

1 large head broccoli, cut-up
   fine
1 large head cauliflower, cut
   up
3 cups red or green grapes, cut
   in half

4 green onions, chopped
½ pound bacon, cooked and
   crumbled (may use bacon
   bits)
¼ cup slivered almonds or
   sunflower seeds

DRESSING:
1 cup mayonnaise
½ cup sugar

1 tablespoon vinegar
1 teaspoon lemon juice

Toss salad; marinate in refrigerator for 2 hours.

Variation: Use ¾ cup raisins instead of grapes.

Clinton's 110th Cookbook

 Minnehaha means laughing water. Longfellow, in his poem, "Hiawatha," made Minnehaha Falls in Minneapolis world famous. As Hiawatha proposed to Minnehaha, he "heard the Falls of Minnehaha calling to him through the silence."

Lush Lettuce Salad

1 head lettuce
2-3 green onions or chives
1 cup chow mein noodles
2-3 tablespoons sesame seeds

6 ounces cashews
Bacon, fried and broken, or
  Bacos

DRESSING:
4 tablespoons sugar
1 teaspoon salt
1/2 teaspoon pepper

1/2 cup cooking oil
2 tablespoons apple cider
  vinegar

Combine dressing ingredients. Mix salad with dressing just before serving.

Centennial Cookbook

Pea and Peanut Salad

1 (10-ounce) package frozen
  green peas (thawed)
2 cups Spanish peanuts
1/2 cup Miracle Whip

1/2 cup sour cream
2 tablespoons lemon juice
1 teaspoon Worcestershire
  sauce

Mix uncooked peas and peanuts. Mix salad dressing, sour cream, lemon juice, and Worcestershire sauce together and blend into peas and peanuts. Refrigerate covered with plastic wrap for 2 hours. Serves 8-10.

People Pleasers

Wild Rice Salad

1 cup wild rice	1 cup sliced fresh mushrooms
3 cups water	1/2 cup olives
1 teaspoon salt	1 cup mayonnaise
2 cups diced turkey (ham or shrimp)	1/2 cup sour cream
	1/2 teaspoon mustard
1 cup sliced water chestnuts	Pepper to taste

Cook rice in water and salt for 40 minutes until tender. Drain and add next 4 ingredients. Mix next 4 ingredients for dressing and add to wild rice mixture. Serves 12.

Martha Chapter #132 OES Cookbook

Wild Rice Salad

1 cup uncooked wild rice	1 (10-ounce) package frozen peas, thawed, drained
1/4 cup thinly sliced green onions	1 jar marinated artichoke hearts, drained
1/2 cup chopped green peppers	1 envelope Good Seasons Italian dressing mix
1/2 pint cherry tomatoes, halved	

Cook rice according to directions. Mix with rest of the ingredients.

Variations: May use 1 can sliced water chestnuts; 1/2 avocado; 1-2 cups chicken or ham.

A Dish to Pass

Northwoods Chicken Salad

1 cup uncooked wild rice
5½ cups chicken broth
Juice of ½ lemon
1 chicken breast (2 halves)
   cooked, cooled and cut into
   bite-size pieces

3 green onions, sliced
½ red pepper, diced
2 ounces sugar pea pods, cut
   into 1-inch pieces
1 cup cashews

DRESSING:
2 large cloves garlic, minced
1 tablespoon Dijon mustard
½ teaspoon salt
¼ teaspoon sugar

¼ teaspoon freshly ground
   pepper
¼ cup herb vinegar
⅓ cup olive oil

Rinse wild rice. Combine with chicken broth in 3-quart sauce-pan. Cover and bring to boil. Reduce heat and simmer for 45 minutes, drain. Cool in bowl. Add lemon juice, chicken, onion, and red pepper. Blend all dressing ingredients and toss with rice mixture. Refrigerate at least 2 hours before serving. Stir in pea pods and cashews. Serves 5-6.

The Clovia Recipe Collection

Shrimp Salad

1 (10-ounce) package frozen
   salad shrimp
1 cup diced stuffed olives
1 cup raw rice, cooked and
   cooled

½ cup chopped green
   pepper
½ cup diced celery
1 cup small cauliflower buds
Salt and pepper to taste

Mix all ingredients in order given.

DRESSING:
1 cup mayonnaise
2 tablespoons salad oil
1 tablespoon vinegar
2 tablespoons sugar

1 tablespoon grated onion
½ tablespoon mustard
1 tablespoon lemon juice

Mix ingredients and toss over salad ingredients. Refrigerate for 3 hours or overnight.

Potluck Volume II

Marco Polo Salad

1 pound spaghetti
3/4 cup olive oil
2 cloves garlic, crushed
1 tablespoon basil
1 tablespoon oregano
1 teaspoon salt
1 teaspoon coarsely-ground
    pepper
1/2 cup half-and-half

1 green pepper, cut julienne
1 red pepper, cut julienne
1/2 cup parsley, chopped
2/3 pound Jarlsberg cheese, cut
    julienne
1/2 cup pecans, toasted and
    chopped
3/4 cup or 1/4 pound fresh
    grated Parmesan cheese

Cook spaghetti until al denté. Drain and toss with 2 tablespoons of the olive oil. Set aside. Mix together garlic, the rest of the olive oil, basil, oregano, salt and pepper. Pour half-and-half into mixture, whisking at the same time. Toss into pasta. Add green and red pepper, parsley, Jarlsberg cheese, and pecans; toss together. Sprinkle Parmesan cheese on top. Serve at room temperature. Makes 8-10 servings.

Our Favorite Recipes

Martha Chapter Turkey Salad

Meat from a 14-pound turkey,
    cubed
2 quarts diced celery
2 quarts green grapes, cut in
    halves
18 hard-boiled eggs, cut up
1 jar pimiento, cut up

1 pint whipping cream
1 quart Miracle Whip
1/4 cup white vinegar
1/4 cup sugar
1 (12-ounce) can chow mein
    noodles or shoestring
    potatoes

Mix turkey, celery, grapes, eggs, and pimento.

Dressing: Whip cream. Fold in Miracle Whip, which has been mixed with vinegar and sugar. Salt to taste. Fold dressing into turkey mixture and store covered overnight. Add chow mein noodles or shoestring potatoes. Serves a crowd.

Martha Chapter #132 OES Cookbook

Minnesota is the second biggest supplier of turkeys in the US.

Deluxe Chicken Salad

1 (7-ounce) box small ring
  macaroni
2 cups chicken, cut bite-size
1 cup green grapes, cut in
  half
1 cup celery, cut fine

1/2 cup sweet pickle, chopped
  fine
Salt to taste
1 cup mayonnaise mixed with 1
  cup whipped topping
1/2 cup cashew nuts

Boil macaroni; drain, rinse and cool. Mix all cut-up ingredients and salt, and add to macaroni. Mix lightly with creamed mixture and nuts. Serve on lettuce leaf.

Sears Through the Years Cookbook

Mock Chicken Salad

1 can chicken rice soup
1 (3-ounce) package lemon
  Jell-O
1 can tuna, drained
1 cup chopped celery

1 1/2 cups Cool Whip
1/2 cup nuts
1/2 cup salad dressing
Stuffed green olives, sliced on
  top (optional)

Heat soup to boiling; stir in Jell-O until dissolved. Cool mixture until it starts to jell. Add remaining ingredients. Chill until firm. Serve on lettuce leaf.

First United Methodist Church Cookbook

Salad on a Shoe String

1 cup grated carrots
1 cup chopped celery
1/4 cup chopped onion

1 (6-ounce) can tuna, drained
1 cup salad dressing
1 can shoestring potatoes

Mix all ingredients except potatoes well, and chill. Just before serving, fold in shoestring potatoes. May substitute other meat for tuna—ham, chicken, or turkey.

The Ultimate Potato Cookbook

Tuna Garden Loaf

2 envelopes unflavored
  gelatin
1/2 cup cold water
1 can condensed cream of
  celery soup
1/4 cup lemon juice
1 tablespoon prepared
  mustard
1 teaspoon salt

Dash of pepper
1 cup mayonnaise
2 (6 1/2 or 7-ounce) cans tuna,
  flaked
1 cup chopped celery
1/2 cup grated cucumber
1/4 cup chopped green
  pepper
Pimento strips for garnish

Soften gelatin in cold water. Heat soup just to boiling; add gelatin and stir to dissolve. Stir in lemon juice, mustard, salt and pepper. Chill till partially set. Blend in mayonnaise. Fold in flaked tuna, celery, cucumber, and green pepper. Pour into 8 1/2 x 4 1/2 x 2 1/2-inch loaf pan. Chill till firm. Unmold; trim with pimento strips. Makes 8 servings.

People Pleasers

Saint Paul began as a French village on the banks of the Mississippi River known as "Pig's Eye Landing." Pierre "Pig's Eye" Parrant was a retired fur trader who owned a saloon near the Lowertown landing. When Father Lucien Galtier arrived in 1841 and built a chapel dedicated to Saint Paul, he asked that the city's name be changed accordingly. Minneapolis was named from Dakota and Greek words meaning "city of waters." It is the state's largest city with 2.5 million residents.

Citrus Tuna Salad

1 (6-ounce) box lemon Jell-O
1/4 teaspoon onion salt
1/4 teaspoon salt
1/8 teaspoon white pepper
2 cups boiling water
1/2 cup orange juice
2 cups chopped celery

1 cup sliced stuffed olives
2 cans white water pack tuna,
  drained
2 cups green grapes, halved
1/2 cup slivered almonds
2/3 cup cream
3 tablespoons salad dressing

Combine Jell-O, onion salt, salt, and white pepper. Add boiling water and stir well. Cool to room temperature, then add orange juice. Refrigerate. When it starts to congeal add celery, olives, tuna, grapes, and almonds. Whip cream and fold into it the salad dressing. Fold into salad mixture. Put into 12 individual salad molds and refrigerate overnight.

Dorthy Rickers Cookbook: Mixing & Musing

Veggie Lovers' Salad

Delicious! Special flavor is given to this salad by the nutmeg.

1/2 package rainbow rotini
1 cup carrots, chopped
1 cup cucumber, chopped
1 cup frozen peas
1 stem fresh broccoli,
  chopped

1/2 cup onions, chopped
1/2 cup celery, cut
3/4 cup ripe olives, sliced

DRESSING:
1 cup salad dressing
1/2 cup sugar
1/4 cup cider vinegar

1/4 - 1/2 teaspoon nutmeg
Salt and pepper

Cook noodles according to package directions. Rinse with cold water and drain. Add noodles to chopped vegetables. Pour dressing over and refrigerate. Makes large salad.

Old Westbrook Evangelical Lutheran Church Cookbook

Spring Salad

Great with ham, roast beef, lamb or even barbecued chicken.

10-12 small red potatoes, unpeeled
1 pound fresh asparagus, cut into 1 to 2-inch lengths
5-6 carrots, peeled and thinly sliced
3/4 cup canola oil
6 tablespoons red wine vinegar

1 tablespoon sugar
1/2 cup chopped parsley
1 tablespoon dried basil (or fresh basil if you have it)
2 cloves garlic, chopped fine
Salt and freshly ground pepper
4 tablespoons chopped green onion

Cook potatoes in salted water until tender; drain and set aside. Steam asparagus just until tender; drain and set aside. Cook carrots for 5 minutes, until tender; drain and set aside. Put all vegetables in a large bowl and chill. In a blender, combine oil, vinegar, sugar, parsely, basil, and garlic. Whirl until smooth. Add salt and pepper to taste. (Check flavor and add more vinegar, sugar, salt or pepper if you wish.) Add onions; toss with vegetables. Cover and chill. Serve cold or at room temperature. Yield: 4-6 servings.

Recipes of Note for Entertaining

Bonnie's Potato Salad

2 pounds red potatoes
3 tablespoons onion, sliced paper thin
3 hard-boiled eggs, coarsely chopped
1 green pepper, seeded and finely chopped
2 stalks celery, chopped

2 tablespoons sliced ripe olives
2 tablespoons pimento, finely chopped
1 tablespoon finely chopped Italian parsley
2 tablespoons chives

Boil unpeeled potatoes in salted water for 25-30 minutes or until fork inserts easily. Slice into 1/4-inch slices. Add onion to warm potatoes. Mix together eggs, pepper, celery, pimento, ripe olives, and parsley. Add to potatoes and onions. Add mayonnaise to moisten. Season to taste.

Herbs in a Minnesota Kitchen

German Potato Salad

1 cup diced bacon (1 pound)
1 cup diced celery
1 cup chopped onions
3 teaspoons salt
3 tablespoons flour
2/3 cup sugar

2/3 cup vinegar
1/2 teaspoon pepper
1 1/3 cups water
8 cups cooked, sliced
   potatoes

Fry bacon and drain. Put 4 tablespoons fat back in pan. Add celery, onions, salt, and flour. Cook gently. Add sugar, vinegar, pepper, and water. Bring to a boil. Pour over potatoes and bacon in 3-quart baking dish. Cover and bake in 350° oven for one hour.

The Queen of Angels Anniversary Cookbook

Corned Beef Potato Salad

Serve in hollowed-out tomatoes for a beautiful presentation.

2 tablespoons vinegar
1 1/2 teaspoons celery seed
1 1/2 teaspoons mustard seed
6-8 potatoes, cooked, peeled
   and cubed
3 teaspoons sugar
2 1/2 cups cabbage, finely
   shredded

1 1/2 cups corned beef,
   chopped
1/4 cup dill pickle, finely
   chopped
1/3 cup green onion, sliced
1 cup mayonnaise
1/4 cup milk

Combine the first 3 ingredients and set aside. Place the potatoes (still warm) in a large bowl. Drizzle with the vinegar mixture. Sprinkle with sugar. Toss and chill thoroughly.

Add the cabbage, corned beef, pickle, and onion. Combine the mayonnaise and milk. Blend and pour over the salad. Toss to coat completely. Makes 8-10 servings.

Recipes from Minnesota with Love

Stuffed Pickled Pepper

12 medium-sized green
  peppers
2 cups finely chopped
  cabbage
1/4 cup grated fresh or
  prepared horseradish
1 cup chopped peeled onions
1/2 cup chopped green
  peppers
1/2 cup chopped sweet red
  peppers

1/2 cup chopped celery
1/2 teaspoon dry mustard
1 tablespoon mustard seeds
1/2 tablespoon celery seeds
1/4 cup salt
1/4 cup (packed) brown
  sugar
1 pint cider vinegar
1/2 teaspoon cayenne
1 teaspoon paprika

Wash all vegetables thoroughly before chopping; drain peppers; cut off tops and save; remove seeds and membranes. Cover tops and peppers with water and bring to boiling; boil gently 10 minutes, or until almost tender. Drain and let cool. Combine chopped vegetables. Mix remaining ingredients; pour over vegetables and mix well. Stuff into peppers; do not pack too tightly. Place top on each pepper. Tie in place with string. Serve whole as a salad, or slice and use as garnish. Good with ham, game, roast pork, and with baked beans.

People Pleasers

Kentucky Fried Coleslaw

2 1/2 pounds cabbage,
  shredded
1 carrot, shredded
1/2 medium onion, chopped
1 green pepper, chopped (if
  desired)

1/4 cup oil
1 cup Miracle Whip
1/4 cup tarragon vinegar
1/2 teaspoon salt
1 cup less 2 tablespoons
  sugar

Mix together cabbage, carrot, onion and green pepper. Set aside. Mix together oil, Miracle Whip, vinegar, salt and sugar; stir and pour over cabbage mixture.

Recipes and Memories

Chinese Salad

1 package chicken flavor, Ramen noodle soup mix

1 package shredded coleslaw mix

1 small package (1/2 cup) sunflower seeds

1 small package slivered almonds

3 chopped green onions and tops

Break up noodles. Mix with other salad ingredients.

DRESSING:

1/2 cup vegetable oil

3 teaspoons vinegar

2 tablespoons sugar

1/2 teaspoon salt

1/4 teaspoon pepper

Season packet from soup mix

Put ingredients in a jar and mix. Shake vigorously, as sugar is hard to dissolve. Pour over mixture about 1-2 hours before serving. Keeps well in the refrigerator.

Red Oak Grove Lutheran Church Family Cookbook

Best-Ever Cole Slaw Dressing

1 cup sugar

1 cup salad oil

1 teaspoon salt

1 small onion, diced

1/2 cup vinegar

1 teaspoon celery seed

1 teaspoon dry mustard

Beat ingredients together until very creamy. Store in covered pint jar in refrigerator. Keeps very well.

Great Cooks of Zion Church

Oriental Chicken Cabbage Salad

DRESSING:

3 tablespoons sugar
1/2 cup vegetable oil
3 tablespoons wine vinegar
1 teaspoon salt (optional)

1/2 teaspoon pepper
1/2 package Ramen seasoning
   mix

SALAD:

1 whole chicken breast, cooked, cut and slivered
2 tablespoons sesame seeds
2 ounces slivered toasted almonds
1/2 head cabbage, shredded fine

1 carrot, shredded fine
2 green onions, chopped fine
1 (3-ounce) package chicken-flavored Ramen noodles

Blend dressing ingredients together. Combine all salad ingredients in a bowl except Ramen noodles. Add dressing to salad and refrigerate until serving time. Shortly before serving, add uncooked noodles which have been broken into small pieces. Toss lightly. This recipe is especially good if chicken breast has been grilled with a teriyaki or mesquite marinade/glaze.

Feeding the Flock

Mustard Ring Salad

The Sodality ladies ham dinner was memorable for this delicious salad. Simply delicious with ham!!

3/4 cup sugar
Pinch of salt
2 tablespoons dry mustard
3/4 cup vinegar (fill with water
  to equal 1 cup)
4 eggs, beaten
1 envelope gelatin

1/2 cup water (to dissolve
  gelatin)
1 cup whipping cream
  (whipped)
1 - 1 1/2 cups shredded
  cabbage

Mix sugar, salt, mustard, and vinegar/water mixture; mix well and add beaten eggs. Dissolve gelatin in water in double boiler and stir until melted; add eggs mixture and cook until creamy, stirring constantly. Cool. Fold in whipped cream and cabbage. Pour into greased mold or tube pan and refrigerate.

Lutheran Church Basement Women

Fresh Apple Salad

8 cups chopped tart red apples,
  unpeeled
1 (20-ounce) can pineapple
  chunks, drained and juice
  reserved

2 cups seedless green grapes
1-2 teaspoons poppy seed
1 1/2 cups toasted pecans

DRESSING:
Reserved pineapple juice
1/4 cup butter
1/4 cup sugar
1 tablespoon lemon juice

2 tablespoons cornstarch
2 tablespoons water
1 cup mayonnaise

Combine pineapple juice, butter, sugar, and lemon juice in a small saucepan. Heat to boiling. Combine cornstarch and water to make a thick paste. Add to the hot mixture. Cook until thick and smooth. Cool COMPLETELY before adding mayonnaise. Combine salad ingredients (except pecans) and add dressing. Refrigerate until ready to serve. Add pecans right before serving.

Feeding the Flock

Taffy Apple Salad

This tastes like caramel apples!

1 (8-ounce) package crushed pineapple
1 egg, beaten
1/2 cup sugar
1 teaspoon flour
2 tablespoons apple cider vinegar

1 (8-ounce) carton Cool Whip, thawed
3/4 cup chopped peanuts
4 apples

Drain juice from pineapple and combine with egg, sugar, flour, and vinegar in medium saucepan. Cook and stir over medium heat until thickened. Cool completely. Fold in Cool Whip and 1/2 cup peanuts. Peel, core and slice apples. Fold apples and pineapple into cooled mixture. Garnish with remaining peanuts. Serves 8.

A Taste of Kennedy Cook Book

Mandarin Orange Jell-O Salad

2 (3-ounce) packages orange Jell-O
1 pint orange sherbet

2 (11-ounce) cans mandarin oranges, drained, reserve juice of 1 can

Add enough water to reserved mandarin orange juice to make 2 cups of liquid. Heat to boiling and dissolve Jell-O. Add sherbet immediately. Stir until dissolved. Remove from heat and add mandarin oranges. Pour into 1 1/2-quart mold or individual molds and chill until firm. Serves 8.

Recipes from St. Michael's

Bloomington's Mall of America is the Midwest's #1 tourist destination. A 4.2 million-square foot, 400-store, 78-acre self-contained city is the biggest shopping center in history. No other place in the world can you find Bloomingdale's, Macy's, Nordstrom and Sears under one roof.

Mandaran Orange and Almond Salad

1/2 head of lettuce, shredded
1 cup celery, chopped
1 tablespoon parsley, minced
2 green onions and tops,
  sliced
1 can mandarin oranges,
  drained

1/2 teaspoon salt
2 tablespoons sugar
2 tablespoons vinegar
1/4 cup salad oil
Few dashes Tabasco Sauce
Pepper
1/4 cup carmalized almonds

Place lettuce, celery, parsley, green onions, and oranges in salad bowl. Shake together salt, sugar, vinegar, salad oil, Tabasco, and pepper. To carmalize almonds, put 2 tablespoons sugar in skillet; cut 1/4 cup almonds crosswise. Add almonds to sugar. Stir constantly over low heat until sugar melts, turns brown and collects on almonds. Remove from heat and break apart. Toss all ingredients together. Makes 6 servings.

A Thyme For All Seasons

Raspberry Jell-O Salad

1 (6-ounce) package raspberry
  Jell-O
2 1/2 cups boiling water
1/2 cup sugar
2 (10-ounce) packages frozen
  raspberries, not drained
2 tablespoons lemon juice
1 pint whipping cream
1 (8-ounce) package cream
  cheese

3/4 cup powdered sugar
1 teaspoon vanilla
Salt (dash)
2 cups graham cracker
  crumbs
2 tablespoons butter
2 tablespoons sugar

Dissolve Jell-O in hot water. Add sugar, raspberries, and lemon juice. Chill until partially set (not stiff). Whip cream. Blend in cream cheese, powdered sugar, vanilla, and dash of salt. Mix graham cracker crumbs, butter, and sugar. Line large glass bowl with 1/3 of crumbs, 1/2 raspberry Jell-O, and 1/2 cream cheese mixture. Repeat layers and top with crumbs.

Great Cooks of Zion Church

Quick Jell-O Salad

1 (3½-ounce) box dry lime
  Jell-O
1 can crushed pineapple,
  drained

1 small carton cottage cheese
1 small container Cool Whip

Mix all ingredients together and chill. It's ready to be served.

Bethany Lutheran Church Celebrating 125 Years

Paper Cup Frozen Fruit Salad

2 cups commercial sour
  cream
2 tablespoons lemon juice
½ cup sugar
⅛ teaspoon salt
1 (8-ounce) can crushed
  pineapple, well drained

1 banana, diced
4 drops red food coloring
¼ cup chopped pecans
1 (1-pound) can pitted bing
  cherries, well drained

Combine sour cream, lemon juice, sugar, salt, drained crushed pineapple, banana pieces and enough red food coloring to give a pink tint. Lightly fold in nuts and cherries; spoon into fluted paper muffin cups (large size) which have been placed in 3-inch muffin pans; freeze. Cover with plastic wrap and store in freezer.

Remove from freezer about 15 minutes before serving to loosen paper cups. Peel off paper cups and place on salad greens. Yield: 12 large paper muffin cups.

Salem Cook Book II

Fruit Salad

1 can mandarin oranges
1 (1-pound) can apricot
  halves
1 (1-pound) can peach slices
1 (1-pound) can pineapple
  chunks

1 small package vanilla instant
  pudding
1 small carton strawberries,
  frozen
3 bananas, sliced

Drain juices from all fruits, except pineapple (save the pine-apple juice). Put drained fruits together in large bowl. Sprinkle with pudding. Put partially-thawed strawberries on top. Let stand overnight. When ready to serve, pour pineapple juice over bananas. Drain and put in salad. Mix and serve. Will keep 2-3 days.

First United Methodist Church Cookbook

Gertie's Cranberry Salad

1 large package strawberry
  Jell-O
2 cups boiling water
1 package frozen
  strawberries

1 can whole cranberry sauce
1 small can crushed
  pineapple

Dissolve Jell-O in the boiling water. Add the frozen strawber-ries, cranberry sauce and pineapple. Mix well. Chill until set.

Recipes from the Flock

Apricot Salad

1 package vanilla pudding
1 can apricots, reserve juice
1 can mandarin oranges

1 (8-ounce) carton Cool
  Whip

Cook pudding with 2 cups apricot juice (if you don't have enough juice, add water). Cool. Add oranges (drained) and cut-up apricots; add Cool Whip. Mix well and chill.

Sharing our Best / Bergen Lutheran Church

Frozen Party Salad

1 cup Miracle Whip Salad
  Dressing
1 (8-ounce) package cream
  cheese
1 (13½-ounce) can drained
  pineapple tidbits (1 cup)
½ cup maraschino cherries
1 (1-pound) can chopped
  drained apricots (1 cup)

2 tablespoons confectioners'
  sugar
Few drops red food coloring
2 cups Kraft miniature
  marshmallows
1 cup heavy cream, whipped

Gradually add salad dressing to soften cream cheese, mixing until well blended. Stir in fruit, sugar, and food coloring. Fold in marshmallows and whipped cream. Pour into 9x5-inch loaf pan. Freeze. Unmold on platter.

People Pleasers

Pear Mousse

1 large can pears
1 large package lemon Jell-O

1 (8-ounce) cream cheese
1 (8-ounce) Cool Whip

Drain pears, reserve juice. Heat juice to boiling and add the Jell-O. Cool. Place pears and cream cheese in blender and blend till smooth. Fold in cooled Jell-O mixture and Cool Whip till smooth. Place in serving dish and refrigerate. Garnish with fresh fruit of any kind.

Treasured Recipes from Treasured Friends

Vegetables

The North Shore offers adventurous hiking trails offering splendid
views of gorges and waterfalls. Lutsen.

Cheesey Potatoes

Excellent reheated in microwave.

10-12 potatoes, cooked, peeled, cut into 1-inch cubes
1 green pepper, cut into 1-inch squares
1 small jar pimentoes, chopped and drained
1/2 pound Cheddar cheese, cubed
1/2 pound American cheese, cubed
1/2 cup margarine or butter
8 tablespoons butter or margarine
8 tablespoons milk
Salt and pepper to taste

Mix together in a 9x13-inch buttered pan. Bake at 350° for one hour. Stir several times during baking.

A Thyme For All Seasons

Cheezy Hashbrowns

2 pounds hashbrowns
1/2 cup melted butter
1 teaspoon salt
Dash pepper
1/2 cup chopped onion
1 (10³/4-ounce) can cream of chicken soup
1 (10³/4-ounce) can cream of mushroom soup
1 (12-ounce) carton sour cream
2 cups grated Cheddar cheese

TOPPING:
2 cups crushed cornflakes   1/4 cup melted butter

Combine all hashbrown ingredients. Mix topping ingredients and sprinkle on hashbrown mixture. Bake at 350° for one hour in 9x13-inch greased pan. Serves 12-16.

Anoka County 4H Cook Book

Golden Parmesan Potatoes

6 large potatoes
1/4 cup flour
1/4 cup Parmesan cheese

3/4 teaspoon salt
1/8 teaspoon pepper
1/3 cup butter

Peel potatoes and cut into quarters. Combine flour, cheese, salt and pepper in bag. Moisten potatoes with water and shake a few at a time in bag until coated with cheese mixture. Melt butter in 9x13-inch baking pan and place potatoes in pan. Bake at 375° for about one hour. Turn once during baking.

First United Methodist Church Cookbook

Refrigerator Mashed Potatoes

We used this at Potato Day several times, using 250 pounds red and white mashing potatoes—served about 350 people!

5 pounds red potatoes
2 (3-ounce) packages cream
  cheese
1 cup sour cream

1 teaspoon salt
1/4 teaspoon pepper
2 tablespoons butter

Peel and cook potatoes. Drain and mash. Add cream cheese, sour cream, salt, pepper, and butter. Beat all together at low speed with electric mixer. Place in covered container and store in fridge.

To serve, place desired amount in baking dish; dot with butter. Cover and heat in microwave or oven until hot. Can make patties if desired. Roll in crushed bread crumbs and fry on both sides.

The Ultimate Potato Cookbook

The state bird of Minnesota is the loon. If you hear its haunting cry, you know you're in a place of unspoiled beauty—the Land of the Loon.

Hasselback Potatoes

1/4 cup butter
6 baking potatoes
1 teaspoon salt

2 tablespoons grated cheese
Melted butter, set aside

Peel potatoes and place in cold water. One at a time, prepare the potatoes as follows: Dry the potato and place in a deep serving spoon. Set spoon on counter. Using a sharp knife and starting near the handle end of spoon, slice across potato just until the knife encounters the edge of spoon, don't go through. Repeat, making slices about 1/8-inch apart. Return potato to the cold water and repeat with remaining potatoes. Butter a 9x13-inch pan. Preheat oven to 425°. Arrange dried potatoes cut-side-up in buttered baking dish and brush with 1/2 of butter; sprinkle with salt. Bake 30 minutes, then brush with remaining butter and cheese and bake until potatoes are done.

One Hundred Years of Sharing

Spunky Twice-Baked Potatoes

7 large baking potatoes
1/2 - 3/4 cup milk
1 (3-ounce) package cream
  cheese, softened
6 tablespoons butter
1/8 teaspoon garlic powder

1/8 - 1/4 teaspoon white
  pepper
Salt
6 ounces Cheddar cheese,
  shredded

Scrub, dry, pierce and bake potatoes at 425° for one hour. About 10 minutes before potatoes are done, blend milk, cream cheese, butter, garlic powder, and pepper until smooth. Add more milk or butter if necessary to get the right consistency. Heat in a saucepan; do not boil.

When potatoes are done, remove and immediately slice lengthwise, leaving shell intact. Spoon out cooked potato into large bowl; salt to taste. With electric mixer, beat potatoes slightly, and gradually add cream cheese mixture. Spoon mixture into shells of 6 potatoes; top with cheese. Heat in oven for about 20 minutes or microwave on high power until cheese is melted. Makes 6 servings.

From Minnesota: More Than A Cookbook

Deluxe Corn Dish

1 (16½-ounce) can
  cream-style corn
1 (16½-ounce) can
  whole-kernel corn
2 eggs, slightly beaten
1 cup sour cream

½ cup melted butter
½ box Jiffy Corn Muffin
  Mix
Salt and pepper
1 cup grated Cheddar cheese

Combine all ingredients, except cheese. Mix, and put in buttered casserole. Bake at 350° for one hour. (Do not cover.) Before serving, top with cheese and put foil over it, so it melts.

Our Heritage Cookbook

Scalloped Corn

1 tablespoon butter
1 tablespoon flour
½ cup milk
Salt to taste

2 cups corn
¼ teaspoon paprika
2 eggs, separated

Melt butter in saucepan until it bubbles. Add flour and mix. Then add milk and cook until thick. Add salt, corn, and paprika. Add well beaten egg yolks. Fold in stiffly beaten egg whites. Bake in greased casserole dish until firm (about 40-50 minutes).

Recipes and Memories

Honey Glazed Pineapple Carrots

3 cups carrots, peeled
1/2 cup water
1/2 cup brown sugar
2 tablespoons butter

1 tablespoon honey
1/3 cup crushed pineapple
Chopped chives or parsley for
garnish

Cut the carrots into 2-inch strips. In a microwave-safe dish, combine the carrots and water. Microwave on HIGH for 4-6 minutes, until carrots are tender.

Add brown sugar, butter, honey, and pineapple. Mix well and microwave for an additional 2 minutes. Sprinkle with chopped chives or parsley as garnish. Makes 6 servings.

Recipes from Minnesota with Love

Carrot Ring With Peas

2 cups cooked, riced carrots
1/4 teaspoon pepper
1 teaspoon melted butter
1 scant cup milk

1 teaspoon salt
1 teaspoon grated onion
3 eggs, lightly beaten

Blend well. Pour into greased ring mold and set in pan of wrm water. Bake 35 minutes at 375°.

PEA RING:
1 can peas (or frozen)   2 tablespoons butter

Heat peas with butter and fill center of carrot ring.

Our Favorite Recipes /Aurdal Lutheran Church

Minnesota Logginberries

Better known as baked beans.

2 cups dried navy beans
Pinch of baking soda
1/2 pound diced bacon or salt
  pork
4 tablespoons brown sugar
3 tablespoons molasses

1/2 teaspoon dry mustard
1 medium onion, chopped
2 tablespoons ketchup
1/2 teaspoon salt
Water

Soak beans overnight in water to cover. Then, add pinch of soda to beans and boil for 10 minutes. Drain and add the rest of the ingredients with enough water to cover. Pressure-cook at 15 pounds for 30 minutes, or bake, covered, at 350° for 6-8 hours or until tender. Serves 6-8.

Winning Recipes from Minnesota with Love

Calico Bean Bake

1/2 pound bacon
1/2 pound hamburger
1 cup chopped onions
1/2 cup catsup
1 tablespoon vinegar
1 tablespoon dry mustard

1 (1-pound) can red kidney
  beans
3/4 cup brown sugar
2 teaspoons salt
1 (1-pound) can Lima beans
1 (1-pound) can pork-n-beans

Brown bacon, hamburger, and onion. Drain. Add remaining ingredients. Mix and bake covered at 350° for 45 minutes; uncover casserole and bake for an additional 15 minutes.

Variation: 1/2 cup B-B-Q Sauce may be added.

Our Family's Favorites

The John Beargrease Sled Dog Marathon, a 500-mile race from Duluth to Grand Portage and back in early January, draws mushers and spectators from throughout the world.

Peas and Cucumbers in Sour Cream

3 cups peas, fresh or frozen
2 medium cucumbers
1 cup dairy sour cream
  (at room temperature)

3 tablespoons finely chopped
  dill
Salt and pepper

Cook peas in boiling salted water until barely tender; drain. Peel cucumbers, quarter, scoop out seeds and dice. Cook cucumbers quickly, about 2 minutes, in just enough boiling water to cover. Do not overcook; cucumbers should remain crisp. Drain immediately.

Just before serving, combine cooked cucumber and peas in top of a double boiler. Combine sour cream, dill, salt, and pepper to taste. Heat slowly over hot—not boiling—water until the vegetables are heated through. Serves 6.

From Minnesota: More Than A Cookbook

Broccoli and Cheese Bake

¼ cup onion, chopped
¼ cup celery, chopped
2 cups wild rice, cooked
1 can mushroom soup

1 (8-ounce) jar Cheez Whiz
  (plain)
1 box chopped broccoli,
  thawed

Sauté onion and celery. Mix with cooked rice and spread around the bottom and sides of a greased casserole. Mix together soup, Cheez Whiz and broccoli; pour into rice. Bake 20-30 minutes at 350°.

One Hundred Years of Sharing

Broccoli Casserole

1 (20-ounce) package chopped
  broccoli
2 eggs, beaten
3/4 cup mayonnaise
1 can cream of mushroom
  soup
18 Ritz crackers, crushed
1/4 cup butter
1 small package grated
  Cheddar cheese

Thaw and put broccoli in a 9x13-inch baking dish. Mix eggs, mayonnaise, and mushroom soup, and pour over broccoli. Put Ritz cracker crumbs and cheese on top. Dot with butter. Bake at 350° for 30-40 minutes. This can be made a day ahead, stored in refrigerator and cooked the next day.

The Centennial Society Cookbook

Broccoli-Onion Deluxe

1 pound fresh broccoli or 2
  (10-ounce) packages frozen
  cut broccoli
2 cups frozen whole small
  onions, or 3 medium onions,
  quartered
4 tablespoons butter or
  margarine
2 tablespoons all-purpose
  flour
1/4 teaspoon salt; dash
  pepper
1 cup milk
1 (3-ounce) package cream
  cheese
2 ounces (1/2 cup) shredded
  sharp process American
  cheese
1 cup soft bread crumbs

Slit fresh broccoli spears lengthwise. Cut into 1-inch pieces. Place broccoli and onion in 1 1/2-quart casserole. In saucepan melt 2 tablespoons of the butter; blend in flour, salt and dash of pepper. Gradually add milk, stirring constantly. Cook and stir until thick and bubbly. Reduce heat; blend in cream cheese until smooth. Pour sauce over vegetables and mix lightly. Top with shredded cheese. Cover and chill. Melt rest of butter, toss with crumbs; cover and chill crumb topping separately.

Before serving, bake casserole, covered at 350° for 30 minutes. Sprinkle crumbs around edge. Bake, uncovered, until heated through, about 30 minutes. Serves 6.

The Clovia Recipe Collection

Purple Passion Cabbage

1/2 cup chopped onion	1/3 cup sugar
2 tablespoons butter or margarine	1 tablespoon lemon juice
	1/3 cup cider vinegar
2 pounds red cabbage, shredded	2 teaspoons salt
	Pepper

Sauté onion in butter until soft. Add remaining ingredients and cook for 20-30 minutes or until cabbage is tender. Best if made the day before serving and reheated. Makes 6-8 servings. Fat 3 grams per serving/Vit C/Fiber/Cruciferous.

Minnesota Heritage Cookbook II

Colcannon

2 pounds russet potatoes	1/2 cup milk
3/4 pound cabbage	1/4 cup margarine
3/4 cup water	Chives

Peel potatoes and cut into 1 1/2 -inch pieces. Cook till done. Mash with potato masher (not electric mixer). Cover and set aside. Thinly slice cabbage and cook (low) with the 3/4 cup water till all water is absorbed. Stir while cooking. Heat milk, margarine, and chives to boiling. Remove from heat. Stir to melt margarine. Combine the cabbage and potatoes. Pour in the milk mixture and mix well.

Treasured Recipes from Treasured Friends

Tangy Beet Casserole

2 tablespoons horseradish (do not use horseradish sauce)	1/4 cup water
	1 pound cooked beets, peeled and cut in bite-sized slices
1 small onion, chopped fine	
1/2 teaspoon salt	1/4 cup dried fine bread crumbs
Pinch white pepper	
1/2 cup mayonnaise	2 tablespoons butter, melted

Mix horseradish, onion, salt, pepper, mayonnaise, and 1/4 cup water. Arrange beets evenly over bottom of buttered 8x8-inch Pyrex casserole. Pour horseradish mixture over beets. Mix bread crumbs with butter and sprinkle over top. Bake at 375° for 20 minutes, or until crumbs are nicely browned. Serves 4.

Chickadee Cottage Cookbook 2

Beets with Horseradish

Great for beet lovers and it can be done in the microwave!

HORSERADISH SAUCE:

3 tablespoons fresh
  horseradish, grated
2 tablespoons mayonnaise
2 tablespoons sour cream

1/2 teaspoon Dijon mustard
1/2 teaspoon white wine
  vinegar

Combine horseradish, mayonnaise, sour cream, mustard, and vinegar.

BEETS:

8 medium beets, washed and
  trimmed of all but 2 inches
  of stem
3/4 cup water
1 tablespoon unsalted butter

1 tablespoon prepared
  horseradish sauce
3 tablespoons half-and-half
Salt and pepper to taste
Parsley or dill for garnish

Place beets in 2-quart microwave casserole. Add water and cover. Cook on high for 18-22 minutes, turning dish once every 6 minutes, until tender. Uncover, cool, remove skins, trim ends and slice into 1/4-inch slices.

Wipe out casserole, add butter and melt on high for 30 seconds. Stir in the horseradish sauce, half-and-half, salt and pepper. Add beets, turning to coat with mixture. Cover and cook on high for 1 1/2 minutes or until heated through. Garnish with parsley or dill and serve. Serves 4.

When Friends Cook

Onions Celeste

6 Vidalia onions, sliced
1/4 cup margarine
1 can cream of chicken soup
1/2 cup milk

Salt and pepper, to taste
6 ounces Swiss cheese,
  grated
7 slices white bread

Cook onions (1/2 at a time) in margarine until transparent, about 10-15 minutes over medium heat, stirring frequently. Transfer to buttered casserole. Cover with mixture of soup, milk, and seasonings mixed together. Next put on grated cheese. Top with slices of white bread—crusts removed and dipped in melted butter or margarine on one side. Cut slices in half diagonally or crosswise, and place buttered-side-up on casserole. Bake at 350° for 35-45 minutes. Flip over to serve.

Duluth Woman's Club 70th Anniversary Cookbook

Walla Walla Onion Pie

4 sweet onions, sliced
1 tablespoon olive oil
3 tablespoons butter
2 eggs
1 cup half-and-half
2 tablespoons flour
1 teaspoon salt

1/8 teaspoon pepper
Pinch of nutmeg
2 ounces Swiss cheese,
  grated
1 (9-inch) pie shell, baked
Chopped parsley

Sauté onion in oil and butter over low heat until golden yellow. Beat eggs together; add half-and-half, flour, salt, pepper, and nutmeg. Mix; add onion and half the grated cheese. Pour into crust. Sprinkle with remaining cheese on top. Garnish with parsley. Bake at 375° for 25-30 minutes. Serves 4.

A Taste of Faith

Minnesota's Iron Range shares natural resources with the delicate balance of nature, history and technology. In winter, the Range becomes a snowmobiler's paradise with over 2,000 miles of well-marked, groomed trails.

Indian Squash

1 large winter squash
1/2 teaspoons salt
2 teaspoons sugar
3 tablespoons soft butter

1 1/2 teaspoons water
3 tablespoons light or dark
  molasses

Cook halved and seeded squash in salt water about 20 minutes. Place halves in baking dish. Make mixture of other ingredients, fill squash and bake in a 350° oven until tender. Makes 2 servings.

Minnesota Heritage Cookbook I

Pecan Squash

We serve it at Chickadee Cottage in the fall when we can get locally grown squash.

4 cups baked winter squash,
  mashed and beaten smooth
1/4 teaspoon white pepper
2 tablespoons brown sugar
1/3 cup melted butter or
  margarine

1/3 cup evaporated milk
1/2 teaspoon nutmeg
1 teaspoon salt
1/2 cup broken pecans
2 tablespoons light or dark corn
  syrup

Combine all ingredients except pecans and corn syrup. Turn into sprayed 1 1/2-quart casserole. Sprinkle pecans on top and drizzle on corn syrup. Bake at 375° about 30 minutes. Makes 6-8 servings.

Chickadee Cottage Cookbook

Summer Squash Casserole

6 cups yellow or green summer
squash, sliced
1/4 cup chopped onion
1 cup condensed cream of
chicken soup
1 cup sour cream

1 cup shredded carrot
1 (8-ounce) package herb
seasoned stuffing mix
1/2 cup melted butter or
margarine

Cook squash and onion in boiling salted water for 5 minutes;
drain. Combine cream soup and sour cream. Fold in squash
and onion. Stir in carrots. Combine stuffing mix and butter.
Spread 1/2 of stuffing mix in bottom of 12 x 71/2 x 2-inch baking
dish. Spoon vegetable mix atop. Sprinkle remaining stuffing
over veggies. Bake at 350° for 25-30 minutes. Yields 6 servings.

Feeding the Flock

Creamed Spinach

*Minnesota's vast iron ranges supply 70% of the iron mined in the
United States. The known deposits of the state's richest ore have been
exhausted. But the Minnesota earth still contains approximately 15
billion tons of valuable low-grade ore. Here is a recipe rich in iron.*

2 packages frozen chopped
spinach
1 medium onion, chopped
8 tablespoons butter, divided
6 tablespoons cream

6-8 tablespoons Parmesan
cheese
Salt and pepper
1/2 cup seasoned bread
crumbs

Cook spinach according to package directions and drain well.
Sauté onion in 6 tablespoons butter until tender. Mix onion
and butter with spinach, cream and cheeese. Salt and pepper
to taste. Put in 1-quart casserole. Mix bread crumbs with 2
tablespoons melted butter. Sprinkle over spinach mixture. Bake
at 350° for 30 minutes. Serves 4-6.

Winning Recipes from Minnesota with Love

Baby Boomers' Best

Homemade baby food for future generations. Freezes well.

1 (16-ounce) can "no salt added" stewed tomatoes
1 small onion, chopped
1 clove garlic, minced

1 carrot, sliced
1 small zucchini, sliced
1 cup barley
1 cup frozen peas

Cook all ingredients together over medium heat for about one hour, until barley is cooked and vegetables are soft. Place portions in baby food grinder, blender or food processor; purée. Makes 10-12 (1/2-cup) servings. Fat 0 grams per serving/Vit A/ Fiber.

Minnesota Heritage Cookbook II

Greek Spinach

A great combination of flavors!

2 pounds fresh spinach
1 tablespoon olive oil
1/2 cup pine nuts (or walnuts)
3 tablespoons chopped basil
2 tablespoons Italian parsley

1 clove garlic, minced
1 small onion, finely chopped
2 tablespoons cider vinegar
Dash of salt

Wash and tear the spinach, removing heavy stems. Heat a large skillet. Add the oil and nuts and saute until golden. Add remaining ingredients. Stir, cover, and cook 2 minutes, until the spinach is barely tender.

Herbs in a Minnesota Kitchen

Pickle Relish

8 medium cucumbers
3 onions
3 green peppers
1 tablespoon salt

1 pint vinegar
1 tablespoon celery seed
2 cups sugar

Grind cucumbers, peppers, and onions. Soak a few hours or overnight with salt. Drain. Add other ingredients and boil together for 10 minutes. Pour into jars and seal.

Our Family's Favorites

Sherried Hot Fruit

Enjoy!!!

1 (16-ounce) can pears
1 (16-ounce) can dark pitted cherries
1 (16-ounce) can pineapple chunks
4 bananas, sliced (more if desired)
1 (16-ounce) can peaches
1/2 cup (1 stick) butter, divided

1/2 cup brown sugar, divided
1 (21/2-ounce) package slivered almonds, divided
1/2 (16-ounce) package macaroons, crumbled
1/4 cup sherry or juice from canned fruit

Drain fruit and cut into bite-sized pieces. In a 3-quart casserole dish, layer fruit, dotting each layer with butter, a sprinkle of brown sugar and almonds. Top with macaroons. Sprinkle with sherry or fruit juice. Bake at 350° for 20 minutes. Serves 10-12.

Recipes of Note for Entertaining

Pasta, Rice, Seafood

Native prairie grasses are preserved in southwestern Minnesota at Blue
Mounds State Park.

Artichoke, Pepper and Olive Vermicelli

One of my favorite dishes.

2 hot banana peppers, sliced in thin rings

1 pound firm ripe Roma tomatoes, peeled and diced

1 tablespoon red wine vinegar

1½ cups pitted and sliced black olives

1 (15-ounce) can artichoke hearts, quartered

2 cloves garlic, minced (optional)

1 quart your favorite spaghetti sauce

¼ cup fresh parsley, finely chopped

1 teaspoon dry oregano or 1 tablespoon fresh

¼ cup olive oil

Salt and pepper to taste

¼ cup fresh basil, finely chopped

1 pound vermicelli pasta

Feta (crumbled) or grated Parmesan cheese for topping

Combine all ingredients, except vermicelli and cheese. Stir until thoroughly mixed. Cover. Refrigerate overnight. Just before serving cook vermicelli as directed on package to al dente. Drain well. Heat sauce to serving temperature. Toss hot spaghetti with sauce; or serve separately so each person can serve themselves. Top with cheese if desired. Makes 6-8 servings.

Note: You can often find hot banana peppers at Farmer's Market. If not available use sweet banana or yellow bell peppers and add red pepper flakes to give zing to the sauce.

Chickadee Cottage Cookbook 2

Herb Garden Pasta

What a treat—pasta and produce fresh from the garden!

1 pound uncooked pasta
1/3 cup olive oil
2 medium zucchini, sliced
2 bell peppers (yellow and red)
1 cup chopped red onion
2 medium tomatoes, cut into wedges

1/4 cup chopped fresh basil
1/4 cup chopped fresh chives
1/4 cup chopped fresh parsley
Salt and pepper
1/2 cup freshly shredded Parmesan cheese

Cook pasta according to package directions; drain. While pasta is cooking, heat oil in skillet. Cook zucchini, peppers, and onion until slightly crisp, stirring occasionally. Add pasta and remaining ingredients. Serves 8.

Herbs in a Minnesota Kitchen

Meatless Lasagna

2 cups fat-free cottage cheese
1 pound tofu, drained
2 eggs

1 box lasagna noodles
1 large jar spaghetti sauce
1 pound Mozzarella cheese, grated

Preheat oven to 350°. Spray 9x13-inch pan with cooking spray. Beat together cottage cheese, tofu, and eggs. Layer bottom of pan with uncooked lasagna noodles. Pour 1/2 jar of spaghetti sauce on noodles; spread. Add 1/2 tofu mixture; spread evenly. Sprinkle with 1/2 of cheese. Repeat layers. Bake for one hour.

A Taste of Faith

A misconception regarding the actual route of the Mississippi River during the signing of a 1783 treaty in Paris created the "Northwest Angle" also known as the "chimney" of Minnesota.

Lazy Lasagne

SAUCE:

1 - 1½ pounds Italian sausage	1 tablespoon dried basil
2 (8-ounce) cans tomato sauce	1 tablespoon dried oregano
2 (6-ounce) cans tomato paste	1 tablespoon sugar
1-2 cloves garlic, minced	1 teaspoon salt
1 cup water	

Brown sausage in Dutch oven; drain well. Add remaining sauce ingredients and simmer to blend flavors.

CHEESE MIXTURE:

1 pound ricotta cheese	2 tablespoons chopped fresh
12 ounces cottage cheese	parsley
½ cup freshly grated	2 eggs, beaten
Parmesan cheese	1 teaspoon salt
¼ - ½ teaspoon pepper	

Combine cheese mixture ingredients and set aside.

1 (8-ounce) package uncooked	1 - 1½ pounds Mozzarella
lasagne noodles or 8-ounce	cheese
sheet fresh pasta	

To assemble, cover bottom of 9x13-inch pan with ¼ of the sauce. Arrange ½ of pasta over sauce. Top with ¼ of sauce, then ½ of cheese mixture, then ½ of Mozzarella. Spread with ¼ more sauce. Repeat layers (pasta, remaining cheese mixture, remaining Mozzarella) and end with sauce. Cover with foil and bake at 375° for 30-35 minutes longer. Let stand 10-15 minutes. Cut into squares to serve. Makes 10-12 servings. Fat 26 grams per serving/Vit A.

Minnesota Heritage Cookbook II

In 1991 the city of Lindstrom constructed a new water tower in its industrial park. One of the local business owners asked the city to consider converting the water tower into a Swedish coffee pot. Completed in the spring of 1993, the design also includes the ability to have "steam" come from the spout of the tower, which will probably only occur during special city celebrations.

Spinach-Wild Rice Quiche

3 eggs, divided
1½ cups hot cooked wild
  rice
3 ounces cheese, grated,
  divided
¾ teaspoon salt

2¼ cups thawed frozen
  spinach, well drained
3 tablespoons skim milk
⅛ teaspoon pepper
1 cup sliced mushrooms

Beat one egg; stir in rice, half the cheese, and salt. Press firmly into an even layer on the bottom of a 9-inch pie, cake, or quiche pan. Beat remaining eggs; stir in spinach, milk, pepper, mushrooms, and remaining cheese. Spoon into pan. Bake at 375° for 30 minutes or until cooked through. Cool 15 minutes before serving. Serves 3.

License to Cook Minnesota Style

Wild Rice Hot Dish

1 pound Jimmy Dean sausage
1 medium onion, chopped
1 teaspoon chopped chives
1/2 cup slivered almonds
2 (4-ounce) cans drained
　mushrooms
1/2 cup butter or margarine
1 cup wild rie (soaked over-
　night)
11/2 cups water
11/2 cups chicken broth
1/2 cup Parmesan cheese

Brown sausage partially done, then add oion, chives, almonds, mushrooms, butter and wild rice. Cook over low heat for 15 minutes. Add water and broth, then boil slowly for 45 minutes. Stir in cheese. May be served immediately or rehaeted in 325 oven for 35 minutes.

Sharing our Best to Help the Rest

Rice and Pecan Casserole

1 pound mushrooms, sliced
4 green onions, sliced
1 clove garlic, minced
1 cup (2 sticks) unsalted sweet
　butter
2 cups uncooked brown rice
1/2 teaspoon dried thyme
　leaves
1/4 teaspoon turmeric
1 teaspoon salt
1/4 teaspoon freshly ground
　pepper
11/2 cups chopped pecans
6 cups beef stock or broth*
Whole pecans
Green onions, tops only,
　sliced

Sauté mushrooms, onions, and garlic in butter in a large Dutch oven until onions are golden, 5-7 minutes. Stir in rice. Cook, stirring with fork, until rice is hot, about 3 minutes. Add thyme, turmeric, salt and pepper. Stir in chopped pecans. Pour in beef stock. (May be prepared ahead to this point and refrigerated.) Heat to boiling. Bake at 400° for one hour and 20 minutes, until liquid is absorbed and rice is tender. Adjust seasoning to taste. Garnish with pecans and onion slices. Serves 10-12.

Note: *3 (10³/4-ounce) cans beef broth mixed with 21/4 cups water can be substituted.

Recipes of Note for Entertaining

Rosa Marina Casserole

1½ pounds ground beef
½ cup onion
¼ cup green pepper
2 cups cut celery
¾ cup Rosa Marina,
  uncooked
¼ cup soy sauce

1 can water chestnuts
1 can cream of mushroom
  soup
1 can mushrooms
2 cups boiling water
1 can fried onion rings

Brown ground beef, onion, and green pepper. Add remaining ingredients (except onion rings). Cover and bake for 45 minutes at 350°. Top with fried onion rings and bake for 15 minutes longer.

Winniehaha's Favorite Recipes

Willm's Wild Rice

1 pound wild rice
1 pound bacon, fried crisp and
  drained
⅓ cup butter

1 cup raisins
½ cup slivered almonds
Salt to taste

Cook wild rice according to package directions until tender. Break bacon into 1-inch pieces. In a saucepan, melt the butter. Add rice, bacon, raisins, almonds, and salt. Stir to mix completely and cook until heated through. Makes 8-10 servings.

Recipes from Minnesota with Love

Wild Rice

1 cup wild rice
1/2 cup onion
1/4 cup butter
1 cup celery
1/4 teaspoon sage
1/4 teaspoon basil
1 tablespoon parsley flakes

1/2 cup slivered almonds,
  browned (optional)
2 (4-ounce) cans mushrooms
  and juice
1 can consommé or chicken
  stock

Wash rice and soak 3 hours or overnight; drain. Put all together in a 2-quart dish and bake at 350° for 1 1/2 hours. Can't be beat! Warm up; add a little water (don't want it too dry).

Potluck Volume II

Wild Rice

Great for before-hockey game party or after-ski party! May be made day before and refrigerated.

1 cup uncooked wild rice
2 1/2 cups water
1 1/2 teaspoons salt
4 tablespoons butter
5 tablespoons flour
1 cup chicken broth

1 1/2 cups evaporated milk
2 cups cooked chicken, diced
3/4 cup mushrooms, sliced
1/4 cup pimiento, diced
1/2 cup green pepper, diced
1/2 cup almonds, sliced

Cook rice with water and one teaspoon salt. Combine butter, flour, and chicken broth. Simmer over low heat until butter melts. Add milk, one teaspoon salt, chicken, mushrooms, pimiento, and green pepper. Mix. Add rice. Place in buttered casserole dish. Cover with almonds. Bake at 350°, uncovered, 30-40 minutes. Makes a large casserole.

A Thyme For All Seasons

Wild rice is Minnesota's state grain. It is the only grain indigenous to North America, and 65% of all natural stands are in Minnesota. "Manomin" was harvested by the Indians from their canoes. The Department of Natural Resources protects the natural stands by allowing them to be harvested only in the traditional Indian way, ensuring that seeds will fall back into the water for the next year's crop.

Grandma Brown's Wild Rice

2 teaspoons salt
2 cups water
1/2 cup long grain rice
1/2 cup wild rice
1/3 cup butter
Garlic salt

MSG (optional)
2 bouillon cubes, dissolved in
  13/4 cups hot water
Parsley
Toasted, slivered almonds

Add salt to water. Bring to a boil and pour over combined rices. Let stand 30 minutes. Rinse rice with cold water. Drain well. Melt butter in skillet; add rice. Cook, stirring frequently, for about 5 minutes. Put in 1-quart casserole, sprinkle with garlic salt and MSG. Add broth. Bake, covered, at 325° for 45 minutes. Add parsley and fluff with fork. Sprinkle with almonds and bake uncovered for 10 minutes longer.

Anoka County 4H Cook Book

Wild Rice Casserole

3/4 cup uncooked wild rice
1 teaspoon salt
Dash of pepper
1 cup fresh mushrooms,
  sliced
1 onion, chopped
1 green pepper, chopped

2 teaspoons butter
1 can cream of mushroom
  soup
1/2 soup can of milk
1 cup grated Cheddar cheese
3/4 cup parsley (optional)

Cook wild rice with salt and pepper. Sauté mushrooms, onions, and green pepper in 2 teaspoons butter. Heat soup and milk, adding cheese so it melts. Add to rice. Stir in parsley, mushrooms, onions, and green pepper. Put in greased casserole and cover. Bake at 325° for one hour, or until rice is tender. Serves 4.

Our Favorite Recipes

Quiche - Shrimp

1 deep dish pie shell (frozen)
1 cup Monterey Jack cheese,
  grated
1½ tablespoons onion,
  minced
Small frozen shrimp, thawed
  and drained

4 eggs
1 pint whipping cream
1 teaspoon sugar
½ teaspoon pepper

Thaw pie shell and prick with holes. Bake at 350° for 15 minutes. In bottom of shell, place the cheese, onion, and shrimp. Lower oven to 250°. Mix eggs, cream, sugar, and pepper; pour into shell. Bake at 250° for 15 minutes; increase oven temperature to 350°. Bake 35-40 minutes or until set and golden brown on top. Let stand a few minutes before cutting.

Treasured Recipes from Treasured Friends

Impossible Seafood Pie

2 (10-ounce) packages broccoli
  or asparagus, thawed and
  drained
3 (6-ounce) packages frozen
  crabmeat and (or) shrimp,
  thawed and drained
½ cup sliced green onions
2 (2-ounce) jars chopped
  pimentoes, drained

1 cup sour cream
1 (8-ounce) package cream
  cheese
1 cup Bisquick
4 eggs
1 teaspoon Nature's
  Seasoning
Dash nutmeg
2 tomatoes

Preheat oven to 350°. Grease 9x13-inch pan. Spread vegetables, seafood, green onions, and pimentoes in the pan. Beat sour cream, cream cheese, Bisquick, eggs, and seasonings, pour over ingredients in pan. Top with thin-sliced tomato and sprinkle with Parmesan cheese. Bake 35-40 minutes at 350°.

Winniehaha's Favorite Recipes

Baked Seafood Au Gratin

1/2 cup butter
3/4 cup flour
4-5 cups milk
1 teaspoon salt
Pepper, to taste
1 teaspoon dry mustard
1 teaspoon celery salt
1 teaspoon onion juice
3 tablespoons dry sherry
1 teaspoon Worcestershire
  sauce

Dash of Tabasco sauce
1 tablespoon lemon juice
1 1/2 cups cheese
3 large or 6 small lobsters
1 package frozen shrimp
1 package scallops
1 bag crab or 1 can crab
1 (8-ounce) can mushrooms

Make a cream sauce using flour, butter, milk, salt, pepper, mustard, onion juice, and celery salt; stir and cook until smooth. Add sherry, Worcestershire sauce, Tabasco sauce and lemon juice. Add cheese; stir until cheese melts and is blended. Combine seafood (cut up into bite-size pieces) and mushrooms. Serve in individual seashells (keep sauce thick) and top with cheese and bread crumbs. Dust with paprika. If served on patty shells or toast, thin sauce.

Our Heritage Cookbook

Tuna Bundles

1 medium onion, chopped
1 small can mushrooms,
  chopped
1/2 stick butter
2 tubes crescent rolls
2 cans tuna, drained

1 1/2 cups shredded Cheddar
  cheese
3/4 cup sour cream
1 can French-style green beans,
  drained

Sauté onion and mushrooms in butter and set aside. Unroll the crescent rolls and put 2 together to make a rectangle, pinching the seam to seal. In a bowl, combine the remaining ingredients and mix well. Add the onion and mushrooms and stir to mix.

To fill crescent rolls, place 1/2 cup mixture in the center of the rectangle. Fold over and use a fork to seal the edges. Bake at 350° for 15 minutes or until golden brown. Makes 8 servings.

Recipes from Minnesota with Love

Baked Lutefisk

Soak 5 pounds of lutefisk in cold water for one hour; drain well. Preheat oven to 400°. Put lutefisk in an enamel roaster (others will stain) with rack in the bottom. Salt slightly. Do not add water; it will steam in its own juices. Cover roaster with heavy foil and then put the roaster cover on. Place in preheated oven for 20 minutes. If it is fork tender, it is done, and 20 minutes usually does it. Serves 4-5. Serve with melted butter or Creamy White Sauce.

CREAMY WHITE SAUCE:

5 tablespoons butter
5 tablespoons flour
2½ cups milk

2½ cups half-and-half
1 teaspoon salt

Melt butter and add flour. Stir until well blended. Add milk and half-and-half gradually. Cook in double boiler, about 10 minutes, or until thick, stirring constantly.

Red Oak Grove Lutheran Church Family Cookbook

Smothered Fish

Minnesota claims more lakes than any other state. Estimates range between 14,000 and 15,000 depending on how large a lake must be to "qualify." With all of the lakes in Minnesota, there are lots of fishermen and, hopefully, lots of fish to catch and prepare. Try this recipe if you're fishing for compliments.

3 pounds walleye, cod, trout,
  or whitefish (fillets or
  whole)
Salt and pepper
⅓ cup dry sherry
½ pound fresh mushrooms,
  sliced

6 tablespoons butter
½ cup grated Parmesan
  cheese
1 cup sour cream
Paprika

Place fish in a shallow baking dish. Season with salt and pepper. Sprinkle sherry over fish. Sauté mushrooms in 2 tablespoons butter; spread over fish. Combine 4 tablespoons melted butter, Parmesan cheese, and sour cream. Spoon sour cream mixture on top of fish. Sprinkle with paprika. Bake at 350° for 30-40 minutes, or until fish flakes easily when pricked with fork. Serves 4-6.

Winning Recipes from Minnesota with Love

No-Flop Flounder

2 (10-ounce) packages frozen
  spinach, thawed and drained
1 cup dairy sour cream
1 tablespoon flour
1/2 teaspoon salt
1/4 teaspoon nutmeg
Dash of pepper

1 pound flounder or orange
  roughy
2 tablespoons butter
1/4 teaspoon salt
1 1/2 teaspoons paprika
1/3 cup shredded Swiss
  cheese

Combine spinach with sour cream, flour, salt, nutmeg, and pepper; mix well. Spoon into shallow greased casserole or baking dish. Rinse fish; dry with paper towel. Place fish on top of spinach mixture in a single layer. Melt butter; brush on fish. Sprinkle fish with salt, paprika, and cheese. Bake at 375° for 30 minutes. Makes 3-4 servings.

From Minnesota: More Than A Cookbook

Minnesota Lobster

3 quarts water
1 medium-sized onion,
  quartered
Salt to taste
1/2 cup lemon juice

3 stalks celery, chopped
3-4 pounds fish fillets, cut into
  2-inch pieces
1 cup butter, melted, divided
Paprika

Place water, onion, salt, lemon juice, and celery in a 4-quart pot; bring to a boil. Add fish and boil for 5 minutes. Drain fish and place on a baking sheet. Brush with melted butter and sprinkle with paprika. Broil fish for 2 minutes. Sprinkle with paprika and serve with remaining melted butter. Serves 8.

Note: Northern Pike, Lake Trout, Coho Salmon, Steelhead or any other firm deep-water fish may be used.

License to Cook Minnesota Style

Grilled Salmon with Sweet Onion Relish

4 salmon steaks
2 large sweet onions, Walla
   Walla or Vidalia
¼ cup olive oil
1 tablespoon sugar

1 bay leaf
1 sprig fresh thyme
1 tablespoon balsamic
   vinegar

Grill salmon steaks 12-15 minutes, depending on thickness. Sauté onions in olive oil until transparent. Add sugar and herbs. Cook until mixture is caramelized. Add vinegar to taste. Serve sauce over grilled salmon steaks. Serves 4.

When Friends Cook

Poultry

Blocks of ice take on incredible shapes by talented ice carvers in a
contest at St. Paul's Winter Carnival.

Apricot Stuffed Chicken Breasts with Sauce Supreme

1/2 pound dried apricots
1 1/2 cups Marsala wine
1/4 pound prosciutto ham
1 cup soft bread crumbs
1 stalk celery, thinly sliced
1/4 cup chopped green onion
Pinch of rosemary
Pinch of thyme

1/2 teaspoon sage
1/4 pound Gruyere cheese, cut into 12 paper-thin slices
6 whole chicken breasts, skinned, boned, halved and pounded to thickness of 1/4 inch
6 tablespoons dry white wine

Soak apricots in Marsala wine for 2 hours. Drain, reserving liquid for sauce. In a food processor, process apricots with prosciutto until chopped fine. Combine apricot-prosciutto mixture with bread crumbs, celery, green onion and herbs to make a fine stuffing. (The stuffing can be prepared a day ahead and refrigerated until ready to use. Bring to room temperature.) Arrange one slice Gruyere cheese (folded if necessary) on each chicken breast. (Chicken breasts can be readied for stuffing early in day and refrigerated until ready to stuff.) Spread about a heaping tablespoonful of stuffing mixture on top of cheese. Fold in the short ends, and beginning at long edge, roll chicken up jellyroll fashion. Pour white wine into a greased 9x13-inch pan. Arrange chicken breasts seam-side-down. Cover pan with foil and bake at 350° for 30 minutes, until tender.

SAUCE:
1 cup half-and-half, room temperature
1/2 cup sour cream, room temperature
6 tablespoons butter
1/2 pound chanterelles or shiitaki mushrooms, thinly sliced

3 cups peeled, seeded and diced fresh tomatoes
Salt
Freshly ground pepper
Lemon slices for garnish
Parsley for garnish

Whisk half-and-half and sour cream together in a bowl; set aside. Melt butter in a heavy skillet over medium heat. Add mushrooms and sauté until tender, about 5 minutes. Add tomatoes and cook until thickened, about 10 minutes. Add reserved Marsala wine and cook until liquid is reduced to 1/2 cup, stir-

CONTINUED

ring occasionally, about 10 minutes. Remove from heat. Blend in cream mixture. Return to medium heat and stir until thickened to sauce-like consistency. Season with salt and pepper to taste. Arrange 2 chicken rolls on each plate. Spoon sauce over chicken. Garnish with lemon slices and parsley. Serve immediately. Serves 6.

Recipes of Note for Entertaining

Chicken with Almonds and Water Chestnuts

2 tablespoons oil
1 pound raw chicken, boned
  and sliced
1/4 cup split almonds
1/4 teaspoon pepper
1 tablespoon water
1/2 cup fresh or canned sliced
  mushrooms

1/2 cup sliced water
  chestnuts
2 tablespoons soy sauce
1 tablespoon cornstarch
2 tablespoons water

In a wok, heat oil and add chicken, almonds, and pepper; stir-fry until the chicken is browned. Add one tablespoon water, mushrooms, water chestnuts, and soy sauce. Stir-fry. Cover, lower heat and simmer 4 minutes. Combine cornstarch and 2 tablespoons water. Add to chicken mixture. Cook and stir until sauce thickens. Serves 4. Can be served with rice or chow mein noodles.

Kitchen Keepsakes

Chicken with Peanuts

1/2 cup water
1/2 cup dry sherry
1/2 cup soy sauce
2 tablespoons dark corn
  syrup
1 tablespoon vinegar
4 teaspoons cornstarch
Oil
6 large chicken breasts, boned,
  skinned and cut into 1/2-inch
  cubes

1 cup peanuts, salted or
  unsalted
1/2 - 3/4 cup green onions,
  sliced
3 garlic cloves, minced
1/2 teaspoon ground ginger
1 teaspoon crushed red
  pepper

Stir together water, sherry, soy sauce, corn syrup, vinegar, and cornstarch. Blend thoroughly and set aside.

Add oil to wok. Stir-fry chicken 2-3 minutes until chicken turns white. Make a well in center of chicken. Add peanuts. Stir-fry approximately 30 seconds. Push mixture up sides of wok. Add onions, garlic, ginger, and crushed red pepper to middle. Stir-fry one minute.

Stir sauce and add to center of wok. Bring to boil without stirring, about one minute. Cook additional minute or until thickened, stirring rest of ingredients with sauce. Serve with white rice. Serves 4.

When Friends Cook

Chinese Chicken

4 tablespoons soy sauce
3/4 cup ketchup
1/2 cup brown sugar
1 cup water

1 1/2 tablespoons vinegar
1 medium onion, diced
1 dash of garlic powder
6 skinless chicken breasts

Mix together. Salt and pepper to taste; pour over chicken. Bake at 375° for 45-60 minutes, until tender. Serve over rice.

Recipes and Memories

Couple's Club Xmas Chicken Divan

8 halved chicken breasts,
  boned
1/4 cup butter
6 tablespoons flour
2 cups chicken broth (2 cubes
  bouillon and 2 cups water)

3 tablespoons dry sherry
1/2 cup whipping cream
1/4 cup Parmesan cheese
2 boxes broccoli or 1 bunch
  fresh (precook for later)
Extra Parmesan

Lightly brown chicken breasts; set aside. In heavy 3-quart pan, melt butter; stir in flour. Add broth; bring to boil, stirring constantly, until thickened. Add sherry, whipping cream and Parmesan cheese. Heat just to boiling point—don't curdle.

In 9x13-inch pan, arrange broccoli and chicken; top with sauce and sprinkle with extra cheese. Bake at 300° for 30 to 40 minutes (if refrigerated, bake for 1 1/2 hours) or until bubbly all over top.

Salem Cook Book II

Cranberry Chicken

1/2 cup all-purpose flour
1/2 teaspoon salt
1/4 teaspoon pepper
6 boneless, skinless chicken
  breast halves
1/4 cup butter or margarine
1 cup fresh or frozen
  cranberries

1 cup water
1/2 cup packed brown sugar
Dash of ground nutmeg
1 tablespoon red wine vinegar,
  optional
Cooked rice

In shallow dish, combine flour, salt and pepper; dredge chicken. In a skillet, melt butter over medium heat. Brown chicken on both sides, remove and keep warm. In the same skillet, add cranberries, water, brown sugar, nutmeg, and vinegar. Cook and stir until the cranberries burst, about 5 minutes. Return chicken to skillet. Cover and simmer 20-30 minutes until chicken is tender, basting occasionally with the sauce. Serve over rice. Yields 4-6 servings.

The Centennial Society Cookbook

Baked Chicken Breasts

3 double breasts of chicken
  skinned
Salt to taste
6 slices of Mozzarella cheese
1/4 cup white wine

1 can cream of chicken soup
2/3 (8-ounce) package herb
  seasoned stuffing
1/2 cup melted butter

Use an ungreased 9x13-inch pan. 1st layer—chicken lightly seasoned with salt. 2nd layer—cover chicken with cheese slices. 3rd layer—mix wine and soup together and pour over above layers. 4th layer—spread stuffing over all and drizzle butter over top. Bake, covered, at 350° for 55 minutes or until done. Serves 6.

Note: Good to use whole cut-up chicken, and water instead of wine.

The Queen of Angels Anniversary Cookbook

Peach Glazed Hens

4 tablespoons peach jam
1 teaspoon soy sauce

Dash of garlic powder
2 game hens

Make glaze of jam, soy sauce, and garlic powder. Bake game hens as usual for 45 minutes; brush with sauce and bake for 15 minutes. Brush again and bake another 15 minutes or till done.

Treasured Recipes from Treasured Friends

Chicken Breasts in Wine

This is delicious served with wild rice. The sauce may be placed in a dish and served with the meal.

6 chicken breasts	3 tablespoons water
1 cup rosé wine	1/4 teaspoon oregano
1/4 cup soy sauce	1/4 teaspoon marjoram
1/4 cup vegetable oil	1 teaspoon ginger
1 teaspoon garlic salt	2 tablespoons brown sugar

Brown chicken breasts slightly. Place in baking dish. Mix rest of ingredients and pour over chicken breasts. Cover with foil and bake for 1 1/2 hours at 375°. Remove foil the last half hour. Turn breasts once during baking.

If you like to do things well in advance of company, skip the pre-browning and pour sauce over chicken and chill for several hours in the refrigerator. Serves 6.

A Thyme For All Seasons

Parmesan Chicken Breasts

Wonderful entrée for entertaining.

8-10 chicken breasts, skinned and boned	1 cup grated Parmesan cheese
3/4 cup oleo or butter, melted	1/2 cup grated Swiss cheese
1/2 tablespoon Dijon mustard	2-3 tablespoons parsley, chopped
1 clove garlic, crushed	1 teaspoon salt
1 1/2 teaspoons Worcestershire sauce	
2 1/2 cups canned dry bread crumbs	

Mix butter, mustard, garlic, and Worcestershire sauce. Dip chicken breasts in mixture and pat into mixture made with bread crumbs, Parmesan cheese, Swiss cheese, parsley, and salt. Tuck ends into a bundle shape and place in a 9x13-inch roasting pan. Drizzle remaining butter mixture over chicken. Bake at 350° for 1 - 1 1/2 hours. Can be prepared ahead. Serve with wild rice casserole.

Our Favorite Recipes

Chicken, Broccoli and Rice Casserole

Delicious!

1/2 cup celery, chopped	1 cup Cheez Whiz
1/2 cup onion, chopped	1 small can water chestnuts,
4 tablespoons margarine	sliced
1 cup rice	1 chicken, boiled and
2 packages frozen broccoli	deboned
1 can cream of celery soup	1/2 cup buttered bread
1 can cream of chicken soup	crumbs

Sauté celery and onion in margarine. Cook and drain rice and broccoli. Mix soups, Cheez Whiz, onions, celery, water chestnuts, and chicken. Place rice in large, flat baking dish. Pour chicken mixture over this. Put broccoli on top of this. Top with buttered bread crumbs. Bake at 350° for about 45 minutes.

Old Westbrook Evangelical Lutheran Church Cookbook

Broccoli and Chicken Hot Dish

1 large package broccoli	1/2 cup mayonnaise
1 chicken, cooked, boned, and	1 teaspoon lemon juice
cut in pieces	1/2 cup grated Cheddar
1 can cream of mushroom	cheese
soup	1 small can shoestring
1 can cream of chicken soup	potatoes

Layer broccoli and chicken in 9x13-inch pan. Mix soups, mayonnaise, and lemon juice and pour over. Sprinkle cheese on top. Bake at 350° for one hour. When nearly done, top with shoestring potatoes. Bake a few minutes more to heat.

Our Favorite Recipes / Aurdal Lutheran Church

Crescent Chicken Casserole

1/2 cup chopped celery
1/2 cup chopped onion
2 tablespoons butter
4 cups chicken breast, skinned
or 3 cups cooked chicken,
chopped
1 (8-ounce) can water
chestnuts, drained

1 can cream of chicken soup
1 (4-ounce) can sliced
mushrooms, drained
2/3 cup mayonnaise
1/2 cup commercial sour
cream
1 (8-ounce) package crescent
rolls

Sauté celery and onion in butter until softened. Heat next 6 items until bubbly, then mix with celery-onion mixture. Put in a 9x13-inch greased pan, then separate crescent rolls into 2 rectangles. Lay over mixture.

TOPPING:
1/2 cup slivered almonds
1 cup shredded cheese

2-3 tablespoons melted butter

Mix ingredients and sprinkle over top. Bake at 350° for 45 minutes.

Potluck Volume II

Chicken Casserole

2 cans cream of chicken soup
1 cup milk
1 (16-ounce) package California vegetables (broccoli, cauliflower and carrots)
3 chicken breast halves, cooked
1 teaspoon garlic powder
8 ounces Mozzarella cheese
1 can onion rings

Heat soup and milk together. In a 9x13-inch cake pan (greased), put vegetables and chicken (cut in pieces). Add soup and milk. Sprinkle with garlic powder. Top with cheese. Cover with foil and bake 45 minutes at 350°. Uncover. Add onion rings. Bake 5-7 minutes more.

Great Cooks of Zion Church

Spring Luncheon Hot Dish

2 cans cream of mushroom soup
2 cans cream of chicken soup
2 (15-ounce) cans evaporated milk
2 small packages slivered almonds
2 small cans mushrooms
2 small jars pimento, cut up
2 cups celery, cut up
4 cups cooked and boned turkey
4 cups chow mein noodles, reserve 1 cup for top

Mix all ingredients; cover with reserved one cup noodles. Spoon into greased casserole dish. Bake for one hour at 350°. Serves 10.

Great Cooks of Zion Church

Chicken Noodle Bake

4 ounces medium noodles
1 cup sliced celery
1/4 cup diced green papper
1/4 cup diced onion
2 tablespoons butter
1 (10 1/2-ounce) can cream of chicken soup
2/3 cup milk

1 1/2 cups shredded sharp American cheese
2 cups cubed cooked chicken
1/2 cup slivered toasted almonds
1/4 cup diced canned pimento
1 cup buttered bread crumbs

Cook noodles in boiling salted water until tender; drain. Cook celery, green pepper and onion in butter until crisp. Add soup, milk and cheese. Layer noodles, chicken, almonds and pimento. Pour soup mixture over all, stir lightly and top with buttered crumbs. Bake, uncovered at 350° for 30-35 minutes. Serves 6.

Salem Cook Book II

Chicken Curry Hot Dish

2 (8-ounce) packages chopped broccoli, cooked and drained
5 cups diced chicken
2 teaspoons lemon juice
2 cans cream of chicken soup
1/2 cup milk
3/4 cup mayonnaise

1/2 teaspoon curry powder, optional
Mild or sharp Cheddar cheese
8 ounces herb stuffing mix
1/2 cup melted butter or margarine

Put cooked broccoli in a greased baking dish. Top with chicken; sprinkle with lemon juice and dot with butter. Cover with chicken soup (mixed with milk, mayonnaise and curry powder). Top with shredded mild or sharp Cheddar cheese. Cover with stuffing mix which has been mixed with the melted butter. Bake at 350° for 30-45 minutes.

Sharing our Best to Help the Rest

Savory Chicken Scallop

4 cups diced cooked chicken
(turkey may be used)
3 cups fine, soft bread
crumbs
1¹/₂ cups cooked rice
³/₄ cup onion, chopped
³/₄ cup celery, diced
1 small jar (¹/₃ cup) pimento,
chopped

³/₄ teaspoon salt
³/₄ teaspoon poultry
seasoning
1¹/₂ cups broth (chicken
bouillon may be used)
1¹/₂ cups milk
4 eggs, slightly beaten
1 recipe Creamy Mushroom
Sauce

Combine all ingredients, except mushroom sauce in large bowl.
Spoon into buttered 9x13-inch baking dish. Bake in 350° oven
for 50-55 minutes or until knife inserted comes out clean. Cut
into squares and serve with Creamy Mushroom Sauce. Makes
12 servings.

CREAMY MUSHROOM SAUCE:
1 can condensed cream of
mushroom soup
¹/₄ cup milk

1 cup diary sour cream
A bit of onion

Combine ingredients in saucepan and heat slowly stirring well.
Do not boil.

Bethany Lutheran Church Celebrating 110 Years

Sally's Chicken

2 tablespoons oil
4-6 chicken breasts
Garlic salt
Butter
Sour cream

2 cans cream of mushroom
soup
¹/₂ cup milk
1 small can French fried
onions

Put oil in the bottom of pan. Lay chicken, skin-side-up. Sprinkle
with garlic salt. Put ¹/₂ teaspoon butter on each piece. Top
with sour cream. Mix milk with soup and pour over chicken.
Top with onions. Bake at 350° for one hour.

Clinton's 110th Cookbook

Sweet as a Peach Chicken

1/4 cup melted butter
1/2 teaspoon cinnamon
1/2 teaspoon nutmeg
1 teaspoon salt

1 (3 - 3 1/2-pound) chicken (8 pieces)
1 (10-ounce) can refrigerated buttermilk biscuits

SAUCE:
1/4 cup butter
1 tablespoon cornstarch
2 tablespoons honey

1/4 teaspoon cinnamon
1 (16-ounce) can peaches, drained

Stir cinnamon, nutmeg, and salt into melted butter. Dip and roll chicken in this butter mixture. Place in baking dish and bake at 350° for one hour.

In heavy 2-quart saucepan, melt 1/4 cup butter for sauce. Add cornstarch and stir, add remaining sauce ingredients. Cook on medium. Heat 4-5 minutes. Boil one minute. Pour sauce over chicken. Place biscuits on top of chicken and bake for 15-20 minutes or until biscuits are golden brown. Yield: 4 servings.

Anoka County 4H Cook Book

Roast Turkey

A seasoned Thanksgiving tradition, can be done with roast chicken also and served all year long.

1/4 pound melted butter
3 cloves garlic, mashed
1/4 teaspoon ginger
1/2 teaspoon seasoned salt

1/8 teaspoon paprika
Flour
1 (10-pound) turkey

Combine the first 6 ingredients, using enough flour to make paste. With hands, rub mixture inside and outside of turkey. Place in a large pan and bake uncovered at 325° for 2 1/2 hours or until brown, basting often. Cover with aluminum foil tent and cook for 2 1/2 hours or more until turkey is done and leg moves easily. May stuff with your favorite dressing. Makes 8-10 servings.

Minnesota Heritage Cookbook I

Minnesota Turkey Tender

10 slices cooked or baked
  turkey breast, warm
1 (6-ounce) box chicken
  flavored stuffing mix
1/2 cup cooked wild rice
2/3 cup roasted sunflower
  seeds

1/2 cup celery, finely chopped
1 cup water
2 teaspoons fresh parsley
1 can cream of chicken soup
1/4 cup milk
1 (2-ounce) jar chopped
  pimento

Cover the bottom of a greased 9x13-inch baking dish with turkey slices. In a medium bowl, combine the stuffing mix, rice, and sunflower seeds, mixing well. In a saucepan, combine the celery and water and simmer for 5 minutes. Add to the stuffing mixture and stir well with a fork. Spread over the turkey. Combine parsley, soup, milk, and pimento and blend. Pour over turkey and stuffing. Bake at 350° for 20 minutes. Makes 6 servings.

Recipes from Minnesota with Love

Aunt Helen's Casserole

This is a Chickadee Cottage favorite.

2 cups diced, cooked chicken
  or turkey (white meat)
1 teaspoon onion (dried is
  fine)
3/4 cup real mayonnaise
1 cup celery, finely chopped
1/4 teaspoon white pepper
1 can cream of chicken soup
1 tablespoon lemon juice
2 cups cooked rice (2/3-cup
  uncooked)

Combine all ingredients in large bowl. Turn into sprayed shallow 1 1/2-quart casserole. Refrigerate at least 2 hours, overnight is fine.

TOPPING:
1/2 cup crumbled, buttered
  cornflake crumbs
1/2 cup slivered almonds

When ready to bake, top with this. Bake at 375° for 30 minutes. Makes 8-10 servings.

Chickadee Cottage Cookbook

Baked Chicken Breasts

6-8 chicken breasts, skin
  removed
4-6 slices Swiss cheese
2 cans cream of chicken soup

1 small can sliced
  mushrooms
2 cups stuffing mix
1 stick margarine, melted

Lay chicken breasts in a greased 9x13-inch pan. Top with Swiss cheese slices. Spread undiluted cream of chicken soup over top. Sprinkle on mushrooms. Mix melted margarine with stuffing mix and spread over chicken mixture. Cover with foil and bake 75 minutes at 350°. Remove foil and bake 15 minutes longer.

Recipes from the Flock

Chicken Minnetonka

Elegant and easy.

2 whole chicken breasts,
  halved, skinned and boned
1/4 cup butter
1 teaspoon dried rosemary,
  crushed

2 teaspoons chopped chives
1/4 teaspoon pepper
1 (8-ounce) can refrigerated
  crescent rolls

SAUCE:
1 tablespoon flour
1 (4-ounce) can sliced
  mushrooms

1/4 - 1/3 cup dry white wine
1/2 cup dairy sour cream

Heat oven to 375°. In skillet, sauté chicken breasts in butter with seasonings until almost done. Separate dough into 8 triangles. Place 4 triangles on large cookie sheet. Put one piece of chicken on each triangle. Put other triangles on top of chicken and seal edges. Bake about 25 minutes until golden brown.

To make sauce, add flour to drippings in skillet; bring to a boil over medium heat. Add mushroom liquid, wine and sour cream, stirring constantly. Stir in mushrooms; heat through. Serve sauce with baked chicken triangles. Serves 4.

From Minnesota: More Than A Cookbook

Broccoli-Chicken Cups

2 (10-ounce) tubes refrigerated
biscuit dough
2 cups (8 ounces) shredded
Cheddar cheese, divided
1 1/3 cups crisp rice cereal
1 cup cubed cooked chicken
1 (10 3/4-ounce) can condensed
cream of mushroom soup,
undiluted
1 (10-ounce) package frozen
chopped broccoli, cooked and
drained

Place biscuits in greased muffin cups, pressing dough over the
bottom and up the sides. Add one tablespoon cheese and cereal
to each cup. Combine chicken, soup, and broccoli; spoon into
cups. Bake at 375° for 20-25 minutes or until bubbly. Sprinkle
with remaining cheese. Yield: 10-12 servings. Enjoy!

Favorite Recipes of Lester Park & Rockridge Schools

Aunt "B's" White Chicken Chili

1 pound chicken pieces
1/4 cup chopped onion
1 tablespoon olive oil
1 cup chicken broth or beer
1 can chopped green chilies
1 teaspoon garlic powder
1 teaspoon cumin
1/2 teaspoon oregano
1/2 teaspoon cilantro
1/4 teaspoon cayenne pepper
1 can white kidney beans,
undrained
1 can black beans, drained
Shredded Monterey Jack
cheese, garnish
Sliced green onions, garnish

Cook chicken and onions in olive oil (break chicken into small
pieces). Add remaining ingredients. Simmer 30 minutes. Garnish with the cheese and onions. Serve with flour tortillas, corn
chips or corn bread. Serves 4.

Favorite Recipes of Lester Park & Rockridge Schools

Public radio in Minnesota has the largest public radio membership support
anywhere. Garrison Keillor's popular "Prairie Home Companion" (now
called "American Radio Company") is one of its innovative programs.

Chicken Hot Dish

2 cups chicken, cooked and
  cut up
1 package (2 cups) Creamettes
  uncooked
1/2 pound Cheddar cheese,
  grated
2 cans mushroom soup
2 cups chicken broth or milk

1/2 green pepper, diced
4 eggs, hard-cooked and
  diced
1 small onion, diced
1 small jar pimento
1 can water chestnuts
Salt and pepper

Oil a 9x13-inch cake pan. Put all ingredients in pan and mix.
Refrigerate overnight. Next day bake 1¹/₄ - 1¹/₂ hours at 350°.
Cover to bake. Uncover last 15 minutes. Serves 10.

The Centennial Society Cookbook

Meats

The sunrise over Lake Superior is quite breathtaking as viewed from Palisade
Head. Near Tettegouche State park.

Beef Burgundy

Crockpot works very well for this recipe.

2 pounds chuck or round
  steak
1 tablespoon Kitchen
  Bouquet
1/4 cup cream of rice cereal
4 medium carrots
2 cups sliced onions
1 clove garlic (optional)

2 teaspoons salt
1/8 teaspoon pepper
1/8 teaspoon marjoram
1/8 teaspoon thyme
1 cup Burgundy, or a dry red
  wine
1 (6-ounce) can mushrooms and
  broth

Trim excess fat from meat. Cut into 1 1/2-inch cubes. Place in
2-quart casserole and toss with Kitchen Bouquet. Stir in cream
of rice cereal. Wash and scrape carrots. Cut into quarters lengthwise, and half crosswise. Add to meat. Add sliced onions. Mix
seasonings together and add to meat. Add Burgundy and mushrooms with broth. Cover tightly. Bake at 350° for about 2 1/2
hours, or until meat is tender. Stir every 30 minutes. Add more
Burgundy and/or beef broth if more liquid is desired. Serve
with noodles, rice or mashed potatoes. Serves 6-8.

Our Favorite Recipes

Mandarin Beef

2 pounds round steak, cut into
  1/2 x 3-inch strips
2 (4-ounce) cans mushrooms
  and liquid
1/4 cup salad oil
1 cup chopped onion

2 cups sliced celery
1/2 cup water
1/4 cup soy sauce
1 (10-ounce) can cream of
  chicken soup

Brown steak in oil. Pour remaining ingredients over. Bake one
hour at 350°. Serve on baked or cooked rice. Serves 6-8.

Note: Recipe is good to use when dinner hour is uncertain.
Turn oven low, 325° or lower, depending when ready to eat.

Kitchen Keepsakes

Cold Peppered Tenderloin
with Creamy Tarragon Caper Sauce

1 (1½ - 2 pound) beef
  tenderloin, at room
  temperature, trimmed and
  tied

1 tablespoon black pepper,
  coarsely ground
1 teaspoon coarse salt
2 tablespoons vegetable oil

Preheat oven to 500°. Pat tenderloin dry and coat all sides with pepper and salt. Place tenderloin in an ovenproof skillet just large enough to hold the meat. Heat the oil over high heat until hot, but not smoking. Brown tenderloin on all sides. Roast tenderloin for 15-20 minutes or until meat thermometer registers 130°. Let cool to room temperature.

SAUCE:

1 egg yolk
2 tablespoons heavy cream
2 tablespoons white wine
  vinegar
1 teaspoon Worcestershire
  sauce
1½ teaspoons Dijon
  mustard
½ cup olive oil

1½ teaspoons fresh tarragon,
  minced
1 tablespoon capers, drained
2 tablespoons scallions,
  minced
2 tablespoons fresh parsley,
  minced
Salt to taste

Blend the yolk, cream, vinegar, Worcestershire sauce, and mustard in blender or food processor. Add oil slowly in a stream with motor running until the mixture is emulsified. Transfer mixture to small bowl and stir in tarragon, capers, scallions, parsley, and salt.

Slice the tenderloin crosswise into ⅓-inch slices. Arrange slices on a platter and spoon the sauce over the meat. Serves 4.

When Friends Cook

The Minnesota Vikings professional football team was franchised in 1960. Because of their gold-trimmed purple and white uniforms, the defensive line became known as "Purple People Eaters." Quarterback Fran Tarkenton was known for his "scrambling" style of play, sometimes running for thirty or forty yards in the backfield before throwing a pass.

Pepper Steak

2 pounds round steak, cubed
2 tablespoons fat
1 can stewed tomatoes
3 tablespoons soy sauce
2 tablespoons flour
1/8 teaspoon pepper
2 teaspoons beef bouillon
  (instant)
1 cup hot water
1 large onion, chopped
1 cup celery, 1-inch size
  pieces
3 green peppers, chopped
1 can sliced mushrooms

Brown cubed meat in fat. Remove meat. Stir tomatoes, soy sauce, flour, pepper, beef bouillon, and water into drippings. Heat to boiling. Turn heat to low and add beef strips, onion, and celery. Cover and simmer about 45 minutes to one hour or until tender. Add green pepper and mushrooms and simmer until pepper is tender. Serve over cooked rice or noodles. If too thick add a little water or white wine.

Sharing Our Best / Home of the Good Shepherd

Crock Pot Swiss Steak

1 - 1 1/2 pounds round steak
Flour
2 teaspoons dry mustard
Salt and pepper, to taste
1 onion, finely chopped
2 carrots, grated
1 stalk celery, finely chopped
1 (16-ounce) can tomatoes
2 tablespoons Worcestershire
  sauce
2 teaspoons brown sugar

Mix flour, mustard, salt and pepper. Brown the Swiss steak that has been coated with seasoned flour. Put the browned meat into a crockpot. Sauté the onion, carrots, and celery. Add the tomatoes, Worcestershire sauce and brown sugar; stir and heat. Pour the heated mixture over the meat in crock pot. Cover. Cook on low 6-8 hours.
Note: If desired, peeled and halved potatoes can be added to the crock pot also. Delicious!

Recipes from St. Michael's

After Church Stew

1¹/₂ pounds lean beef, cut in 1-inch cubes

2 teaspoons salt

¹/₂ teaspoon basil

¹/₄ teaspoon pepper

2 stalks celery, cut in ¹/₂-inch diagonal slices

4 medium carrots, pared and quartered

2 medium onions, cut in ¹/₂-inch thick slices and separated into rings

1 (10³/₄-ounce) can tomato soup

¹/₂ soup can water

3 medium potatoes, pared and cubed

Place beef cubes (no need to brown them) in a 3-quart casserole. Sprinkle evenly with salt, basil, and pepper. Top with celery, carrots, and onion. Combine soup and water; pour over meat and vegetables, coating all pieces. Cover tightly and bake at 300° for 3 hours. Add potatoes and bake an additional 45 minutes. Serves 6.

The Clovia Recipe Collection

Individual Beef Wellingtons

1 pound mushrooms, fresh	1/4 teaspoon thyme
1 medium onion	Salt
1/4 cup butter	4 pounds beef rib-eye roast
3 cups bread crumbs	Puff pastry, frozen
1/2 teaspoon pepper	2 eggs, separated

Chop mushrooms, saving 10 caps. Cook chopped mushrooms with chopped onions in butter until liquid evaporates. Stir in bread crumbs and seasonings. Cool. Cut meat into 10 pieces; trim fat. Dry meat. Roll out puff pastry to 1/4-inch thick. Cut pieces large enough to wrap around meat. Place 1/3 cup mix on puff pastry. Top with meat and one mushroom cap. Brush edges of pastry with beaten egg white. Fold pastry over meat. Press to seal. Refrigerate. Thirty-five minutes before serving, pre-heat oven to 400°; brush beaten egg yolk over pastry. Bake 20 minutes for rare, 27 minutes for medium and 30 minutes for well-done. Serves 10.

The Centennial Society Cookbook

Italian Beef

1 (5 - 10-pound) rump roast	1 1/2 teaspoons ground
Peppercorn seeds	oregano
3 cups hot water	1 teaspoon garlic salt
3 beef bouillon cubes	1 green pepper
1 1/2 teaspoons black pepper	

Press peppercorn seeds into roast. Brown at 450° for 30 minutes. Combine hot water, bouillon cubes, pepper, oregano and garlic salt; pour over roast. Bake at 350° for 3 hours, covered. Lightly brown strips of green peppers in butter; pour on top of roast 1/2 hour before done. Slice beef when cool; return to juice. Serve on Italian bread. Juice may be used as au jus.

Great Cooks of Zion Church

French Dip Sandwich Au Jus

3-5 pounds boneless rump
  roast
1 large sweet onion, cut in
  1/4-inch slices
1/4 cup margarine
1/2 cup soy sauce
1 clove garlic

1 1/2 teaspoons Kitchen
  Bouquet sauce
1 package dry onion soup
  mix
4-5 cup water
French rolls
1 cup shredded Swiss cheese

Place roast in a crockpot or slow cooker. Brown the onions in the margarine and place on top of roast. Combine the next 5 ingredients and pour over the roast and onions. Cook on LOW for 8-10 hours. Remove meat and slice. Make sandwiches with bread, meat, and cheese. Put au jus in small bowls and dip sandwiches.

Treasured Recipes from Treasured Friends

Barbecued Beef

1 beef roast
1 onion, chopped
1 (14-ounce) bottle catsup
2 tablespoons prepared
  mustard

6 tablespoons white vinegar
6 tablespoons sugar
Salt and pepper to taste
1 tablespoon Worcestershire
  sauce

Boil beef roast until well cooked and it shreds with a fork. Mix other ingredients, then add to shredded beef. Simmer together for 45 minutes.

The Queen of Angels Anniversary Cookbook

The third largest structural memorial in the US, the Iron Ore Miner Statue, is dwarfed only by the Statue of Liberty and the St. Louis Gateway Arch. This 85-foot, free standing bronze and steel statue pays tribute to all the men who worked in the early ore mines of the Mesabi, Vermilion, and Cuyuna Ranges.

Main Street Main Dish

1 (3½ - 4-pound) beef blade
  pot roast
Flour
Vegetable oil
Salt and pepper
2 cups sliced onion
¼ cup water
¼ cup catsup
⅓ cup dry sherry
1 clove garlic, minced

¼ teaspoon dry mustard
¼ teaspoon dried marjoram
¼ teaspoon dried rosemary
¼ teaspoon dried thyme
1 medium bay leaf
1 (8-ounce) can sliced
  mushrooms, drained
2 tablespoons flour
2-3 cups water

Trim excess fat from meat. Dredge meat in a little flour. In large skillet, brown meat on both sides in a little oil. Sprinkle generously with salt and pepper; add onion. Stir ¼ cup water, catsup, sherry, garlic, and seasonings together; add to skillet. Add mushrooms. Cook, covered, over low heat or bake at 325° for 2 hours.

Remove meat to serving platter. Discard bay leaf. Sprinkle 2 tablespoons flour into drippings in skillet; cook and stir until mixture thickens. Boil and stir one minute. Gradually add water until gravy is desired consistency. Serves 6-8.

From Minnesota: More Than A Cookbook

Barbecued Beef on Buns

1 (3-pound) boneless beef
  chuck roast
1 medium onion, chopped
1/2 cup chopped celery
Water
1 1/2 cups ketchup
1/4 cup packed brown sugar
1/4 cup vinegar
2 tablespoons dry mustard

2 teaspoons salt
2 teaspoons Worcestershire
  sauce
1 teaspoon chili powder
1/2 teaspoon paprika
1/2 teaspoon garlic salt
Few drops hot pepper sauce
Hamburger buns

Place beef, onion, and celery in a Dutch oven; add water to almost cover meat. Bring to a boil; reduce heat. Cover and simmer for 2 1/2 - 3 hours or until meat is tender.

Remove meat; strain and reserve cooking liquid. Trim and shred meat; return to Dutch oven. Add 2 cup of strained cooking liquid (save remaining cooking liquid) and chill. Skim and discard fat. Add ketchup, brown sugar, vinegar, and seasonings. Cover and simmer for one hour, stirring ocassionally. If mixture becomes too thick, add additional reserved cooking liquid. Serve on hamburger buns. Yield: 15-20 servings.

Favorite Recipes of Lester Park & Rockridge Schools

Korean Barbequed Beef
(Bulgogi)

1 pound lean beef (sirloin or
  tenderloin)
2 tablespoons sugar
4 tablespoons soy sauce
2 tablespoons sesame oil
1 teaspoon ground sesame
  seeds

4 tablespoons green onion,
  chopped
1/2 - 3/4 teaspoon garlic
  powder
1/2 - 3/4 teaspoon black
  pepper

Thinly slice beef across grain into 3-inch slices. Combine rest of ingredients and add to beef slices. Marinate for at least 15 minutes. May be oven broiled or pan-fried. Serve with rice.

Bethany Lutheran Church Celebrating 125 Years

Bar-B-Que Beef

1 (5 - 6-pound) rump roast
2-3 tablespoons liquid smoke
1 (28-32 ounce) catsup
1/4 cup brown sugar
1 tablespoon Worcestershire
  sauce

1/2 tablespoon liquid smoke
1/2 teaspoon salt
1 teaspoon garlic salt,
  optional
1/2 teaspoon Tabasco sauce

Rub roast on all sides with liquid smoke. Wrap in foil and bake at 325° for 20-30 minutes per pound. Cool and slice as thin as possible. Return to foil. Mix remaining ingredients to make sauce and pour over the sliced meat. Close the foil and let meat stand overnight in the refrigerator. Reheat at 275° for one hour in foil package.

Vaer saa god Cookbook

Iron Miners' Pasty

Cornish miners introduced pasties to the Range.

PASTY DOUGH:

1 teaspoon salt	1 egg
3 cups flour	1 tablespoon vinegar
1 cup shortening	Water

Combine salt and flour; cut in shortening. Place egg and vinegar into a measuring cup; add water to fill to one cup. Blend dry and liquid ingredients until a soft dough is formed. Add additional flour if dough is too soft. Divide dough into 6 parts and roll into 6 individual circles.

FILLING:

6 cups cubed potatoes	1 1/2 pounds coarsely ground beef
2 cups cubed carrots	1 teaspoon salt
2 cups cubed rutabaga	Pepper to taste
2 tablespoons instant chopped onion, or 1/4 cup fresh minced onion	

Combine vegetables and beef; season to taste. Divide filling onto the 6 circles, placing the filling on half of each circle. Brush the edges of each circle with water and fold half the circle over the filling. Crimp the edges to seal well. Do not prick. Place on an ungreased baking sheet and bake at 375° for one hour.

License to Cook Minnesota Style

Cheez Whiz-Corned Beef Casserole

1 (14-ounce) package noodles	1 can cream of celery soup
1 (8-ounce) jar Cheez Whiz	1 can corned beef, diced
1 can cream of chicken soup	1 cup milk
1 can cream of mushroom soup	1/2 cup chopped onion
	1/3 cup buttered bread crumbs

Cook and drain noodles well. Add all other ingredients. Bake at 350° for 45 minutes to an hour.

Sharing our Best / Bergen Lutheran Church

Campfire Supper

SAUCE:

1/2 cup vinegar	2 tablespoons melted butter
1/2 cup ketchup	1 teaspoon prepared mustard
2 tablespoons Worcestershire sauce	Juice of 1 lemon
	Salt and pepper

Blend sauce ingredients together. Cut 6 squares of heavy-duty aluminum foil.

2 pounds ground beef	1 medium-sized potato, sliced lengthwise
Salt and pepper	
1 medium-sized onion, sliced	2 stalks celery, cut into 3-inch lengths
2 carrots, cut into strips	

Shape beef into 6 seasoned patties. Place each patty onto the center of a foil piece. Cover each patty with onion, carrot strips, potato slices, and celery sticks. Divide the sauce between the patties. Seal the foil pouches tightly. Place 4 inches from hot coals for about 30 minutes or until done.

License to Cook Minnesota Style

Fellowship Hot Dish

A good dish to take to a potluck or to a family on moving day.

1 pound spaghetti or fettuccini noodles, cooked and drained
2 eggs
1/4 cup milk
1 (32-ounce) spaghetti sauce
1 large onion, chopped fine
2 stalks celery, chopped fine
1/2 green pepper, chopped fine
2 teaspoons garlic, chopped fine
2 pounds ground beef, browned
1 tablespoon Italian seasoning
2 cups shredded Mozzarella cheese
20 or so pieces sliced pepperoni

Beat eggs and milk; toss with spaghetti. Spread in a greased 9 x 13-inch pan. Top with sauce. Sauté chopped onion, celery, green pepper, and garlic. Mix with well browned ground beef. Add Italian seasoning. Spread mixture over sauce. Sprinkle with cheese. Decorate with pepperoni slices. May also use cherry tomatoes and/or green pepper slices. Bake at 350° for 30 minutes. Let stand 5 minutes. Cut into squares. Serves 10-12.

Recipes from St. Michael's

Wild Rice Hamburger Hot Dish

1 cup dry wild rice
1 pound hamburger
3 tablespoons beef bouillon
1 large onion, chopped
1/2 cup chopped carrots
1 cup chopped celery
1 can chopped water chestnuts
1 can mushroom pieces
1 can cream of mushroom soup

Cook rice in salted water until almost done. Fry the hamburger until brown. Add the rice and remainder of ingredients. Mix together, and bake for 30 minutes in a 325° oven.

Wannaska Centennial

Hamburger Kraut Hot Dish

1½ pounds hamburger
1 small onion, chopped
1 (15-ounce) can sauerkraut
1 can cream of mushroom
  soup
1 can cream of celery soup

¾ cup water
5 ounces uncooked egg
  noodles
Slices American or Velveeta
  cheese

Brown hamburger and onion. Place in 9x13-inch pan. Cover with sauerkraut. Heat soups and water. Pat dry noodles over kraut. Cover with soup mixture. Bake covered in 350° oven for 45 minutes. Top with cheese slices and return to oven until melted.

One Hundred Years of Sharing

Cedric Adams' Low Calorie Casserole

There was a day when Minnesotans' bedtimes were geared to Cedric Adams' nighttime news. Cedric was a popular WCCO radio person-ality, who was often on a diet. He touted this dish, which has contin-ued through the years to be talked of as "The very best diet casserole."

1 medium head cabbage
1 pound lean ground beef

1 small onion, chopped
1 can tomato soup

Chop cabbage and parboil for 3 minutes. Drain. Brown beef with onion. Drain well. Alternate layers of cabbage with the meat and onion mixture in a 2-quart casserole. Pour soup, un-diluted, on top. Pierce layers with a fork several times, so soup runs through the layers. Bake, uncovered, 30 minutes at 350°. Serves 4-6. Serve with low calorie cottage cheese, sprinkled with chopped chives and parsley.

Variations: Some versions of this dish don't parboil the cab-bage, add a small amount of rice (about ¼ cup) and use tomato juice or whole tomatoes instead of the tomato soup.

Dorthy Rickers Cookbook: Mixing & Musing

Pizza Hot Dish

1 pound hamburger
1 onion, chopped
8 ounces sliced pepperoni
1/3 cup margarine, melted
6 ounces ready-cut bite-size
  spaghetti, cooked
1 each (15-ounce and 6-ounce)
  can tomato sauce
1/2 teaspoon basil and
  oregano

8 ounces Swiss cheese,
  grated
1 pound Mozzarella cheese,
  grated
1 (4-ounce) can mushrooms,
  drained
3/4 cup chopped olives

Brown hamburger and onion. Drain. Add pepperoni. Put melted margarine in a 9x13-inch pan. Add cooked spaghetti and toss together. Add tomato sauce and seasonings. Then add in order: 1/2 hamburger, 1/2 cheeses, mushrooms, olives, 1/2 hamburger, 1/2 cheeses. Bake at 400° 25 minutes. Serves 8-10.

Sharing our Best to Help the Rest

Cashew Casserole

8 ounces egg noodles
1 1/4 pounds ground beef
1 large onion, chopped
2 ribs celery, chopped
1 can cream of mushroom
  soup

1 can cream of celery soup
1 soup can milk
1/2 pound Velveeta cheese
1 cup stuffed olives, sliced
Cashews (1/2 can)

Cook noodles and drain. Brown ground beef, onions, and celery in small amount of fat. Heat soups, milk, and cheese and stir until smooth. Mix with noodles, meat mixture and sliced olives. Grease 9x13x2-inch pan. Spread mixture in pan and sprinkle with cashews. Bake at 350° until hot and bubbly, about 45 minutes to one hour.

Note: Can use 9-ounce package of fresh fettuccini. This can be made a day ahead of time but DO NOT put the cashews on top until you are ready to bake it.

Sharing Our Best / Home of the Good Shepherd

Spaghetti Pie

1 (8-ounce) package spaghetti, cooked and drained (vermicelli)
2 tablespoons butter, melted
2 eggs
1/3 cup Parmesan cheese
3/4 cup cottage cheese
1 pound hamburger
1/2 cup Italian sausage
1 quart Ragu sauce
2 cups Mozzarella cheese

Stir together first 4 ingredients and pour into greased 9x13-inch pan. Pat mixture down. Spread cottage cheese over spaghetti. Brown and drain hamburger and sausage. Mix with sauce. Pour over cottage cheese. Spread Mozzarella on top. Let sit for 6 hours, or overnight, in refrigerator. Cover with foil. Bake at 350° for 55-60 minutes.

Kompelien Family Cookbook

Cheeseburger Pie

1 pound ground beef
1/3 cup evaporated milk
1/3 cup catsup
1/3 cup fine dry bread crumbs
1/4 cup chopped onion
1/2 teaspoon dried oregano, crushed
3/4 teaspoon salt
1/8 teaspoon pepper
Plain pastry
4 ounces American cheese, shredded (1 cup)
1 teaspoon Worcestershire sauce

Combine first 8 ingredients. Prepare pastry to line one 8-inch plate. Fill with the meat mixture and bake at 350° for 35-40 minutes. Toss cheese and Worcestershire sauce and sprinkle on top. Bake 10 minutes more. Remove from oven. Let stand 10 minutes before serving. Trim with pickles, if desired. Serves 6.

People Pleasers

Today, Northeastern Minnesota is the only area in the lower 48 states where wolves still thrive. The International Wolf Center in Ely enlightens visitors about the myths and realities of these curious creatures.

Layered Tostada Bake

1 pound ground beef
1/2 cup chopped onion
1 (1 1/4-ounce) envelope taco
  seasoning mix
1 (8-ounce) can tomato sauce
1 (16-ounce) can refried beans
  (can use hot chili beans)
1 (4-ounce) can whole green
  chilies, drained, seeded and
  chopped

2 eggs
1 egg beaten
1 cup Bisquick baking mix
1/2 cup cornmeal
1/4 cup milk
2 tablespoons oil
1 cup dairy sour cream
2 cups shredded Cheddar cheese

Heat oven to 375°. Grease oblong baking dish (12 x 7 1/2 x 2). Cook and stir ground beef and onion in skillet until beef is brown; drain. Stir in seasoning mix, tomato sauce, beans, chilies. Mix 1 egg, baking mix, cornmeal, milk, and oil until moist, beat vigorously 30 seconds. Spread dough in dish. Spoon beef mixture over dough. Mix sour cream, 1 beaten egg and cheese. Spoon over beef mixture. Bake 30 minutes. Let stand 10 minutes before cutting. Garnish with green pepper rings, if desired. Makes 6-8 servings.

People Pleasers

Potato Pizza

1 package frozen hash brown
  squares
1 pound browned ground
  beef
1 (15-ounce) jar Prego

1 can Cheddar cheese soup
  (undiluted)
1 (8-ounce) package Mozzarella
  cheese

Spray a 9x13-inch pan lightly with Pam. Line with frozen hash browns. Mix ground beef, Prego, and Cheddar cheese soup. Heat through. Pour over hash browns. Cover with foil and bake at 375° for 45 minutes. Take foil off and cover with Mozzarella. Bake 15 minutes more. Let stand 10 minutes before serving.

    If desired, you can add a pizza topping of your choice to the hamburger mixture.

The Ultimate Potato Cookbook

Quick Tater Tot Bake

1 pound hamburger
1 small onion, chopped
Salt and pepper, to taste
1 (16-ounce) package frozen
  tater tot potatoes

1 can cream of mushroom soup,
  undiluted
1/2 can milk or water
1 cup (4-ounce) shredded
  Cheddar cheese

Brown hamburger and onion. Drain. Season with salt and pepper. Place in greased 1 1/2 - 2-quart casserole. Top with potatoes. Combine soup and milk or water. Pour over potatoes. Sprinkle with cheese. Bake at 325° for 30-40 minutes.

Kompelien Family Cookbook

Beef-Potato Hot Dish

1 large onion, chopped	1 can vegetable soup
1 pound ground beef	3/4 cup water
4 medium potatoes, sliced thin	Salt and pepper to taste
2 carrots, thinly sliced	1 can mushroom soup

Brown onion and beef in large skillet. Alternate layers of potatoes, carrots, vegetable soup mixed with water and meat in large baking dish. Add salt and pepper. Cover casserole with mushroom soup. Bake at 350° for 1 - 1½ hours. Yields 8 servings. (This hot dish has been used at many dinners, etc.)

Bethany Lutheran Church Celebrating 125 Years

Beef 'n' Potato Bake

4 cups frozen hash brown potatoes (thawed)	½ teaspoon garlic salt
3 tablespoons oil	1 (10-ounce) package frozen mixed vegetables
¼ teaspoon pepper	1 cup shredded Cheddar cheese
1 pound ground beef	
3/4-ounce package brown gravy mix	Canned French fried onion rings
1 cup water	

In shallow 1½-quart baking dish, combine potatoes, oil, and pepper. Press firmly to bottom and sides of dish. Bake shell uncovered at 400° for 15 minutes. Brown beef and drain. Add gravy mix, water, and garlic salt. Bring to slow boil. Add vegetables and cook on medium for 5 minutes. Add ½ cup cheese; place into potato shell. Bake uncovered at 350° for 15 minutes. Sprinkle with remaining cheese and onion rings; return to oven for 5 minutes.

The Oke Family Cookbook

Minnesota is famous for its many beautiful lakes and rivers. The name Minnesota is a Sioux Indian name meaning "sky-tinted water."

Perfectly Marvelous Mishmash

1 pound lean ground beef
1 (20-ounce) bag frozen Italian
  vegetables
1/2 - 3/4 cup Minute rice
1/4 teaspoon garlic salt

1/4 teaspoon basil (optional)
Salt and pepper
Sliced fresh tomatoes
1 can mushroom soup
Shredded Cheddar cheese

In greased 2-quart casserole, break up beef, not browned. Mix vegetables with rice, garlic salt, basil, salt and pepper. Put this mixture over meat. (The packaged Italian vegetable combination in the grocer's freezer includes sliced carrots, zucchini, cauliflower, and lima beans. If you have garden vegetables, you will want to make up your own "Italian combo." I used just carrots, zucchini and limas. Don't use any potatoes.)

Cover with sliced fresh tomatoes, peeled. Spread over all one can mushroom soup, undiluted. Refrigerate casserole overnight or a few hours. Bake, covered, at 350° for 2 hours. The last half hour top with generous sprinkling of shredded Cheddar.

Dorthy Rickers Cookbook: Mixing & Musing

Sour Cream Meat Loaf and Mashed Potatoes

2 eggs
1 (8-ounce) carton sour
  cream
1/4 cup milk
1/2 cup fine dry bread
  crumbs
1/4 cup finely chopped onion
2 tablespoons snipped
  parsley
1 tablespoon Worcestershire
  sauce

1 tablespoon Dijon-style
  mustard
1/4 teaspoon salt
1/4 teaspoon pepper
1 1/2 pounds lean ground
  beef
1 (.75-ounce) package brown
  gravy mix
1 recipe mashed potatoes

In a large bowl combine eggs, 1/2 cup sour cream, and milk; stir in bread crumbs, onion, parsley, Worcestershire sauce, mustard, salt and pepper. Add beef, mix thoroughly. Pat into a 9x5x3-inch loaf pan. Bake uncovered in a 350° oven for 1 1/4 hours or until meat thermometer registers 170°.

Gravy: Stir together remaining sour cream and gravy mix. Add water as called for on package. Cook according to package directions.

POTATOES:
4 potatoes
2 tablespoons butter
1/4 teaspoon salt

1 dash pepper
2-3 tablespoons milk

Boil potatoes 20-25 minutes; drain. Beat or mash. Add butter, salt, pepper, and milk. Beat until light and fluffy.

A Taste of Kennedy Cook Book

International Falls was the inspiration for Frostbite Falls, the hometown of cartoon characters Bullwinkle Moose and Rocket J. Squirrel—"the sleepy little town where nothing ever happens." International Falls is also the home of the Smokey the Bear statue, which is 26 feet high and weighs 82 tons, and a 22-foot tall thermometer that stands in Smokey Bear Park.

Wild Rice and Meatballs

MEATBALLS:

1/2 cup bread crumbs
3/4 cup milk
1 teaspoon salt
1 teaspoon dry mustard

1 teaspoon Worcestershire
 sauce
2 pounds extra lean ground
 beef

Mix and shape into meatballs; brown.

RICE:

1 cup celery, chopped
1 cup onion, chopped
1 can cream of mushroom
 soup
1 can water

1/4 cup Burgundy wine
1 cup ripe olives, chopped
11/4 cups wild rice
1 cup grated Swiss cheese

Sauté celery and onion; add remaining ingredients except cheese. Bake covered at 350° for 45 minutes. Add cheese and bake 45 minutes more.

Vaer saa god Cookbook

Scandinavian Meatballs

The result is authentically Northern European!

2 eggs
4 Holland rusks, crushed
1/4 cup milk
1 onion, chopped fine
1 tablespoon butter
1/4 cup water

11/2 pounds round steak,
 ground
1/2 pound pork shoulder,
 ground
1 teaspoon salt
1/4 teaspoon allspice

Beat eggs slightly in large bowl. Add the crushed rusks and milk. Sauté the chopped onion in skillet in butter and water for 5-10 minutes (until the onions are transparent). Add to the rusks and mix. Add the meat and spices. Mix. Roll into ball shape and fry in butter.

A Thyme For All Seasons

Norwegian Meatballs

A good reason to use the chafing dish tucked away in your cupboard...

1¹/₄ pounds lean ground beef
³/₄ pound ground pork and veal combined
2 slices soft white bread without crusts
²/₃ cup light cream
2 eggs, lightly beaten
1 small onion, grated
2 small or 1 large clove garlic, minced
1 tablespoon chopped parsley
1 teaspoon salt
¹/₄ teaspoon pepper
¹/₄ teaspoon nutmeg
¹/₄ teaspoon allspice
2 tablespoons margarine
1 tablespoon oil
1¹/₂ quarts beef bouillon
¹/₄ cup flour
1 cup water
Salt and pepper to taste

Mix together beef, pork, and veal in a large bowl. In separate bowl, soak bread in cream for a few minutes, then add to meat. Next add eggs, onion, garlic, parsley, salt, pepper, nutmeg, and allspice. Mix thoroughly, using hands, and shape into 1-inch balls; refrigerate for 30 minutes. Heat margarine and oil in skillet and fry meatballs until lightly browned.

In a large kettle or Dutch oven, heat the beef bouillon. Drop browned meatballs into bouillon and simmer covered for 20 minutes. Mix flour and water together, add to broth and simmer 10 minutes longer. Season to taste with salt and pepper. Makes 8 servings.

Minnesota Heritage Cookbook I

Waikiki Meatballs

2 pounds hamburger or ground
  pork
2/3 cup cracker crumbs
1/3 cup chopped onion

1 egg
1/4 teaspoon ginger
1/4 cup milk

SAUCE:
1/2 cup brown sugar
2 tablespoons cornstarch
1 (20-ounce) can crushed
  pineapple, drained, reserve
  pineapple

1/3 cup vinegar
1 tablespoon soy sauce

Mix together ingredients for meat. Form into balls and brown
in saucepan. In separate saucepan, stir sauce ingredients together until smooth; boil for one minute. Sprinkle crushed pineapple over meatballs and pour sauce over. Simmer until warm,
or keep in crockpot.

Recipes and Memories

Swedish Meat Balls

1 1/2 pounds ground beef
1/2 cup minced onion
1 cup oatmeal
1 tablespoon minced parsely
1 1/2 teaspoons salt

1/8 teaspoon pepper
1 teaspoon Worcestershire
  sauce
1 egg
1/2 cup milk

Mix togehter and shape into walnut-sized balls. Brown in 1/2
cup hot oil. Remove the meat.

GRAVY:
1/4 cup flour
1 teaspoon paprika
1/2 teaspoon salt

1/8 teaspoon pepper
2 cups boiling water
3/4 cup milk

Stir into the fat, the flour, paprika, salt and pepper. Stir in the
water and milk. Heat. Return meat to gravy and simmer 15-
20 minutes.

Wannaska Centennial

Barbequed Meat Balls

1 (13-ounce) can evaporated
  milk
3 pounds hamburger
2 eggs
2 cups quick oatmeal

1 cup chopped onion
2 teaspoons salt
1 teaspoon chili powder
1/2 teaspoon pepper

Mix and shape into golf ball-size balls. Put in single layer in 9x13-inch pan.

MEAT SAUCE:
2 cups catsup
1 cup brown sugar
2 tablespoons liquid smoke,
  optional

1/4 teaspoon garlic powder
1/2 cup chopped onion

Dissolve and pour over meat balls. Bake one hour at 350°.

Finn Creek Museum Cookbook

Barbecue Cups

3/4 pound ground beef
1/2 cup barbecue sauce
2 teaspoons instant onion
Dash garlic powder

1 (10-ounce) package
  refrigerator biscuits
2 ounces grated Cheddar
  cheese

Brown ground beef; drain off excess grease. Add barbecue sauce, instant onion and garlic powder; mix well. Flatten each biscuit and press into a muffin tin. Spoon beef mixture into center of each biscuit cup; then top with grated cheese. Bake at 400° for 10-12 minutes. Makes 10 cups.

People Pleasers

On September 7, 1876, Jesse James and his gang rode into Northfield to rob the First National Bank. The raid was thwarted by the brave townspeople; but Jesse James, Cole Younger, and the gang members rode out of town on what is now known as The Outlaw Trail.

Potato Hamburgers

1 pound lean ground beef
1 cup grated raw potato
3 tablespoons minced onions
1 tablespoon minced parsley

1 egg
1 teaspoon salt
1/4 teaspoon pepper

Mix well. Shape into 1/2-inch thick patties. Place on broiler rack. Brush with your favorite barbecue sauce. Broil three inches from heat until well browned. Turn and broil other side. Baste occasionaly with barbecue sauce (or tomato sauce or cat-sup).

To pan fry, brown on one side, turn and brown on other side. Reduce heat and fry until done.

People Pleasers

Crockpot Spareribs

4 pounds country spareribs
1/2 cup cider vinegar
1 tablespoon soy sauce
1 teaspoon salt
Dash cayenne powder

1 can tomato soup
1/2 cup brown sugar
1 teaspoon celery seed
1 teaspoon chili powder

Layer ribs in pot. Combine all other ingredients and pour over ribs. Cook on medium heat 6-8 hours.

One Hundred Years of Sharing

Barbecued Ribs

About 5 pounds spareribs	Lipton onion soup mix
Salt	2 cups water

Cut ribs into serving pieces. Put ribs in a single layer in a baking pan. Sprinkle lightly with salt. Sprinkle with Lipton soup mix. Add a couple cups of water. Bake in 325° oven until tender. Pick ribs out of pan and drain pan. Save the juice for a base of a great gravy.

SAUCE:

Kraft with Onion Bar-B-Q Sauce	2 tablespoons brown sugar
	1 tablespoon vinegar
1 teaspoon prepared mustard	

Make a sauce of the above ingredients. Dip the ribs in this sauce and lay a single layer in pan. Bake in 325° oven until heated through.

Wannaska Centennial

Barbecued Pork Ribs

I think it's the combination of honey, chicken broth, and wine-based soy sauce which makes for such a pleasing sauce. We wouldn't think of using the bottled stuff after finding this recipe—and the ribs won't taste any better on the grill!

4 pounds ribs (spareribs or country style)	5 tablespoons honey
	3 tablespoons Kikkoman Soy Sauce
1 cup hot chicken broth or bouillon	2 tablespoons catsup
3 tablespoons sugar	1 teaspoon salt

If the ribs are fatty, cover with water and boil for 10 minutes. Remove from water and place in baking dish. Mix remaining ingredients and pour over ribs. Marinate ribs for 2 hours, turning occasionally. Bake at 300° for 2 - 2½ hours, again turning ribs occasionally. Makes 5-6 servings.

A Thyme For All Seasons

Pork Tenderloin

1 (2 - 3-pound) pork
  tenderloin
3 strips bacon
1/2 cup soy sauce
1 tablespoon grated onion

1 clove garlic, minced
1 tablespoon vinegar
1/8 teaspoon cayenne pepper
1/2 teaspoon sugar

Wrap tenderloin with bacon. Fasten with toothpicks. Mix remaining ingredients and pour over meat. Marinate 3 hours or overnight. Turn once. Bake at 300° for 2 hours or until tender, basting often. Serve over rice with juices.

Sharing Our Best / Home of the Good Shepherd

Fantastic Pork Fajitas

1 pound pork strips
1/2 medium onion, peeled and
  sliced
1 green pepper, seeded and
  sliced

2 teaspoons vegetable oil
4 flour tortillas, warmed
Broccoli, pea pods, or any
  favorite vegetable can be
  added

Heat large non-stick skillet over medium-high heat. Add oil; heat until hot. Toss pork strips (easier to cut when meat is partly frozen), onion and pepper slices into skillet; stir-fry quick, 4-5 minutes. Roll up portions of the meat mixture in flour tortillas and serve with salsa, if desired.

Recipes and Memories

Mushroom-Onion Pork Chops

5 or 6 chops
Salt and pepper
1 package dry onion soup
  mix

1 can cream of mushroom
  soup
1/4 can milk

Brown pork chops. Put in a 9x13-inch cake pan. Sprinkle with salt and pepper to taste. Mix onion soup mix and cream of mushroom soup. Thin with milk. Pour over chops. Bake in 350° oven for one hour. Soup sauce makes good gravy.

Note: May use recipe in crockpot.

Recipes from the Flock

Marinated Pork Chops

1/4 cup soy sauce
1/2 cup water
1 clove garlic, sliced
1/4 cup oil

2 teaspoons brown sugar
6 pork chops
Salt

Mix ingredients together and pour over trimmed pork chops. Marinate 3 to 4 hours. Best when cooked on an outdoor grill— 7 minutes on each side.

Salem Cook Book II

Crockpot Pork Chops

Place enough pork chops for your family in the crockpot. Add one can cream of mushroom or cream of chicken soup, salt and pepper. Turn pot on high for 4-5 hours. The chops are so tender, they fall apart, and the soup may be used for gravy.

Kitchen Keepsakes

Trainwreck Pork Chops

1 (8-ounce) can stewed
  tomatoes
1/4 cup instant minced onion
1 teaspoon garlic salt
1 teaspoon crushed oregano
1 teaspoon sugar

1/2 teaspoon pepper
1 (8-ounce) can tomato sauce
1 tablespoon hickory smoke
  barbecue sauce
4 loin pork chops (3/4-inch
  thick)

Break up tomatoes with spoon and add onion, garlic salt, oregano, sugar, pepper, tomato sauce, and barbecue sauce. Pour 1/2 of mixture into shallow 2-quart casserole. Trim fat from chops and arrange in sauce, then pour remaining sauce over top. Bake covered at 350° for one hour. Serve over hot cooked noodles.

Duluth Woman's Club 70th Anniversary Cookbook

Pork Hocks and Sauerkraut

2 pork hocks
Water to cover
1/2 teaspoon salt
1/8 teaspoon pepper

1 medium onion, quartered
2 stalks celery, sliced
3 1/2 cups sauerkraut
Brown sugar

Boil hocks in water with salt, pepper, onion, and celery. Cook until tender, about 3 hours. Remove meat and cool. Trim lean meat off hocks and skim fat off broth. (Can be put in freezer a few minutes to solidify fat for easy removal.) Put broth and sauerkraut in a roaster. Lightly sprinkle with brown sugar. Add meat and cover. Bake at 350° for about 2 hours. Serve with boiled buttered potatoes. Makes 4-6 servings.

Minnesota Heritage Cookbook I

Ham Loaves

2 pounds ground beef
2 pounds ground ham
2 pounds ground pork
4 cups crushed graham
  crackers

4 eggs, beaten
2 1/2 cups milk

Combine above ingredients, mixing well. Divide into 3 regular-size loaf pans. Bake one hour at 325°. Remove from oven and poke holes in meat. Pour over the following sauce that has been heated and blended. Bake one more hour.

SAUCE:
1 can tomato soup
1 cup brown sugar

1/3 cup vinegar
1 teaspoon dry mustard

First United Methodist Church Cookbook

Ham Logs with Raisin Sauce

1 pound ground ham
1/2 pound ground pork
3/4 cup milk
1/2 cup oatmeal (raw)

1 egg
1/2 teaspoon salt
Dash pepper

Combine ingredients; form into 6 logs. Put in baking dish. Cover with the following sauce.

SAUCE:
1/2 cup brown sugar
1 tablespoon cornstarch
3/4 cup cold water

2 tablespoons vinegar
2 tablespoons lemon juice
1/4 cup seedless raisins

Combine brown sugar and cornstarch, gradually add water, vinegar, lemon juice, and raisins. Heat to boiling, stirring. Bake at 350° for 40-45 minutes, basting with the raisin sauce.

People Pleasers

Ham 'n Hash Browns

1 (12-ounce) package frozen
  hash brown potatoes, thawed
1½ cups shredded Cheddar
  cheese
1 cup finely chopped, fully
  cooked ham
½ cup sliced green onions,
  with tops

1½ cups milk
1 teaspoon salt
1 teaspoon dry mustard
Dash of ground red pepper
6 eggs, beaten
Paprika

Heat oven to 350°. Mix all ingredients except paprika in large bowl. Pour into lightly greased 11x7x2-inch baking dish. Sprinkle with paprika. Bake uncovered until knife inserted in center comes out clean (40-45 minutes). Serves 6.

Our Favorite Recipes / Aurdal Lutheran Church

Ham and Potato Scallop

1 can cream of chicken soup
¾ cup milk
Dash of pepper
1 cup diced cooked ham

4 cups sliced potatoes
1 small onion, sliced
1 tablespoon butter

Blend soup, milk, and pepper; add ham. In buttered 1½-quart pan, alternate in layers of potatoes, onion, and sauce. Dot top with butter and sprinkle with paprika. Cover; bake at 375° for one hour. Uncover and bake for 15 minutes longer.

Our Family's Favorites

Fabulous Easy Quiche

16 slices white bread, crusts
  removed and cubed
1 pound ham, cubed
1 pound Cheddar cheese,
  grated
1 1/2 cups Swiss cheese,
  cubed

6 eggs
3 cups milk
1/2 teaspoon onion salt
Pepper

Spread 1/2 of bread cubes in a 9x13-inch baking dish. Sprinkle evenly with ham and both cheeses. Cover with remaining bread cubes. In a bowl, mix eggs, milk, onion salt, and pepper. Pour over bread. Refrigerate overnight.

TOPPING:
3 cups cornflakes, crushed   1/2 cup butter, melted

Combine and spread evenly over quiche. Bake, uncovered, at 375° for 40 minutes. Let stand a few minutes before serving. Makes 4-5 servings.

Recipes from Minnesota with Love

Spam Casserole

2 cups Spam, chopped
2 cups partially cooked
  macaroni
2 cups milk
1 cup cream of mushroom
  soup

1 cup cream of celery soup
1/4 cup chopped onion
1/4 cup chopped green
  pepper
2 cups mild cheese, shredded
2 cups crushed potato chips

Mix all together; place in 9x13-inch greased pan. Top with crushed potato chips. Bake at 350° for one hour.

A Dish to Pass

Minnesota has 87 counties; only one of them—Rock County—doesn't have a natural lake.

Pasties
(Meat and Potato Turnovers)

6 cups sifted flour
3 teaspoons salt
1½ teaspoons baking powder
2 cups shortening or lard
1 - 1½ cups ice water
3 cups thinly sliced potatoes
1½ cups sliced carrots
  (optional)
1½ cup chopped rutabaga
  (optional)

3 cups chopped onion
Salt and pepper
2 pounds beef sirloin, round or
  flank steak, cut in ½-inch
  pieces
¾ pound pork butt, ground
  or chopped (optional)
½ cup butter melted with
  ½ cup water

Mix flour, 3 teaspoons salt and baking powder in a large bowl. Add shortening and cut in with a pastry blender. Add ice water, a little at a time, until dough can be easily handled. Divide dough into 6 pieces, wrap in waxed paper and refrigerate for 30 minutes.

For each pasty: Roll out dough into a 9-inch circle. Layer potatoes, carrots, rutabaga and onion; sprinkle with salt and pepper. Add beef, pork, more salt and pepper, ending with a second layer of potatoes. Fold in half, moistening edge with cold water, and seal edges. Crimp edge with a fork. Place on greased cookie sheet. In the top of each pasty, cut a small hole with a sharp knife.

Bake pasties in 425° preheated oven for 15 minutes. Turn oven to 350° and bake 35-45 minutes or until they are nicely browned. After ½ hour of baking, remove from oven and spoon the butter-water mixture into the hole, return to oven and complete baking. Serve hot or cold. Pasties freeze and reheat well. Yield 6 large pasties.

Minnesota Heritage Cookbook I

Pizza Manicotti

1 pound Italian sausage
1 (28-ounce) can whole tomatoes, undrained and cut up
1 (15-ounce) can pizza sauce
2¹/₂ cups shredded Mozzarella cheese
1 (15-ounce) package ricotta cheese
¹/₂ cup quartered pepperoni slices
¹/₂ cup snipped fresh parsley or 2 tablespoons dried
1 egg
1 (8-ounce) package manicotti shells, uncooked
6 green pepper rings, optional
¹/₄ cup black olives, sliced

Brown sausage until no longer pink; drain. Add tomatoes and pizza sauce; mix well and set aside. In mixing bowl, combine 1 ¹/₂ cups Mozzarella cheese, ricotta cheese, pepperoni, parsley, and egg. Stuff each uncooked manicotti shell evenly with mixture. Arrange stuffed shells in a 9x13-inch baking dish. Spoon tomato mixture over shells. Arrange pepper rings over tomato mixture. Sprinkle evenly with olive slices. Cover with plastic wrap. Refrigerate 12 hours or overnight. Heat oven to 350°. Remove plastic wrap, cover with foil, and bake 50 minutes to one hour or until hot and bubbly. Remove foil and sprinkle with remaining one cup Mozzarella cheese. Recover for 5 minutes or until cheese is melted. Makes 8 servings.

Potluck Volume II

Sausage Dinner in a Pumpkin Shell

1 small (12 - 14-inch)
   pumpkin
1 pound bulk pork sausage,
   cooked and drained
1 cup brown, wild or white rice,
   cooked

1 (4-ounce) can mushrooms
1 (10¹/₂-ounce) can cream of
   mushroom soup

Cut a fairly large lid from the top of pumpkin. Scoop out seeds and stringy portions and wash inside and out. Combine sausage, rice, mushrooms and soup. Mix together and put into pumpkin. Put pumpkin shell lid in place. Set in large shallow baking pan. Add 2 cups water to the pan and bake at 350° for 2 hours. To serve, spoon out foods on top and cut squares of pumpkin from the opening down. Serves 4-6.

A Dish to Pass

Herbed Lamb Stew

1 tablespoon oil
1 pound lean lamb leg or
   shounder, cut into ¹/₂-inch
   cubes
2 tablespoons flour
2 cups water
1 (8-ounce) can tomato sauce
1 cup chopped onion
1 clove garlic, minced
¹/₈ teaspoon salt/pepper

1 cup peeled, diced potatoes
1 cup frozen peas
1 cup sliced carrots
1 cup sliced mushrooms
1 cup sliced zucchini or
   squash
2 tablespoons parsley
1 tablespoon fresh chopped
   oregano leaves or ³/₄ teaspoon
   dried

In Dutch oven, heat oil to medium heat. Add lamb; sauté until slightly brown. Reduce heat, add flour and stir constantly until thick. Slowly add water, tomato sauce, onion, garlic, salt, pepper, and blend well. Cover and cook over low heat for 30 minutes; stir occasionally. Add vegetables, parsley, oregano. Cook 30 more minutes. Yield: 6 servings.

Anoka County 4H Cook Book

Venison Mushroom Simmer

2 pounds venison steak, cut
  into thin strips
2 tablespoons shortening
1 medium onion, chopped
1 clove garlic, minced
1/4 cup soy sauce
1 (4-ounce) can undrained
  mushroom pieces

2 beef bouillon cubes
1/2 teaspoon salt
Dash of pepper
2 1/2 cups water
1/4 cup cornstarch

In large skillet or wok, brown meat in shortening. Add onion and garlic; cook until tender. Add soy sauce, mushrooms, bouillon, salt and pepper, and 2 cups of water. Cover and simmer until tender, 30-40 minutes. Combine cornstarch with 1/2 cup water and stir into meat mixture. Cook and stir until thickened. Serve over rice or noodles. Makes 6 servings.

Maple Hill Cookbook

There are nature trails all over Minnesota. In Aitkin County alone, there are over 650 miles of marked, groomed public snowmobile trails. The Taconite Trail, Minnesota's first and longest snowmobile trail, runs 170 miles from Grand Rapids to Ely and connects to hundreds of smaller trails—just one link in an interconnecting 1,600-mile network in Northeastern Minnesota. Spring through fall, the trails are open for hiking, mountain biking, hunting, and horseback riding.

Indian Tacos

INDIAN FRY BREAD:

1/4 cup sugar
2 cups flour
3 teaspoons baking powder
1 teaspoon salt

1 cup water (or enough to make a soft dough, start with 1/2 cup)

INDIAN TACO TOPPINGS:

1 pound ground buffalo meat (or ground beef)
2 (16-ounce) cans refried beans
1-2 packages taco seasoning to taste

Grated Cheddar cheese
Shredded lettuce
Chopped tomatoes
Guacamole, sour cream and salsa

Mix Fry Bread ingredients together. Pat out Fry Bread dough in flour and fry in 1-2 inches of oil at 350° until brown. Brown ground meat. Stir in refried beans and taco seasoning. Spread on top of Fry Bread. Top with cheese, lettuce, and tomatoes. Guacamole, sour cream, and salsa may be served on the side.

Favorite Recipes of Lester Park & Rockridge Schools

Corned Bear Salad

2 cups cooked corned bear, diced
3 medium potatoes, cooked, cooled, diced
1 medium green pepper, chopped

3 hard cooked eggs, sliced
1 small red onion, minced
1/4 cup minced parsley
Lettuce leaves

DRESSING:

1/2 cup olive oil
2 tablespoons red wine vinegar
1 tablespoon sour cream
1 teaspoon Dijon-style mustard

1/2 teaspoon prepared horseradish
1 small clove garlic, minced
Few drops hot pepper sauce
Salt and pepper to taste

In large bowl, beat dressing ingredients well. Add remaining ingredients except lettuce. Toss lightly to coat well. Serve on lettuce leaves.

Bears in My Kitchen

Drunken Bear

4 tablespoons bear lard**
1 pound bear loin, cut into
   3/4-inch cubes*
1/4 teaspoon marjoram
1 teaspoon parsley
1/2 teaspoon curry powder
1 medium onion, chopped
4 stalks celery, sliced
1/2 pound fresh mushrooms,
   sliced

1 ounce 100-proof vodka
4 medium tomatoes, diced
1 ounce sherry
1 (16-ounce) carton sour
   cream
Rice pilaf
Anise seeds

In large skillet melt 2 tablespoons bear lard. Add bear loin and brown quickly. Add spices, cover and simmer 45 minutes or until meat is tender. In another skillet melt 2 tablespoons bear lard. Add onion, celery, and mushrooms and sauté 10 minutes. When meat is tender, add vegetables to meat skillet. Pour vodka over mixture and light with a match. When flame dies out, add tomatoes and sherry and mix well. Simmer 2 minutes. Add sour cream, mix well and heat just to boiling. Spoon over rice pilaf. Sprinkle 1/2 teaspoon anise seeds over the top and serve.

   *If you don't have bear on hand, may substitute beef, pork or venison. **May substitute shortening.

Bears in My Kitchen

Bear with Chocolate

Don't let the chocolate in this recipe scare you off!! It makes a wonderful brown gravy and doesn't taste a bit like Hostess Cupcakes!

1/4 cup olive oil	1 cup beef bouillon
4 servings bear round steak	6 peppercorns
Salt	4 allspice berries
3 cloves garlic, chopped	1 ounce unsweetened baking
1 bay leaf	chocolate
6 tablespoons wine vinegar	1/2 pound fresh morels
1 cup dry red or white wine	4 slices fried bread

In Dutch oven, heat oil and brown steaks. Remove from pan. Add salt, garlic, bay leaf, vinegar, wine, bouillon, peppercorns and allspice to pan. Cover and cook 5 minutes. Put steaks back and complete cooking, about one hour. Remove meat and keep warm. Strain sauce and place back in pan. Add chocolate. Bring to boil and simmer 5 minutes. Add morels and simmer 15 minutes. To serve, place a slice of fried bread on serving plate, top each with a steak and cover with the sauce.

Bears in My Kitchen

Cakes

Phelps Mill in west central Minnesota.

Fresh Peach Cake

1 cup sifted plus 1/4 cup
  unsifted flour
1 1/2 teaspoons baking
  powder
1/2 teaspoon salt
1/4 cup plus 3 tablespoons
  granulated sugar
7 tablespoons unsalted butter
1 egg

1/4 cup milk
1/2 teaspoon grated lemon
  peel
10 large ripe peaches, halved,
  pitted, peeled and quartered
3/4 cup slivered almonds
1/4 cup light brown sugar
1/4 cup apricot preserves
1 tablespoon water

Preheat oven to 400°. With pastry brush, spread a light coating of melted or softened butter inside a 12-inch round by 2-inch deep baking dish or pan. Sprinkle in spoonful of flour; shake dish to distribute it; tap out excess.

Sift one cup of flour, baking powder, salt and 1/4 cup granulated sugar in small bowl. With fingers or a pastry blender, work in 1/4 cup butter until mixture resembles coarse meal. Beat egg with milk and add to flour mixture along with lemon peel. Stir just until batter is blended. Spread batter evenly in prepared dish. Arrange peaches over top of the batter, rounded-side up. Sprinkle fruit with remaining 3 tablespoons sugar. Bake for 35 minutes.

While cake is baking, whirl the almonds in blender to fine powder. Mix almonds with remaining 3 tablespoons butter, 1/4 cup flour and brown sugar. Take cake from oven. Border the top of cake with almond mixture. Put cake back in oven for another 10 minutes. Press the apricot preserves through a sieve into saucepan. Add the tablespoon of water and cook for 2 minutes, until preserves melt. Remove cake from oven. Brush tops of peaches with the preserves.

Note: When batter is assembled, it will be thick. However, the batter puffs up as it bakes.

The Centennial Society Cookbook

The little town of Rose Hill has come to be known as Nodine, after being renamed by two very hungry government surveyors who couldn't find a place to eat there.

Red Cake

1/2 cup shortening	2 1/2 cups cake flour
1 1/2 cups sugar	2 tablespoons cocoa
1 teaspoon vanilla	1 teaspoon baking soda
2 eggs	1 cup buttermilk
2 ounces (1/4 cup) red food coloring	1 teaspoon vinegar

Heat oven to 350°. Grease and flour 13x9-inch pan. Beat shortening, sugar, and vanilla until smooth. Add eggs and food coloring. Combine flour, cocoa, and soda in small bowl. Add alternately with buttermilk and vinegar. Pour into pan. Bake 25-35 minutes or until top is brown/red. Frost with White Frosting.

WHITE FROSTING:

3 tablespoons flour	1 cup butter (not margarine)
1 cup milk	1 teaspoon vanilla
1 cup sugar	

Cook flour and milk over medium heat until thick, stirring constantly. Cool completely. Beat sugar, butter, and vanilla. Beat into cooled milk mixture until fluffy.

The Clovia Recipe Collection

Walnut Apple Cake with Poured on Caramel Icing

1 cup oil	3/4 teaspoon soda
2 eggs	1/2 teaspoon salt
1 1/2 cups sugar	2 cups diced apples, peeled or unpeeled
1 1/2 teaspoons vanilla	1 cup chopped nuts
2 cups flour	

Mix oil, eggs, sugar, and vanilla. Add flour, soda, and salt. Add apples and nuts. Bake in sprayed 9x13-inch baking pan at 350° for 50-60 minutes. Ice while hot with following ingredients which have been boiled together for 2 1/2 minutes.

1 stick butter (1/2 cup)	3/4 cup brown sugar
3 tablespoons milk	

Chickadee Cottage Cookbook

Mom's Spice Cake

1¼ cups brown sugar	1½ teaspoons cinnamon
1 cup white sugar	¾ teaspoon nutmeg
¾ cup soft shortening	¾ teaspoon cloves
3 eggs, beaten thoroughly	1 teaspoon salt
2¾ cups flour	1½ cups buttermilk
1½ teaspoons soda	

Cream together the sugars and shortening until fluffy. Beat in the eggs. Sift the dry ingredients together and stir in alternately with the buttermilk. Pour into a greased and floured 9x13-inch oblong pan. Bake at 350° for 35-40 minutes or until cake tests done. Cool.

BROWN SUGAR FROSTING:

1 cup brown sugar	4 tablespoons butter
12 tablespoons cream or half-and-half	1 teaspoon vanilla

Combine brown sugar and cream. Boil for exactly 3 minutes. Remove from heat and add butter and vanilla. Beat mixture until the gloss leaves. If mixture gets too stiff, add a little cream.

Treasured Recipes of Chippewa County

Prairie Beer Cake

1/2 cup butter, softened
1 egg
2 cups flour
1/2 teaspoon cinnamon
1/2 cup chopped walnuts or
   pecans
1 cup chopped dates

1 cup beer
1 cup brown sugar, packed
1/4 teaspoon salt
1 teaspoon soda
1/2 teaspoon nutmeg

Mix together. Pour into greased 10-inch tube pan or Bundt pan. Bake at 350° for 1 hour or until done. Cool in pan. Turn out carefully; cool completely. Cover and refrigerate overnight. Serve plain, dusted with powdered sugar or with lemon glaze.

From the Recipe File of Agnes Gaffaney

The Best Peanut Butter Cake

2 cups all-purpose flour
1/4 cup whole wheat flour
2 cups packed brown sugar
1 cup peanut butter
1/2 cup butter or margarine,
   softened
1 teaspoon baking powder

1/2 teaspoon baking soda
1 cup low-fat milk
1 teaspoon vanilla
3 eggs
1 cup chocolate or carob
   chips

Heat oven to 350°. Grease bottom only of 9x13-inch pan. Combine flours, brown sugar, peanut butter, and butter in large mixer bowl; mix at low speed until crumbly. Reserve one cup. To remaining mixture in bowl, add baking powder, soda, milk, vanilla, and eggs; blend at low speed until moistened. Beat for 3 minutes at medium speed. Spread batter in pan; sprinkle with reserved crumbs, then chocolate chips. Bake for 35-40 minutes. Makes 18 servings. Fat 18 grams per serving with chocolate chips.

Minnesota Heritage Cookbook II

The Kensington Rune Stone, on exhibit in Alexandria, tells of early exploration by Swedes and Norwegians, and is dated 1362—which is 130 years before Columbus discovered America. Because so many Swedish, Danish, Finnish, and Norwegian settlers came to Minnesota, it is often called the Second Scandinavia.

Higgins Cake

2 cups flour
2 cups sugar
1 (20-ounce) can crushed
  pineapple in own juice
  (don't drain)

1 teaspoon vanilla
2 eggs
2 teaspoons soda
1/2 cup chopped nuts

Mix all of the above. Bake at 350° for 40-45 minutes in a 9x13-inch greased pan.

FROSTING:
1/2 stick margarine
1 (8-ounce) package cream
  cheese

1/2 cup chopped nuts
1 teaspoon vanilla
1 3/4 cups powdered sugar

Mix well and spread over slightly warm cake.

Recipes and Memories

Pumpkin Cake in a Jar

This dessert treat is baked and presented in a wide-mouth canning jar. Because the jar is sealed, the cake keeps indefinitely. It can be made well ahead of time.

2/3 cup shortening	1/2 teaspoon baking powder
2 2/3 cups sugar	1 teaspoon ground cloves
4 eggs	1 1/2 teaspoons salt
2 cups fresh or canned pumpkin	1/2 teaspoon allspice
	1 teaspoon cinnamon
2/3 cup water	2 teaspoons soda
3 1/2 cups flour	1 cup chopped walnuts

Cream shortening and sugar, adding sugar slowly. Beat in eggs, pumpkin and water. Sift together flour, baking powder, salt, cloves, allspice, cinnamon, and soda. Add to pumpkin mixture and stir well. Add nuts. Pour batter into 8 greased pint-size, wide-mouth jars (with lids and rings for sealing), filling half-full. Place jars on cookie sheet.

Bake upright in preheated 325° oven about 45 minutes. Cake will rise and pull away from sides of jar. When done, remove one jar at a time. While still warm, place 8 wax paper circles cut to fit inside canning jars on top end of cake. Wipe sealing edge of jar. Place lid on jar and close tightly with ring. Turn jar upside down. Cake will loosen at this time. Leave jars upside down until sealed (lid will remain flat when pressed in center.)

To serve: Open jar, slide a knife around inside of jar to loosen cake and remove from jar. Warm cake in oven if desired. Slice and serve with whipped cream.

Duluth Woman's Club 70th Anniversary Cookbook

A strange magnetic phenomenon near Two Harbors caused compasses to go berserk and sent many a ship crashing into the perilous reefs. The famous Split Rock Lighthouse towering 50 feet high, has kept watch there since 1910.

Pumpkin Pie Cake

1 (29-ounce) can pumpkin
1 large can evaporated milk
3/4 cup white sugar
3/4 cup brown sugar
4 eggs
2 teaspoons cinnamon
1 teaspoon ginger
1/2 teaspoon nutmeg
1/2 teaspoon salt
1 yellow cake mix
1 cup melted margarine
1 cup chopped nutmeats

Beat all ingredients except cake mix, margarine, and nutmeats. Pour pumpkin mixture in an ungreased 9x13-inch pan. Mix cake mix and margarine like pie crust to make crumbs and sprinkle over pumpkin mixtre. Sprinkle on chopped nut meats. Bake for one hour at 350° (no longer). Cool and serve with Cool Whip.

Martha Chapter #132 OES Cookbook

Chocolate Sheet Cake

2 cups sugar
2 cups flour
1 teaspoon soda
2 sticks margarine
1 cup water
4 tablespoons cocoa
2 eggs
1/2 cup buttermilk
1 teaspoon vanilla

Mix sugar, flour, and soda. Bring to a boil margarine, water, and cocoa, then pour over the dry ingredients. Add eggs, buttermilk, and vanilla. Pour in greased jellyroll pan. Bake 20-25 minutes in 400° oven.

ICING:

1 stick margarine
4 tablespoons cocoa
5-6 tablespoons buttermilk
3 3/4 cups powdered sugar
1 teaspoon vanilla
1 cup nuts (optional)

Mix margarine, cocoa, and buttermilk and bring to boil. Remove from heat; add remaining ingredients and pour over hot cake.

Feeding the Flock

Oatmeal Harvest Cake

1 1/2 cups boiling water
1 cup oatmeal
1/2 cup shortening
1 cup brown sugar
1 cup white sugar

2 eggs, well beaten
1 1/3 cups flour
1 tablespoon cinnamon
1 teaspoon baking soda
1/2 teaspoon salt

CRUMB TOPPING:
2 tablespoons soft butter
3 tablespoons brown sugar
3 tablespoons white sugar
4-6 chopped Heath candy
    bars

3 chopped Hershey bars
1/2 cup nuts

Pour boiling water over oatmeal. Let stand 20 minutes. Cream shortening, brown sugar, and white sugar. Add eggs. Then add flour, cinnamon, soda, and salt. Pour into greased 9x13-inch pan.

Crumble together butter, brown sugar, sugar, Heath bars, Hershey bars, and nuts. Sprinkle on top of cake mixture. Bake cake and topping for 30 minutes at 350°.

Favorite Recipes of Lester Park & Rockridge Schools

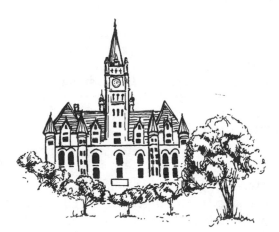

Amaretto Fudge Cake

1³/₄ cups flour
1¹/₂ cups sugar
³/₄ cup cocoa
1¹/₂ teaspoons baking soda
1¹/₂ teaspoons baking
  powder
¹/₂ teaspoon salt
2 eggs

²/₃ cup skim milk
¹/₂ cup plus 2 tablespoons
  amaretto
¹/₂ cup applesauce,
  unsweetened
2 teaspoons vanilla
¹/₂ cup boiling water

Spray a 9-inch springform pan with nonstick vegetable cooking spray. Combine all ingredients and beat 2 minutes (batter is thin). Bake at 325° for 12 minutes.

TOPPING:

¹/₄ cup miniature chocolate
  chips

¹/₄ cup almond slices

Combine and sprinkle on cake. Continue baking for 40-45 minutes (total of 50-60 minutes). Cool 30 minutes; loosen sides and remove. Makes 12-15 servings. Cover the cake (it keeps well and is better the second day).

Vaer saa god Cookbook

Black Bottom Cupcakes

1 (8-ounce) package cream
  cheese
1 egg
¹/₄ cup granulated sugar
1 (6-ounce) package chocolate
  chips
1¹/₂ cups flour
1 cup granulated sugar

¹/₄ cup cocoa
1 teaspoon soda
¹/₂ teaspoon salt
1 cup water
1 tablespoon vinegar
¹/₂ teaspoon vanilla
¹/₃ cup oil

Beat cream cheese, egg, and ¹/₄ cup sugar; add chocolate chips. Set aside. For batter, combine dry ingredients and set aside. Combine water, vinegar, vanilla, and oil, and beat well with a fork. Add all at once to dry ingredients. Fill paper-lined muffin tins ¹/₂ full with chocolate batter and top with a spoonful of cream cheese mixture. Bake at 350° for 30 minutes. Yield: 15 servings.

Anoka County 4H Cook Book

Zucchini Chocolate Cake

1/2 cup margarine
1/4 cup oil
1 3/4 cups white sugar
2 eggs, beaten
2 1/2 cups flour
4 tablespoons cocoa
1 teaspoon baking soda

1/2 teaspoon baking powder
1 teaspoon cinnamon
1/2 cup sour milk
2 cups zucchini, peeled and
  grated
1 teaspoon vanilla

Preheat oven to 325°. Cream margarine, oil, and white sugar. Beat in eggs and set aside. Sift dry ingredients and add alternately with sour milk to creamed mixture. Add zucchini and vanilla. Beat everything in large bowl well. Grease a 9x13-inch pan or use Pam on bottom. Pour batter into greased pan. Spread evenly.

TOPPING:
1 cup chopped walnuts
1/2 cup brown sugar, packed

1 cup chocolate chips

Mix ingredients well and spread evenly on the cake batter before baking. Bake at 325° for 40-45 minutes or until done.

Potluck Volume II

Rhubarb Torte

We've lost count of how many times this has been requested and printed in the Daily Globe.

FIRST LAYER:

1 cup flour	Pinch of salt
2 tablespoons sugar	1/2 cup butter

Combine ingredients and press in 8x10-inch pan. Bake at 325° for 20 minutes.

SECOND LAYER:

1¼ cups sugar	2¼ cups cut rhubarb
2 tablespoons flour	3 egg yolks
1/3 cup milk	

Cook until thick; pour over baked crust.

THIRD LAYER:

3 egg whites	1/4 teaspoon cream of tartar
6 tablespoons sugar	

Beat egg whites, sugar and cream of tartar. Spread atop cooked rhubarb mixture. Brown in 325° oven for 10-15 minutes.

Dorthy Rickers Cookbook: Mixing & Musing

Cranberry Torte

1 cup sugar	1/2 teaspoon baking powder
1 egg	1/2 teaspoon salt
1½ cups flour	1 teaspoon vanilla
1/4 cup oleo	1½ cups whole cranberries
1/2 cup milk	

Mix ingredients except cranberries. Fold in cranberries (may be frozen). Put in a 9x9-inch pan and bake at 350°. Serve cake warm with Butter Sauce.

BUTTER SAUCE:

1 cup sugar	1/2 cup butter or oleo
1 cup cream or evaporated milk	1 teaspoon vanilla

Simmer until sugar is dissolved. A very special Christmas favorite. If any is left, both cake and sauce freeze well.

Vaer saa god Cookbook

Edelweiss Torte

Simple, but delicious . . . make two, freeze one.

1/2 bar German sweet chocolate	1 cup sugar
1/2 cup butter	1/2 cup flour
3 eggs, beaten	1 1/2 teaspoons vanilla

Melt chocolate and butter in a small pan over low heat. Beat eggs with a whisk until light and foamy. Gradually beat in sugar, flour, and vanilla to eggs. Add butter and chocolate. Pour into a well buttered 9-inch pie pan. Bake at 325 - 350° for 25-30 minutes. (Do not overbake . . . will sink slightly in middle). Serve warm or cold. Top with whipped cream and chocolate slivers. Freezes beautifully! Makes 6-8 servings.

A Thyme For All Seasons

Glazed Apple Cake

1/2 cup sugar	1/3 cup milk
1/3 cup margarine	1 1/2 cups flour, sifted
1 egg, beaten	5 medium apples, peeled and sliced
1 teaspoon vanilla	1 tablespoon sugar
1 1/2 teaspoons baking powder	1 tablespoon cinnamon
1/4 teaspoon salt	Raisins and nuts (optional)

Cream sugar and margarine. Add egg and vanilla. Mix baking powder and salt with flour. Add milk and flour alternately to sugar mixture. Spread in jellyroll pan. Cover batter with apple slices sprinkled with one tablespoon sugar and one tablespoon cinnamon. Sprinkle with raisins and nuts. Pour on glaze and bake at 350° for approximately 45 minutes.

GLAZE:

3/4 cup sugar	6 tablespoons margarine
1 tablespoon cornstarch	3/4 cup water

Mix all ingredients in saucepan and cook until clear.

Our Favorite Recipes

Minneapolis is so cold that the city has its own Habitrail system for people during the winter.

Rhubarb Cheesecake

An early spring favorite.

CRUST:

1 cup flour   1/4 cup sugar
1/2 cup butter or margarine

Mix flour, butter, and sugar. Pat into sprayed 10-inch pie plate or 9-inch springform pan.

RHUBARB LAYER:

3 cups rhubarb, cut in   1/2 cup sugar
   1/2-inch pieces   1 tablespoon flour

Combine rhubarb, sugar, and flour; toss lightly and spoon into crust. Bake at 375° for 15 minutes.

CREAM LAYER:

1/2 cup sugar   2 eggs
12 ounces cream cheese,
   softened

With electric mixer beat cream cheese with sugar until fluffy. Beat in eggs one at a time, then pour over hot rhubarb layer. Bake at 350° 30 minutes or until set.

TOPPING:

8 ounces sour cream   1 teaspoon vanilla
2 tablespoons sugar

Combine ingredients; spread over hot cheesecake. Chill. Makes 12 servings.

Chickadee Cottage Cookbook 2

Creamy Cheesecake

GRAHAM CRACKER CRUST:

1 1/3 cups graham cracker
  crumbs
1/3 cup original margarine,
  melted

1/3 cup white sugar

Preheat oven to 350°. In a medium mixing bowl, using a large fork, stir together graham cracker crumbs, margarine, and sugar. Press crust mixture into bottom of springform pan. Set aside.

CHEESECAKE:

2 (8-ounce) packages
  Neufchatel cream cheese,
  softened
2 cups low-fat vanilla yogurt
2 large eggs

2 large egg whites
1 cup white sugar
4 tablespoons white flour
1/4 cup chocolate syrup (ice
  cream topping)

In a large mixing bowl, using a large fork, stir Neufchatel cheese and yogurt together. One at a time add eggs and egg whites, stirring until smooth after each egg addition. Add sugar and flour, mixing until well combined. Remove 1/3 cup of batter and place in small mixing bowl. Add chocolate syrup to 1/3 cup batter and blend well. Pour white cheese mixture over graham crust, spreading evenly. Add chocolate cheese batter on top. Using knife, swirl chocolate and white batters together creating a marbled design.

Bake for one hour then turn off oven. Let cheesecake sit in oven for one additional hour. Remove from oven, placing pan on rack to cool completely. Cover with aluminum foil and refrigerate 3 hours or more before serving. When ready to serve, remove foil and sides of springform pan. Using knife dipped in hot water, cut into serving-size wedges. Dip knife in hot water before and after each cut to prevent cake from sticking to knife. Store leftovers covered in refrigerator.

Bake Yourself Happy

Minneapolis, the "City of Water," features 22 lakes and 170 parks woven together by an astonishing 55-mile system of paved paths. One of the safest cities in the nation, Minneapolis is ranked among the top three most livable cities in the nation.

Caramel-Apple Sundae Cheesecake

1/3 cup butter or margarine
1 cup sugar, divided
4 eggs
1 1/4 cups flour
2 (8-ounce) packages cream
  cheese, softened
2 tablespoons flour

1/2 cup sour cream
1 cup apples, peeled and
  chopped
3/4 teaspoon cinnamon
1/2 cup caramel topping (for ice
  cream)
1/4 cup chopped pecans

Combine butter and 1/3 cup sugar until light and fluffy. Blend in one egg. Add 1 1/4 cups flour; mix well. Spread dough onto bottom and sides of 9-inch springform pan. Bake at 450° for 10 minutes.

Combine cream cheese, 1/3 cup sugar, and 2 tablespoons flour, mixing at medium speed until well blended. Add 3 eggs, one at a time, mixing well after each addition. Blend in sour cream. Toss apples in remaining sugar and cinnamon. Stir topping into cream cheese mixture. Pour over crust. Swirl 1/4 cup caramel topping into cream cheese mixture. Bake at 350° for one hour. Loosen cake from rim of pan; cool before removing rim of pan. Chill. Top cheesecake with remaining topping and pecans. Makes 10-12 servings.

Centennial Cookbook

German Chocolate Cheesecake

GRAHAM CRACKER CRUST:

1½ cups graham cracker
  crumbs

2 tablespoons brown sugar
¼ cup butter, melted

Combine crumbs, sugar, and melted butter. Press mixture onto bottom and sides of 9-inch springform pan. Chill.

COCONUT TOPPING:

¼ cup plus 1 tablespoon
  brown sugar
¼ cup plus 1 tablespoon
  butter

¼ cup plus 1 tablespoon
  half-and-half cream
¾ cup shredded coconut
¾ cup chopped walnuts

Combine sugar, butter, half-and-half, coconut, and walnuts in saucepan. Bring to boil and boil 3 minutes. Cool and use to spread on cake.

CAKE:

1 cup semi-sweet chocolate
  pieces
16 ounces cream cheese,
  softened
⅔ cup brown sugar, packed
2 tablespoons unsweetened
  cocoa

5 eggs
1 teaspoon vanilla
1 teaspoon almond flavoring
Graham Cracker Crust
Coconut Topping

Melt the chocolate in top of double boiler. Place cream cheese in bowl and beat until fluffy. Gradually beat in brown sugar and cocoa. Add eggs, one at a time, beating after each addition. Beat in melted chocolate, vanilla, and almond flavoring. Turn into prepared springform pan and bake at 350° for 45 minutes. Cool and refrigerate overnight. Remove from springform pan and spread with Coconut Topping. Makes 12 servings.

Winning Recipes from Minnesota with Love

The boundary between Minnesota and North Dakota is formed by the Red River which was once part of Lake Agassiz. This lake was a gigantic body of water that was larger than all the Great Lakes combined, and covered northwest Minnesota, part of North Dakota, and went into Canada.

Old Fashioned Jellyroll

4 eggs, separated
1 teaspoon vanilla
3/4 cup sugar

3/4 cup flour
1 teaspoon baking powder
Jelly/ice cream

Beat egg yolks and vanilla until light. Add sugar gradually to egg yolks, beating until creamy. Sift flour with baking powder. Add gradually to egg mixture. Beat until smooth. Whip the egg whites until stiff. Lightly fold whites into the batter. Grease a 10x15-inch jellyroll pan. Line with foil, grease with butter, lard or oleo. Spread the batter evenly in the pan. Bake at 375° for 13-15 minutes, until top springs back when touched and cake shrinks from side of pan. Loosen the edges and turn out at once on a towel sprinkled with powdered sugar. If foil has stuck, peel off. Work fast. Cake cannot cool for easy rolling. Spread with jelly and roll up, or you can roll up the cake without jelly. Cool, then unroll and spread with jelly or softened ice cream. Roll up in towel. Refrigerate jellyroll before cutting. Freeze ice cream roll and serve with fudge sauce.

Finn Creek Museum Cookbook

Cookies and Candies

Lindberg man/boy statue. St. Paul.

Swedish Farmer Cookies

1 cup sugar
1 cup butter
1 egg, beaten
1/4 teaspoon salt
1 teaspoon vanilla

1/2 teaspoon coconut
   flavoring
2 cups flour
1 teaspoon soda

Mix well in order given. Shape into 2 rolls. Wrap in waxed paper. Chill for several hours. Cut into 1/4-inch slices. Bake at 350° until edge of cookies begin to brown.

One Hundred Years of Sharing

White Sugar Cookies

1 cup sugar
1 cup powdered sugar
1 cup butter
1 cup oil
2 eggs
1 teaspoon soda

1 teaspoon cream of tartar
1 teaspoon salt
1 teaspoon vanilla
4 cups flour plus 4 tablespoons
   flour

Cream sugar, powdered sugar, butter and oil. Add beaten eggs, soda, cream of tartar, salt and vanilla; add flour. Chill dough; roll in balls, and flatten with glass dipped in sugar. Bake at 350°.

Salem Cook Book II

Snowball Cookies

1 cup butter or margarine   2¹/4 cups flour
¹/2 cup powdered sugar   ¹/2 cup walnuts, chopped fine
1 teaspoon vanilla

Cream butter or margarine until light. Add powdered sugar and continue creaming. Add vanilla and mix. Add flour and blend. Stir in walnuts. Shape into small balls. Place on ungreased cookie sheet. Bake about 15 minutes at 350°. While still warm, roll in additional powdered sugar. Cool on a rack and then roll again in powdered sugar.

Recipes from St. Michael's

Ten Minute Sugar Cookies

1 cup white sugar   2 cups flour
¹/2 cup softened butter   ¹/2 teaspoon soda
1 egg   ¹/2 teaspoon salt
2 tablespoons lemon juice

Roll into small balls. Flatten with glass dipped in sugar. Bake at 375° for 10 minutes.

From the Recipe File of Agnes Gaffaney

White "Melt in Your Mouth" Cookies

1 cup butter   4 cups flour
2 cups sugar   3 teaspoons cream of tartar
1 cup oil   1 teaspoon soda
2 eggs   2 teaspoons vanilla

Cream butter and sugar. Add oil and eggs. Combine dry ingredients and add gradually. Add vanilla. This is a soft dough. Make balls, press with sugared glass. Bake at 375° for 10 minutes (watch carefully).

Recipes from the Flock

Aggression Cookies

The more you knead, mash, squeeze, and beat the general bejunior out of the dough, the better you feel and the better the cookies taste!

3 cups brown sugar
3 cups butter or margarine,
  or 1¹/2 cups each)

6 cups oatmeal
1 tablespoon baking soda
3 cups flour

Put all ingredients in a huge bowl. Mash, knead, and squeeze. Form dough into small balls, midway between filbert size and walnut size. Put on ungreased cookie sheet.

    Butter the bottom of a small glass, dip it in sugar, and mash the balls flat. You may need to butter the glass bottom once or twice, but you need to re-dip it in sugar for each ball. Bake at 350° for 10-12 minutes.

A Taste of Faith

Filled Cookies and Filling

FILLING:
2 teaspoons flour
¹/2 cup sugar

¹/2 cup chopped raisins
¹/2 cup chopped figs

Mix and cook until thick, being careful not to burn. Cool.

¹/3 cup shortening
1 cup sugar
1 cup eggs
¹/2 cup milk

1 teaspoon vanilla
3¹/2 cups flour
¹/2 teaspoon salt
4 teaspoons baking powder

Mix and roll out thin; cut with round cookie cutter. Put a teaspoon of filling on a cookie and top with another, and press around edges to keep filling in while baking. Bake at 350°, about 12-15 minutes.

Sears Through the Years Cookbook

Buck Hill Cookies

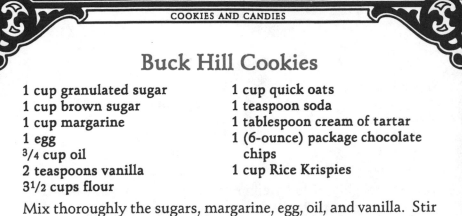

1 cup granulated sugar
1 cup brown sugar
1 cup margarine
1 egg
3/4 cup oil
2 teaspoons vanilla
3 1/2 cups flour

1 cup quick oats
1 teaspoon soda
1 tablespoon cream of tartar
1 (6-ounce) package chocolate
    chips
1 cup Rice Krispies

Mix thoroughly the sugars, margarine, egg, oil, and vanilla. Stir in remaining ingredients. Cover and chill dough. Drop by rounded teaspoonfuls 2 inches apart onto greased baking sheet. Bake at 350° for 8-10 minutes. Makes 5-6 dozen.

Martha Chapter #132 OES Cookbook

Crunchy Round-Trip Cookies

Still just as crisp on the way home.

1 cup granulated sugar
1 cup packed brown sugar
1 cup margarine, softened
1 cup vegetable oil
2 eggs
1 teaspoon vanilla
3 1/2 cups all-purpose flour
1 teaspoon cream of tartar

1 teaspoon baking soda
1 teaspoon salt
1/2 cup chopped nuts
1 cup flaked or shredded
    coconut
1 cup rolled oats
1 cup Rice Kirspies

Blend sugars, margarine, oil, eggs, and vanilla. In separate bowl, stir dry ingredients together; add to first mixture and blend well. Stir in nuts, coconut, oats, and cereal. Chill dough. Heat oven to 350°. Drop by teaspoonsfuls onto ungreased cookie sheets. Press down with a fork until very thin. If dough is sticky, chill fork in ice water and wipe dry. Bake 10-12 minutes. Makes 7 dozen.

From Minnesota: More Than A Cookbook

Molasses Crinkles

³/4 cup shortening
1 egg, beaten
2¹/4 cups flour
¹/4 teaspoon salt
1 teaspoon ginger
¹/2 teaspoon nutmeg

1 cup brown sugar
¹/4 cup molasses
2 teaspoons soda
1 teaspoon cinnamon
¹/2 teaspoon cloves

Mix thoroughly. Chill well or overnight. Shape in balls. Dip one side in sugar. Place sugared side up on pan. Bake at 350°. Makes 3 dozen big cookies. Good to put chocolate kisses on some.

From the Recipe File of Agnes Gaffaney

Norwegian Macaroons

1¹/4 cups flour
1¹/4 teaspoons baking soda
1 cup sugar
1 cup melted butter
1 egg, beaten

1 cup coconut
1³/4 cups oatmeal
¹/2 cup chopped nuts
About 6 squares white almond
   bark

Stir dry ingredients together. Add the melted butter, the beaten egg, coconut, oatmeal and nuts. Drop by teaspoon on cookie sheet and press down with fork or roll into balls; flatten with a glass. Bake at 350° until light brown, about 10-12 minutes. Frost with white almond bark. Makes 70-80 small cookies.

Sharing our Best / Bergen Lutheran Church

Best Ever Cookies

2 cups brown sugar
2 cups white sugar
2 cups butter
4 eggs
3 cups flour
2 teaspoon soda
2 teaspoon salt
2 teaspoons vanilla

3 cups quick oatmeal
3 cups regular oatmeal
1 (6-ounce) package chocolate chips
1 (6-ounce) package butterscotch chips
2 cups coconut
1 cup chopped nuts (optional)

Cream sugars and butter. Add eggs, mix well. Add all dry ingredients (you will need to use your hands). Add all other ingredients. Chill; make into balls. Bake at 350° for 15-20 minutes.

Note: Okay to freeze balls. For fresh baked cookies, select the amount you need. If frozen, bake a little longer.

A Dish to Pass

Chewy Chocolate Oatmeal Cookies

1/2 cup Hershey's cocoa
1/2 cup margarine or butter, melted
1 (14-ounce) cup Eagle Brand sweetened condensed milk
2 eggs, beaten
2 teaspoons vanilla

1 1/2 cups quick-cooking oatmeal
1 cup biscuit baking mix
1/4 teaspoon salt
1 (12-ounce) package Hershey's vanilla milk chips (or peanut butter)

Preheat oven to 350°. In large bowl, stir cocoa and margarine until smooth. Stir in remaining ingredients until well blended. Let dough stand 10 minutes. Drop by heaping teaspoonfuls onto lightly greased cookie sheet. Bake 7-9 minutes; remove from baking sheets. Cool completely. Store tightly covered.

Winniehaha's Favorite Recipes

The Mesabi Iron Range is 100 miles long. Within the range is the one-mile by three-mile long Hull-Rust-Mahoning open-pit mine—the biggest hole ever dug by man.

Strawberry Cookies

1 cup sweetened condensed
  milk
1 tablespoon sugar
1 teaspoon vanilla
2 packages strawberry gelatin,
  divided
1 pound coconut, ground
1/4 pound ground almonds

Mix all ingredients together (save 1/2 package gelatin). Shape into strawberries. Roll in remaining gelatin and decorate with green leaves made from frosting. (Use lemon Jell-O for wedding bells.) Makes 54 balls.

From the Recipe File of Agnes Gaffaney

Cornflake Cookies

1 (6-ounce) package
  butterscotch chips
1/2 cup peanut butter
3-3 1/2 cups cornflakes

Melt chips, then add peanut butter. When mixed, add cornflakes. Drop by teaspoonfuls onto waxed paper.

Kitchen Keepsakes

Butterfinger Cookies

1 1/2 cups sugar
1 cup shortening
2 eggs
1 teaspoon vanilla
2 1/3 cups flour
1 teaspoon baking soda
1 teaspoon salt
2 (20-ounce) butterfinger
  bars

Cream sugar and shortening. Add eggs and vanilla. Mix in dry ingredients. Chop candy bars and mix in. Drop on cookie sheet and bake at 350° for 10-15 minutes.

Centennial Cookbook

The 45-foot Glockenspiel Tower in Ulm is one of only a few free-standing carillon clock towers in the world.

"Turkey" Cookies

These are great to eat at Thanksgiving or just to eat for fun!

1 package round chocolate
stripe cookies (turkey tail)
1 cup chocolate frosting
(glue)
24 miniature peanut butter cups
(body)

24 pieces corn candy (turkey
gobbler)
48 chocolate chips (turkey
legs)

Cut approximately 1/8 inch off bottom of cookies to make flat base. Using the chocolate frosting as glue, glue on remaining ingredients as follows. 1) Glue largest side of peanut butter cup over the hole in the middle of the cookie for body. 2) Glue corn candy in the middle of the peanut butter cup as gobbler. 3) Glue chocolate chips on bottom of peanut butter cup for legs. Turkey will stand up. Makes 24 turkeys.

A Taste of Kennedy Cook Book

Lemonade Cookies

Very refreshing.

1 cup margarine or butter
1 cup sugar
2 eggs
3 cups flour
1 teaspoon baking soda

1 (6-ounce) can frozen
lemonade concentrate,
thawed
Sugar

Cream butter and one cup sugar. Add eggs; beat until fluffy. Sift flour and baking soda. Add alternately to cream mix with 1/2 cup of lemonade concentrate. Drop from a teaspoon, 2 1/2 inches apart, on ungreased cookie sheet. Bake in hot oven (400°) 8 minutes, or until lightly browned around the edges. Brush hot cookies with remaining lemonade concentrate. Sprinkle with sugar. Remove to cooling racks. Makes 4 dozen small cookies.

This is a soft cookie. Best stored in a flat pan—only a double layer.

Our Favorite Recipes

Hoot Owl Cookies

The cutest cookies you've ever seen.

2 1/2 cups flour
2 teaspoons baking powder
1/2 teaspoon salt
3/4 cup butter
1 cup brown sugar
1 egg

1 teaspoon vanilla
1 1/2 squares unsweetened
   chocolate
1/4 teaspoon baking soda
Chocolate chips (garnish)
Whole cashew nuts (garnish)

Sift together flour, baking powder, and salt. Cream butter and gradually add brown sugar. Beat in egg and vanilla. Gradually blend in dry ingredients. Melt unsweetened chocolate and when cool, add soda to it. Remove 2/3 of dough to floured surface. Blend chocolate into remaining dough.

Roll half of light dough to a 10 x 4 1/2-inch strip. Shape half of dark dough into a roll 10 inches long; place on strip of light dough. Mold sides of light dough around dark. Repeat with remaining dough. Wrap each roll in foil and chill at least 2 hours. Cut dough into slices 1/4-inch thick. Place two slices together on a greased baking sheet to resemble an owl. Pinch a corner of each slice to form ears. Place a chocolate chip in the center of each slice for eyes; press a whole cashew nut between slices for a beak. Bake at 350° for 8-12 minutes. Cool on wire racks. Makes 4 dozen.

Winning Recipes from Minnesota with Love

Apricot Half Moons

1/2 cup butter	1 cup flour
1 (3-ounce) package cream cheese	

Cream butter, cream cheese and flour. Form dough into ball and place in refrigerator for short time. When dough is chilled, roll out quite thin and cut with round cookie cutter or large glass. The dough rolls out very easily. Place on each cookie a tiny spoonful of apricot filling. Fold dough over to form a half moon and seal edges by pressing down with a fork. Bake at 350° for 15-20 minutes, until delicately browned. Sprinkle while hot with granulated sugar. Makes about 30.

FILLING:

12 ounces dried apricots	1 cup sugar
2 1/2 - 3 cups water	

Cut the dried apricots into small pieces. Cover with water and sugar. Cook, watching carefully so it doesn't stick to pan. Stir and cool. This amount of filling is enough for about 3 double batches of the cookies. It can be stored in the refrigerator for weeks, even months, and used for fillings for rolls as well as these pastries.

These pastries may also be made with date or mincemeat filling and sprinkled with a cinnamon and sugar mixture.

Dorthy Rickers Cookbook: Mixing & Musing

Rosettes

2 eggs	1 cup milk
1 tablespoon sugar	1 cup flour
1/4 teaspoon salt	Oil for frying

Beat eggs and add other ingredients and mix well. Heat oil. Dip rosette iron in batter and fry in hot oil. When cool, shake in a bag with sugar. Makes about 40 rosettes.

Sears Through the Years Cookbook

Marble Brownies

1 package lite (reduced calorie) brownie mix
1 (8-ounce) package Philly Free fat-free cream cheese, softened
1/3 cup sugar
1 egg
1/2 teaspoon vanilla
1 cup semi-sweet chocolate chips

Prepared brownie mix as directed on package. Pour into greased 9x13-inch pan. Beat cream cheese and sugar. Add egg and vanilla; mix well. Pour cream cheese mixture over brownie mixture; cut through batter with knife for marble effect. Sprinkle with chips. Bake at 350° for 35-40 minutes or until cream cheese mixture is lightly browned. Cool, cut into squares. 30 pieces = 66 calories; 2.7 g fat.

Recipes from St. Michael's

Joan's Brownies

1 cup margarine
1 cup water
1/4 cup cocoa
2 cups flour
2 cups sugar
1/2 teaspoon salt
1/2 cup buttermilk
2 eggs
1 teaspoon soda
1 teaspoon vanilla

Put margarine, water, and cocoa in a saucepan and bring to a boil. Pour over flour, sugar, and salt which have been combined in a mixing bowl. Beat with a mixer and add buttermilk, eggs, soda, and vanilla. Pour into a greased 11x17-inch pan. Mixture will be thin. Bake at 400° for 20 minutes.

FROSTING:

1/2 cup margarine
1/4 cup cocoa
1/3 cup buttermilk
2 1/2 cups powdered sugar
1 teaspoon vanilla
Salt

Bring margarine, cocoa, and buttermilk to a boil. Pour over powdered sugar, vanilla, and salt. Beat with a mixer. Pour over hot brownies.

Bethany Lutheran Church Celebrating 125 Years

Cafe Brownies

1 cup sugar
1 stick margarine, melted
1 teaspoon baking powder

4 eggs, beaten
1 cup chocolate syrup
1 cup flour

FROSTING:
1 cup sugar
1/4 cup milk
1/4 cup margarine

1/2 cup mini-marshmallows
1/2 cup chocolate chips

Mix brownie ingredients, and bake at 350° in 9x13-inch pan until edges begin to pull away from pan. Stir sugar, margarine and milk together in small saucepan, until it comes to a boil. Add marshmallows and boil for no more than one minute. Remove from heat, and add chocolate chips. Stir briskly until marshmallows and chips are melted. Pour over brownies and let cool before cutting.

Wannaska Centennial

Chocolate Mint Brownies

1 cup flour
1/2 cup butter or margarine,
  softened
1/2 teaspoon salt
4 eggs

1 teaspoon vanilla
1 (16-ounce) can chocolate
  flavor syrup
1 cup sugar

Combine ingredients and beat at medium speed for 3 minutes.
Pour into greased 9x13-inch pan. Bake at 350° for 30 minutes.
(Brownie top appears wet.) Cool completely.

FILLING:

2 cups confectioners' sugar
1/2 cup butter or margarine,
  softened

1 tablespoon water
1/2 teaspoon mint extract
3 drops green food coloring

Combine ingredients and beat until creamy. Spread over cool
brownies; refrigerate until set.

TOPPING:

1 (10-ounce) package mint
  chocolate chips

9 tablespoons butter or
  margarine

Melt chocolate chips and butter over low heat in small saucepan. Let cool 30 minutes to lukewarm; stir occasionally. Spread
over filling. Chill before cutting. Store in refrigerator.

Feeding the Flock

Chocolate Cream Cheese Brownies

1 (4-ounce) package German
    sweet chocolate
2 tablespoons butter or
    margarine
3 eggs
1 teaspoon vanilla
³/4 cup sugar

1/2 cup flour
1/2 teaspoon baking powder
1/4 teaspoon salt
1 (3-ounce) package cream
    cheese
1/2 teaspoon vanilla
1/4 cup sugar

Melt chocolate and butter together and cool. Beat 2 eggs, vanilla, and ³/4 cup sugar together in small bowl until thick. Sift together flour, baking powder, and salt; then add to the egg mixture and beat well. Blend in cooled chocolate mixture. Set aside. Cream cheese and sugar until fluffy. Blend in one egg. Spread half of chocolate mixture into greased and floured 8x8-inch pan. Pour cheese mixture over. Top with rest of chocolate mixture and swirl to marble. Bake at 350° for 40-45 minutes. Cut in squares when cool.

Centennial Cookbook

Polka Daters

1 (8-ounce) package chopped
    dates
1 cup hot water
1¹/4 cups sugar
1 cup butter
2 eggs

1³/4 cups flour
1¹/2 teaspoon baking soda
1 teaspoon vanilla
1 (6-ounce) package chocolate
    chips
1/2 cup nuts

Mix dates and hot water. Set aside to cool. Beat sugar, butter, and eggs until smooth. Stir in flour and baking soda. Mix in dates, vanilla, and 1/2 of chips. Spread in a greased jellyroll pan. Top with remaining chocolate chips and nuts. Bake 30 minutes at 350°.

A Dish to Pass

Saucepan Brownies

2 squares unsweetened
chocolate*
1/2 cup margarine
1 cup water
2 cups sugar
2 cups flour

1/2 teaspoon salt
2 eggs
1/2 cup plain yogurt or sour
cream
1 teaspoon soda

Heat oven to 350°. Bring unsweetened chocolate, margarine, and water to boil in small saucepan, stirring frequently. Cool slightly. Mix sugar, flour, and salt in mixing bowl; stir in chocolate mixture. Add eggs and beat until smooth. Stir in yogurt and soda. Pour into greased jellyroll pan (also works well in a 13x9-inch pan or layer cake pans.) Bake 20-25 minutes. Cool completely and frost.

*Six tablespoons cocoa plus 2 tablespoons vegetable oil can be substituted for the 2 squares unsweetened chocolate.

FROSTING:
1 cup sugar
1/3 cup milk
5 tablespoons margarine

1 cup semi-sweet chocolate
chips

Bring sugar, milk, and margarine to boil. Boil one minute, stirring constantly. Remove from heat and beat in chocolate chips until smooth. Spread on cooled brownies.

The Clovia Recipe Collection

Choc-Marshmallow Bar

1/2 cup butter or margarine
3/4 cup flour
2 eggs
2 tablespoons cocoa

3/4 cup white sugar
1 teaspoon vanilla
1/2 bag mini-marshmallows

Combine all but mini-marshmallows and mix well. Spread in 9x13-inch pan and bake at 350° for 15 minutes. Remove from oven and spread with mini-marshmallows. Return to oven for 3 minutes. Cool and prepare topping. Spread topping over marshmallows.

TOPPING:
1 cup chocolate chips
1 cup crunchy peanut butter

2 cups Rice Krispies

Melt chips and peanut butter together, then stir in Rice Krispies.

First United Methodist Church Cookbook

Mock Mocha Bars

1 white cake mix
1 (3-ounce) package instant
  coconut cream pudding mix

2 eggs
2 cups milk

Mix cake mix, pudding mix, eggs, and milk together. Spread in a large well-greased and floured jellyroll pan. Bake at 350° for 20 minutes. Cool.

2 cups powdered sugar
1/4 cup peanut butter
1/4 cup melted margarine

1/4 cup hot milk
2 cups chopped peanuts

Beat all ingredients, except peanuts, until smooth; spread on bars. Sprinkle with peanuts.

Recipes from the Flock

Pizza Bars

1 cup brown sugar
1/2 cup margarine
1 egg
1 teaspoon vanilla

1 1/4 cups flour
1/2 teaspoon baking soda
1/2 teaspoon salt
2 cups oatmeal

Cream together sugar and margarine. Add egg and vanilla. Mix well. Sift flour, soda, and salt; add oatmeal; add to first mixture. Mix well and press into 10x15-inch pan. Bake 10-15 minutes in 350° oven. Do not overbake.

TOPPING:

1 package caramels
3 tablespoons water or cream
1 cup chocolate chips

1 cup chopped walnuts
1 cup M&M's
3 blocks almond bark

Melt caramels and cream. Spread over baked mixture. Sprinkle with mixture of chips, nuts, and M&M's. Melt bark. Drizzle over top. Cut into squares.

Kompelien Family Cookbook

Frosted Apple Bars

2 1/2 cups flour
1 tablespoon granulated sugar
1 teaspoon salt
1 cup shortening
2 egg yolks (add milk to make 2/3 cup liquid)
2 egg whites

1 1/2 cups crumbled cornflakes
8-10 pared apples, sliced thin
1 1/2 cups granulated sugar
1 1/4 teaspoons cinnamon
1 cup powdered sugar
3 or 4 teaspoons water

Sift flour, sugar, and salt together. Cut in shortening. Add egg yolks and milk. Chill and then roll out 1/2 of dough to fit a 12x15-inch jellyroll pan. Sprinkle cornflakes over dough. Add apples. Mix sugar and cinnamon and sprinkle over apples. Roll out other 1/2 of dough and place on top of apples. Pinch edges together. Beat egg whites until frothy and spread over crust. Bake at 350° for one hour. Remove from oven. Mix powdered sugar and water together, and drizzle over hot crust.

Anoka County 4H Cook Book

Fruit Squares

1 cup soft butter
1¹/₂ cups sugar
4 eggs

2 cups flour
1 tablespoon lemon juice
1 can pie filling (your choice)

Preheat oven to 350°. Grease jellyroll pan. Cream butter and sugar. Add eggs one at a time. Add flour and juice. Spread batter into pan. Score dough into 24 squares and drop pie filling into center of each square. Bake for 35-40 minutes. Sprinkle with powdered sugar.

Maple Hill Cookbook

Pumpkin Bars

4 eggs
1 cup salad oil
2 cups sugar
1 (15-ounce) can pumpkin
2 cups flour
2 teaspoons baking powder

1 teaspoon baking soda
1/2 teaspoon nutmeg
1/2 teaspoon salt
2 teaspoons cinnamon
1/2 teaspoon ginger
1/2 teaspoon cloves

Preheat oven to 350°. Mix first 4 ingredients together well and add the others. Mix well; pour into a greased 12x8-inch pan. Bake at 350° for 25-30 minutes. Cool and frost.

FROSTING:
1 (8-ounce) package cream
   cheese, softened
3/4 stick butter

1 tablespoon cream or milk
1 teaspoon vanilla
4 cups powdered sugar

Mix all ingredients and frost bars.

Old Westbrook Evangelical Lutheran Church Cookbook

Almond Bars

1 cup butter
2 cups flour
1/2 cup powdered sugar
1 (8-ounce) package cream
   cheese
2 eggs

1/2 cup granulated sugar
1 teaspoon almond flavoring
1 1/2 cups powdered sugar
1/4 cup butter
1 1/2 tablespoons milk
1 teaspoon almond flavoring

Mix the first 3 ingredients for crust and pat into a 9x13-inch pan. Bake at 350° for 20-25 minutes. Using mixer, mix well softened cream cheese, eggs, granulated sugar, and 1 teaspoon flavoring. Pour over hot crust. Bake another 20-25 minutes at 350°; cool. Mix the last 4 ingredients for frosting and frost cooled bars.

Great Cooks of Zion Church

Apricot Bars

3/4 cup butter
1 cup sugar
2 cups flour

1/2 teaspoon salt
1/2 teaspoon baking soda

Cream butter, sugar, flour, salt, and baking soda together. Spread 3 cups into a 10x15-inch pan. Bake 10 minutes at 400°.

FILLING:
1 small jar apricot jam
1/2 cup chopped walnuts

1 1/2 cups oatmeal

Spread over first mixture. Sprinkle remaining crumbs over the apricot filling. Bake at 400° for 15-20 minutes.

Kompelien Family Cookbook

Apricot Bars

3/4 cup butter or margarine
1 cup sugar
1 egg
2 cups all-purpose flour
1/4 teaspoon baking powder

1 1/3 cups shredded coconut
1/2 cup chopped walnuts
1/2 teaspoon vanilla extract
1 (12-ounce) jar apricot
    preserves

In a large bowl, cream butter and sugar. Add egg. In a separate bowl combine flour and baking powder gradually. Add to butter mixture. Add coconut, walnuts, and vanilla. Place 2/3 of dough into a 13x9-inch greased baking pan. Spread with apricot preserves. Crumble rest of dough over the preserves. Bake at 350° for 30-35 minutes until golden brown. Cool and cut into bars. Yields 36 bars.

Red Oak Grove Lutheran Church Family Cookbook

Quick Lemon Bars

1 package Betty Crocker Angel
   Food Cake Mix

1 can lemon pie filling
1 cup coconut

Mix cake and pie filling; mix well. Add coconut. Put in greased jellyroll pan and bake at 350°. Cool and put on glaze frosting (powdered sugar and lemon juice).

Winniehaha's Favorite Recipes

Little Debbie Bars

Prepare one devil's food cake mix as directed on package. Divide into 2 jellyroll pans (10½ x 15½ x 1) and bake 20 minutes at 350°.

FILLING:

5 tablespoons flour
1 cup milk
½ teaspoon salt
1 cup sugar

½ cup Crisco
½ cup margarine
1 teaspoon vanilla

Blend flour, milk, and salt. Cook until thick, then cool. Cream at high speed the sugar, Crisco, and margarine. Gradually add cooled mixture and vanilla. Beat 7 minutes at high speed. Put filling on one cake; put other cake on top.

FROSTING:

1⅓ cups sugar
6 tablespoons margarine

⅓ cup milk
½ cup chocolate chips

Boil sugar, margarine, and milk for one minute. Take off heat and stir in chocolate chips until melted. Let cool for 15 minutes. Stir often. Frost cake on top only. Keep in refrigerator; it is best cooled.

Variation: Twinkie Bars—substitute yellow cake mix for devil's food: then serve with or without frosting.

The Queen of Angels Anniversary Cookbook

Walnut Strips

CRUST:

1/2 cup shortening	1 cup flour

Mix and pat into bottom of 9x13-inch pan. Bake 12-15 minutes.

FILLING:

2 eggs	1/2 teaspoon salt
1 1/2 cups brown sugar	1/2 cup chopped walnuts
2 tablespoons flour	1/2 cup coconut (optional)
1/4 teaspoon baking powder	1 teaspoon vanilla

Mix in order given and spread on crust. Return to oven and bake 15-20 minutes.

FROSTING:

2 tablespoons butter	1 teaspoon lemon juice
2 tablespoons warm orange juice	1 1/2 cups powdered sugar

Beat together till creamy and spread on cake. Cut in squares. Bake for 30 minutes at 350°.

Lutheran Church Basement Women

Sunflower Nut Bars

CRUST:
3/4 cup butter
3/4 cup brown sugar
1 cup flour

1 cup oatmeal
1 teaspoon soda
1/2 teaspoon salt

FILLING:
35 caramels
3-4 tablespoons cream or
  half-and-half

3 tablespoons butter

TOPPING:
1 (6-ounce) package chocolate
  chips

1 1/2 cups sunflower nuts

Mix crust ingredients together. Pat mixture into greased 9x13-inch pan and bake 10 minutes at 350°. Melt filling ingredients in double boiler; pour over crust and top with topping mixture. Bake 10-15 minutes more. Makes 18-24 bars.

A Taste of Kennedy Cook Book

Mystery Bars

3 eggs
2 cups sugar
1 cup cooking oil
2 cups unpeeled zucchini,
  coarsely grated and packed
2 cups flour

1 tablespoon cinnamon
2 teaspoons soda
1/4 teaspoon baking powder
1 tablespoon (yes) vanilla
1/2 cup nuts (optional)
1/2 cup raisins (optional)

Beat eggs; add sugar, oil, and zucchini. Sift in flour, cinnamon, soda, and baking powder. Add vanilla, nuts, and raisins. Bake in greased and floured jellyroll pan or 9x13-inch pan at 350° for 20-35 minutes. Cool. Frost with Cream Cheese Frosting.

CREAM CHEESE FROSTING:
4 tablespoons melted butter or
  margarine
6 ounces cream cheese,
  softened

3 cups powdered sugar
1 teaspoon vanilla

Mix well. Frost bars.

Kitchen Keepsakes

Fancy Caramel Oatmeal Bars

64 caramels
1/2 cup plus 2 tablespoons
  milk
2 cups rolled oats
2 cups all-purpose flour
1 1/2 cups packed brown
  sugar
1 teaspoon baking soda
1 teaspoon salt
1 1/2 cups margarine,
  softened
2 cups chocolate chips
1 cup chopped pecans

Melt caramels in milk; set aside to cool slightly. Heat oven to 350°. Mix oats, flour, brown sugar, soda, salt, and margarine together. Press half of mixture into 15x10-inch pan. Bake 10 minutes. Sprinkle chocolate chips and nuts evenly over baked crust. Drizzle with caramel mixture; top with remaining crust mixture. Bake 10-15 minutes longer. Makes 5 dozen.

From Minnesota: More Than A Cookbook

Keebler Bars

Keebler Club Crackers
2/3 cup sugar
1/2 cup brown sugar
1 stick butter
1 cup crushed graham
  crackers
1/4 cup milk
2/3 cup peanut butter
1/2 cup chocolate chips
1/2 cup butterscotch chips

Put one layer of crackers in bottom of greased 9x13-inch pan. Combine sugar, brown sugar, butter, graham crackers, and milk in saucepan. Boil for 5 minutes and pour over crackers. Cover with another layer of crackers. Melt together peanut butter, chocolate chips, and butterscotch chips. Pour over crackers. Cool and cut. Enjoy!

Favorite Recipes of Lester Park & Rockridge Schools

Cereal Bars

5 cups cereal (Special K, flakes
  or Chex)
1 cup sugar
1 cup white syrup

1 1/2 cups peanut butter
1/2 cup chocolate chips
1/2 cup butterscotch or peanut
  butter chips

Put cereal in large bowl. Bring to boil the sugar and syrup; remove from heat when it starts to boil. Add peanut butter and mix with cereal. Put in 9x13-inch pan. Melt chips together and frost bars.

Clinton's 110th Cookbook

Byerly's Butterscotch-Nut Bars

1 1/2 cups flour
3/4 cup packed brown sugar
1/2 cup butter or margarine
1 (6-ounce) package
  butterscotch chips
1/2 cup light corn syrup

2 tablespoons butter or
  margarine
1 tablespoon water
1 (12-ounce) can mixed, salted
  nuts or salted peanuts

Preheat oven to 350°. Combine flour and brown sugar; cut in butter with pastry blender until mixture resembles coarse meal. Press into greased 9x13-inch baking pan. Bake for 10 minutes; remove from oven. Combine butterscotch chips, corn syrup, butter, and water in heavy saucepan; heat and stir over medium heat until smooth. Stir in nuts; spread over crust. Return to oven; bake 10 minutes longer. Cool; cut into bars. Makes 24 (1 1/2 x 3-inch) bars.

The Centennial Society Cookbook

Flour milling in Minnesota started at a small grist mill at St. Anthony Falls constructed by troops at Fort Snelling in 1823. Minnesota won the contest for the best flour in the world at the Paris 1900 World's Exposition. Because of its flour mills and dairy products, Minnesota is called the Bread and Butter State.

Crispy Chunky Oat Bars

2 large eggs
1/2 cup canola oil
1/2 cup corn syrup
1 cup dark brown sugar, firmly
  packed
2 teaspoons pure vanilla
  extract
2 cups uncooked regular
  oatmeal

2 cups unbleached flour
1 teaspoon baking soda
1/2 teaspoon salt, optional
1/2 cup chopped nuts
1/2 cup chopped dates
1 cup milk chocolate chips

Preheat oven to 350°. In a large mixing bowl, using a large fork, vigorously stir eggs, oil, and syrup together. Mix in brown sugar and vanilla until well combined. Set aside. In second bowl, combine oatmeal, flour, baking soda, and salt. Mix well. Stir mixture into egg—oil/syrup/sugar/vanilla mixture. Add chopped nuts, dates and milk chocolate chip; stir to mix well. Pour batter in prepared 13x9-inch pan.

Bake for 25 minutes until golden brown and firm to touch. Cool, cut into squares and serve. Cover and store leftovers in refrigerator to retain freshness.

Bake Yourself Happy

7 Layer Bar

1 stick butter
1 cup graham cracker
  crumbs
1 cup flaked coconut
1 (6-ounce) package chocolate
  chips

1 (6-ounce) package
  butterscotch chips
1 can Eagle Brand sweetened
  condensed milk
1 cup chopped nuts

In 9x13-inch pan, melt butter. Sprinkle with remaining ingredients in order listed. Bake at 350° for 30 minutes.

From the Recipe File of Agnes Gaffaney

Salted Peanut Bars

3 cups flour
3/4 cup brown sugar

1 cup margarine
1/2 teaspoon salt

Mix like pie crust and pat in a cookie sheet. Bake 10 minutes at 350°.

TOPPING:
1 (12-ounce) package
   butterscotch chips
3 tablespoons butter

3 tablespoons water
1/2 cup white syrup
3 cups peanuts or mixed nuts

Combine chips, butter, water, and syrup and melt over hot water. When melted add peanuts or mixed nuts and spread over crust. Return to oven for 8 minutes longer. Cool and cut into bars.

The Queen of Angels Anniversary Cookbook

Oyen's Christmas Caramels

2 cups sugar
1 1/2 cups white Karo syrup
1/2 cup butter

2 cups cream, divided
Nuts
1/2 teaspoon vanilla

Combine sugar, Karo syrup, butter and one cup cream. Bring to a boil, stirring constantly. After boiling a short time, add the remaining cup of cream. Continue boiling until it reaches the softball stage (240°). Remove from heat. Add nuts and vanilla. Pour into a greased 8x11-inch pan. When cool, cut into desired pieces and wrap in wax paper. Store in a cool place.

Treasured Recipes of Chippewa County

 The world's largest hockey stick is in downtown Eveleth, the home of the United States Hockey Hall of Fame. This "Big Stick" is 107 feet long and weighs over 3 tons. It faces a red, white and blue mural titled, "Hockey's Home," depicting a hockey goaltender and defenseman.

Chocolate Covered Cherries

Definitely worth the effort!

16 ounces powdered sugar
5 tablespoons soft butter
2 tablespoons half-and-half
  cream
1/2 teaspoon vanilla
2 (10-ounce) jars maraschino
  cherries, well drained

8 ounces semi-sweet
  chocolate
1/2 bar paraffin wax, shaved
1 tablespoon butter

Knead first 4 ingredients until smooth. Flatten rounded tea-spoonful of dough in palm of hand, roll dough around cherry. Place on foil-lined baking sheet, refrigerate until slightly firm (about one hour). Melt chocolate, paraffin, and butter in top of double boiler. Hold cherries by stem, or if no stem, stick a tooth-pick into each cherry. Dip cherry in chocolate and return to baking sheet. When all cherries are covered, dip a spoon into chocolate and cover hole from toothpick, making a design on each. Cool. Place in bonbon cups. Store in cool, dry place. Makes 4 dozen.

Winning Recipes from Minnesota with Love

Buttery Almond Roca

Scrumptious.

1 cup butter   8 ounces milk chocolate
1 cup sugar
1 cup toasted almonds,
  halved

Melt butter in a heavy skillet. Add sugar and bring to a boil.
Stir constantly after it comes to a boil. Boil for 5 minutes or
until caramelized. If butter separates from sugar, keep stirring
until butter blends back in. Save a few almonds to grind on
top; stir in the rest of almonds. Pour into 8x8-inch pan lined
with waxed paper. When cool, melt chocolate and spread on
top. Sprinkle with ground almonds. Break into bite-sized pieces.
Keep refrigerated.

Winning Recipes from Minnesota with Love

Pies and Desserts

A beautiful winter scene at Temperance River State Park.

Sour Cream Raisin Pie

3 eggs, separated
1 1/2 cups sour cream
3/4 cup sugar
1/4 cup flour
1 teaspoon cinnamon

1/4 teaspoon cloves
1 cup raisins
1 baked pie shell
3 tablespoons sugar

In top of double boiler blend 3 egg yolks and 1 1/2 cups sour cream. Stir dry ingredients gradually in eggs and cream. Cook until thick. Stir in one cup raisins. Pour in baked pie shell. Top with meringue from 3 egg whites, whipped very stiff with 3 tablespoons sugar. Bake at 350° for 10-15 minutes.

One Hundred Years of Sharing

Unusual laws in Minnesota: It's illegal to tease skunks. Every man in Brainerd is required by law to grow a beard. Double-parkers in Minneapolis can be put on a chain gang. Women who impersonate Santa Claus could face up to 30 days in jail.

Six-Minute Pecan Pie

3 eggs (slightly beaten)
1 cup corn syrup
1 cup sugar
2 tablespoons butter or
  margarine

1 teaspoon vanilla
1 1/2 cups pecans
1 unbaked pie shell

In large bowl stir together first 5 ingredients until well blended. Stir in nuts. Pour into pastry shell. Bake in 350° oven 50-55 minutes, or until knife inserted halfway between center and edge comes out clean. Cool.

The Oke Family Cookbook

Fresh Strawberry Pie

1 cup sugar
1 cup water
3 tablespoons cornstarch
2 tablespoons flour

3 tablespoons strawberry
  Jell-O
2 cups fresh strawberries
1 (9-inch) prepared pie crust

Mix sugar, water, cornstarch, flour, and Jell-O. Microwave 4 1/2 minutes at FULL POWER, until clear and thick. Add fresh strawberries and put in pie crust. Refrigerate. Serve with whipped cream.

Great Cooks of Zion Church

Barbara's Fighting Peach Pie

1 cup sugar
5 tablespoons flour
1 (9-inch) pie shell (unbaked)

3-4 fresh peaches
1 cup whipping cream

Combine the sugar and flour until well blended; put 1/3 of this in the bottom of the pie shell. Peel and pit peaches; place the peach halves (do not slice), pit-side-up, in the shell, using enough to fill shell. Mix the last 2/3 of flour mixture with the cream and pour over peaches. Bake at 425° for 10 minutes; lower oven to 350° and bake for 1 hour 20 minutes.

Treasured Recipes from Treasured Friends

Fresh Peach Dessert

CRUST:

1/2 cup butter   2 tablespoons sugar
1 cup flour

GLAZE:

1 cup sugar   3 tablespoons dry peach or
1 cup water   orange Jell-O
3 tablespoons cornstarch   2-3 cups sliced fresh peaches

Mix ingredients for crust until crumbly. Pat in 9x13-inch pan
and bake at 350° for 10 minutes. Mix dry ingredients for glaze
and gradually add water. Cook until thick. When cool, add
sliced peaches and spread on top of crust. Refrigerate. Cut in
squares and serve with whipped topping.

Winniehaha's Favorite Recipes

Peach Praline Pie

Prepare one unbaked pie shell. Heat oven to 350°.

FILLING:

4 cups canned (drained)   2 tablespoons tapioca
   peaches   1 teaspoon lemon juice
1/2 cup sugar

Mix and let set while you make the topping.

TOPPING:

1/4 cup butter   1/4 cup brown sugar
1/2 cup flour   1/2 cup chopped pecans

Mix with hands until crumbly. Put 1/4 of this on the bottom of
an unbaked pie shell. Put peach mixture on top. Put the rest of
the topping on top of the peach mixture. Bake at 350° for about
50 minutes.

Braham's Pie Cookbook

Peanut Butter Cream Cheese Pie

6 ounces cream cheese,
softened
3/4 cup sifted powdered
sugar
1/2 cup peanut butter

2 tablespoons milk
2 cups Cool Whip
1 (8-inch) graham cracker pie
crust

Beat cheese and sugar till light and fluffy. Add peanut butter
and milk. Beat till smooth and creamy. Fold in Cool Whip and
turn into crust. Chill 5-6 hours or overnight.

Maple Hill Cookbook

Chocolate Banana Pudding Pie

4 squares semi-sweet
chocolate
2 tablespoons milk
1 tablespoon margarine or
butter
1 graham cracker crust
2 medium bananas, sliced

2 3/4 cups cold milk
2 (3.5-ounce) packages Jell-O
vanilla or banana cream instant
pudding*
1 1/2 cups thawed Cool
Whip*

Microwave chocolate, milk, and margarine in medium
microwaveable bowl on HIGH for 1 -1 1/2 minutes, stirring every 30 seconds. Stir until completely melted. Spread evenly in
crust. Refrigerate 30 minutes or until chocolate is firm. Arrange banana slices over chocolate. Pour milk into large bowl;
add pudding mixes. Beat with a wire whisk for one minute.
Let stand 5 minutes. Spoon over bananas in crust. Spread with
whipped topping. Refrigerate 4 hours or until set.

*Can use Jell-O vanilla flavored sugar-free reduced calorie instant pudding and Cool Whip lite.

Potluck Volume II

The Greyhound Bus Lines had its start in Hibbing in 1914.

Grasshopper Pie

20 large marshmallows
1/2 cup milk
18 chocolate cookies, crushed
1/4 cup melted butter
1 cup whipping cream, whipped

1 ounce (1/4 cup) cream de cocoa
1 ounce (1/4 cup) cream de menthe

Melt marshmallows in milk and let cool. Mix cookie crumbs with butter and press into pie tin. Stir liqueurs into whipped cream, then add marshmallow mixture. Pour into crust and let set overnight in refrigerator.

From the Recipe File of Agnes Gaffaney

Rich Chocolate Pie

One of the most requested recipes.

1 baked (9-inch) pie shell
3/4 cup powdered sugar
1/4 pound butter
1/4 pound semi-sweet chocolate

1/2 teaspoon vanilla
3 eggs
Whipped cream (garnish)
Chocolate shavings (garnish)

Cream sugar and butter, blending very well. Melt chocolate in double boiler and beat into mixture. Add vanilla. Add eggs, one at a time, beating well after each addition at high speed. Pour into pie shell. Garnish with whipped cream and chocolate shavings. Refrigerate.

Winning Recipes from Minnesota with Love

With some 15,000 lakes, there are lots and lots of fisherman in Minnesota. And it goes on all the time; in winter, they just saw a hole in the ice and pull 'em out. Some of the best fishing is on a frozen Minnesota lake. Fishing huts are quite cozy and offer a contrast to the open lakes of summer. These winter fishing-folks are likely sitting in their shirt sleeves, playing cards, and catching fish in a style unseen during warm weather ventures.

Amelia Bedelia's Raspberry Pie

CRUST:

1 cup flour	3/4 cup chopped pecans
1/2 cup margarine	1/4 cup powdered sugar

FILLING:

1 1/2 cups sugar

1/4 cup cornstarch

Dash salt

1 1/2 cups water

1 (3-ounce) package raspberry gelatin

1 (8-ounce) package cream cheese

2/3 cup powdered sugar

1 pint fresh raspberries (or 10 ounces frozen drained raspberries)

Cool Whip

Heat oven to 350°. Combine crust ingredients. Press on bottom and sides of 9- or 10-inch pie pan. Bake 8-10 minutes until light brown. Cool.

Combine sugar, conrstarch, salt, and water (can use drained juice). Cook over medium heat until thick and bubbly. Stir in gelatin until dissolved. Cool about 20 minutes.

Mix cream cheese and powdered sugar. Spread on crust. Arrange fresh raspberries on cream cheese layer. Pour gelatin mixture over berries. Refrigerate until firm. Serve with Cool Whip. Makes 8 servings.

Note: Can substitute strawberries and strawberry gelatin.

Favorite Recipes of Lester Park & Rockridge Schools

Cran-Lorraine Pie

SINGLE PIE SHELL:

1 cup shortening
1/2 stick butter
1 tablespoon oil
1/2 teaspoon salt

3 cups flour
1/2 cup buttermilk, less 2
  tablespoons
2 tablespoons vinegar

Mix and roll into pie pan, prick with fork, and bake at 475° for 8 minutes.

FILLING:

2 cups whole cranberry
  sauce (16 ounces)

1 tablespoon cornstarch
1 tablespoon cranberry juice

Combine cranberry sauce and cornstarch and bring to boil. Boil for one minute. Remove from heat and stir in cranberry juice. Cool. Take out 1/4 cup and set aside.

CANDY MIXTURE:

2 cups white vanilla milk
  chips (or white bark)
1 egg

1/4 cup water
1/2 teaspoon almond extract

Melt white chips; beat egg and water slightly. Add small amount of hot chips to egg-water, stir, and return it all back to the heating pan and boil until thick, about 5 minutes. Remove from heat. Add almond extract. Cool.

2 cups whipping cream
2 tablespoons powdered sugar

1 teaspoon vanilla
1/2 teaspoon almond extract

Beat whipping cream, powdered sugar, and flavorings. Mix half with candy mixture. Put half of candy mixture in pie shell. Add cranberry mix. Top with other half of candy mixture. Top with other half of whipping cream. Decorate with the 1/4 cup of cranberry mix. Garnish with sliced almonds.

Braham's Pie Cookbook

Because more popcorn is consumed per capita than anywhere else—an average of four pounds per person per year—Minneapolis-Saint Paul is the Popcorn-Eating Capital of the World.

Summertime Jewel Pie

OATMEAL CRUST:

1¹/2 cups oatmeal toasted for 10 minutes at 350°

¹/2 cup butter, melted
¹/2 cup brown sugar

Mix and pat in pan, bake 350° for 10 minutes. Cool before filling.

JEWEL FILLING:

1 (10-ounce) package frozen strawberries, thawed slightly
1 cup applesauce, sweetened
1 (3-ounce) package strawberry Jell-O

¹/2 cup 7-Up
¹/2 cup mini-marshmallows

Drain strawberry juice in saucepan; add applesauce and heat. Do not boil. Add Jell-O; stir to dissolve. Add strawberries and 7-Up. Let cool until starting to thicken. Put marshmallows in oatmeal crust. Spoon mixture carefully on top, and refrigerate until set. Serve with dollops of whipped cream.

Note: This is a lo-cal pie if the cream is left off.

Braham's Pie Cookbook

Peach Ice Pie

1 (9-inch) pie crust
1¹/4 cups water
1 package lemon or peach gelatin
1 pint vanilla ice cream

¹/2 teaspoon almond extract
1¹/2 cups sliced fresh peaches
Whipped cream

Prepare pie crust and bake; cool. Heat water to boiling in 2-quart saucepan. Remove from heat. Add gelatin; stir until dissolved. Add ice cream, cut into pieces and add to hot liquid. Stir until melted. Blend in almond extract. Chill until thickened but not set (25-35 minutes). Fold in peaches. Turn into pie shell. Chill until firm and top with whipped cream and additional peaches.

The Oke Family Cookbook

Tin Roof Ice Cream Pie

Have an empty 9-inch pie pan ready.

1/4 cup peanut butter
1/4 cup corn syrup
2 cups cornflakes
1 quart ice cream, slightly
   softened

Chocolate syrup
3 tablespoons chopped salted
   cocktail peanuts

Stir together peanut butter and corn syrup in a medium-size mixing bowl. Add cornflakes, stirring until well-coated. Press evenly in 9-inch pie pan. Chill.

Scoop softened ice cream into crust mixture. Freeze until firm. Remove from freezer 10 minutes before serving. To serve, top with chocolate syrup and peanuts.

Braham's Pie Cookbook

Bits 'O Brickle Ice Cream Pie*

PIE:
Prepared 9-inch graham
   cracker pie shell
1/2 gallon vanilla ice cream,
   softened

1/2 (7.8-ounce) bag brickle
   bits

Spoon 1/2 of ice cream into prepared pie shell. Sprinkle bits (1/2 bag) on top. Heap with remaining ice cream. Freeze.

SAUCE:
1 1/2 cups sugar
1 cup evaporated milk
1/4 cup butter

1/4 cup Karo (light)
Dash of salt
Remaining 1/2 bag bits

Combine sugar, milk, butter, syrup, and salt. Bring to boil over low heat; boil one minute. Remove from heat and stir in remaining bits. Cool. Stir occasionally. Chill. Stir sauce well before serving, spoon over pie. Keep remaining sauce. Good! Enjoy!

Favorite Recipes of Lester Park & Rockridge Schools

Buster Bar Dessert

1/2 cup melted butter	2 cups powdered sugar
1 pound Hydrox cookies	2/3 cup chocolate chips
1/2 gallon vanilla ice cream	1 1/2 cups evaporated milk
2 cups Spanish peanuts (or more to suit taste)	1/2 cup butter
	1 teaspoon vanilla

Mix together melted butter and crushed Hydrox cookies. Place in a 9x13-inch pan; refrigerate until firm.

Place ice cream (softened) on top of crust, then peanuts. Mix together powdered sugar, chocolate chips, evaporated milk and butter. Boil this mixture for 8 minutes, then stir and add vanilla. Cool and pour on top layer; freeze.

Salem Cook Book II

Butterscotch Sauce

1 cup light corn syrup	1/2 cup milk
1 cup brown sugar	3 tablespoons butter
Salt	Vanilla

Bring ingredients to full boil. Cook 5 more minutes. Makes one pint.

The Oke Family Cookbook

An-Jell-O Food Dessert
(A Low-Fat Dessert)

1 package angel food cake
mix
1 large package berry-flavored
gelatin

2 (10-ounce) packages frozen
berries (strawberries or
raspberries)
1 large container Cool Whip

Prepare angel food cake following the package directions. Let it cool. Pull apart cake into bite-sized pieces and cover the bottom of a 9x13-inch pan. Prepare Jell-O according to directions and let it set slightly. Cover the angel food layer with thawed berries. When Jell-O has set slightly, blend in Cool Whip with beaters. The mixture should thicken. Cover the berries with the Jell-O/Cool Whip mixture. Chill in the refrigerator for one hour. Enjoy!

Sharing our Best to Help the Rest

Frozen Mint Dream Dessert

1 (1-pound) package Hydrox or
  Oreo filled chocolate cookies
1/2 cup melted butter
1 large can evaporated milk
1 cup sugar
1/2 cup butter

2 squares baking chocolate
1/2 gallon plus 1 pint mint chip
  ice cream, softened
2 cups cream, whipped
Chopped toasted almonds

Crush cookies. Combine with 1/2 cup melted butter. Put in 2 (9x13-inch) cake pans. Chill.

Combine evaporated milk, sugar, 1/2 cup butter, and baking chocolate. Cook in heavy saucepan 10-15 minutes until thick, stirring and watching closely. (Or use microwave.) Let cool.

While filling is cooling, spread ice cream on crumbs, dividing it between the two pans. Freeze again, then spread with the cooled filling. Freeze once more, then top with whipped cream and sprinkle with almonds. Freeze. Let soften out of freezer a while before serving.

Dorthy Rickers Cookbook: Mixing & Musing

Lemon Sherbet Dessert

1 1/2 cups crushed Ritz
  crackers
4 tablespoons sugar
7 tablespoons melted
  margarine

2 quarts vanilla ice cream
1 quart lemon or lime sherbet

Mix first 3 ingredients until crumbly and press into a 9x13-inch pan. Mix ice cream and sherbet until soft and spread over crumbs; freeze.

TOPPING:
4 tablespoons lemon juice, or
  3 tablespoons Realemon
1 cup sugar

6 tablespoons margarine
2 beaten eggs

Mix and cook over low heat until dissolved and thick; cool; then spread over frozen ice cream and freeze.

Vaer saa god Cookbook

Zuccotto

Impressive!

3/4 cup chopped pecans
1 teaspoon oil
Salt
1 (12-ounce) pound cake
1/3 cup amaretto liqueur
3 tablespoons Cointreau
2/3 cup miniature semi-sweet
  chocolate bits, divided

2 cups heavy cream
1/3 plus 2 tablespoons
  powdered sugar, divided
4 teaspoons light corn syrup
2 teaspoons vanilla
2 tablespoons unsweetened
  cocoa powder

Place pecans in a shallow pan. Drizzle with oil and sprinkle lightly with salt; toss to mix. Toast pecans in oven at 375° until golden brown, about 5 minutes, stirring occasionally. Remove from oven and set aside to cool.

Cut pound cake into 1/8-inch slices and cut each slice in half diagonally. Place cake triangles close together on a jellyroll pan. Combine liqueurs in a measuring cup and drizzle evenly over cake. Line a 1 1/2-quart round-bottom bowl with plastic wrap. Place a triangle of cake against the inside of the bowl and repeat until the inside of the bowl is completely lined with cake. If there are gaps, fill in with pieces of moistened cake (reserve some for top). Coarsely chop 1/3 cup plus one tablespoon chocolate bits; set aside.

In a chilled bowl, combine cream, 1/3 cup powdered sugar, corn syrup, and vanilla. Beat until cream is stiff. Fold in 1/2 cup toasted pecans and chopped chocolate bits. Divide mixture into 2 equal parts. Spoon half of the whipped cream mixture into the cake-lined bowl, spreading it evenly over entire cake surface. Leave a well in the center. Melt the remaining chocolate bits. Cool slightly and fold into remaining half of whipped cream mixture. Spoon into cavity, completely filling the center. Even top, trimming pieces of cake. Top mixture with remaining cake pieces and cover bowl with plastic wrap. Refrigerate overnight.

To serve, remove top layer of plastic wrap. Cover bowl with a flat serving dish and invert dessert onto the plate. Lift off bowl, and carefully remove plastic wrap. Refrigerate until serving time.

CONTINUED

Combine 2 tablespoons powdered sugar and cocoa in a jar with a shaker top. Sprinkle mixture over top and sides of unmolded dessert just before serving. Sprinkle with remaining chopped pecans. Cut into wedges and serve. Serves 8-10.

Recipes of Note for Entertaining

Lemon Angel Food Dessert

1 tablespoon unflavored gelatin	Juice of 2 lemons
1/4 cup cold water	6 egg whites
6 egg yolks, beaten	1 angel food cake
1 1/2 cups sugar, divided	1 cup whipping cream

Soften gelatin in water. Beat yolks and add 3/4 cup sugar. Add lemon juice and cook in a double boiler until thick. Remove from heat and add gelatin. Cool. Beat whites, add 3/4 cup sugar gradually. Beat until very stiff. Fold into cooked egg yolk mixture.

Tear angel cake in pieces. In angel food pan or Bundt pan, alternate layers of torn cake and lemon mixture until all is used. Chill several hours or overnight. Unmold and frost with whipped cream. Refrigerate until ready to serve.

Duluth Woman's Club 70th Anniversary Cookbook

Mandarin Orange Dessert

2 sleeves Ritz crackers,
  crushed
1/4 cup butter
1/4 cup sugar
1 (9-ounce) carton whipped
  topping

1 can sweetened condensed
  milk
1 (6-ounce) can frozen orange
  juice concentrate, thawed
2 (11-ounce) cans mandarin
  oranges, drained

Mix cracker crumbs, butter, and sugar. Reserve some of the crumbs for the top. Pat into a greased 9x13-inch pan. Mix whipped topping, sweetened condensed milk, orange juice, and drained oranges. Spoon over crust. Sprinkle remaining crumbs on top. Refrigerate. Makes 12-15 servings.

A Dish to Pass

Cookie Salad

1 cup buttermilk
1 package instant vanilla
  pudding (or French vanilla)
1 (8-ounce) carton Cool Whip
1 can mandarin oranges,
  drained

1/2 - 3/4 bag crushed shortbread
  fudge stripe cookies or Oreo
  cookies
3/4 bag marshmallows (optional)

Mix buttermilk and pudding until creamy and smooth. Blend in Cool Whip, oranges and marshmallows. Add crushed cookies right before serving. Ready to serve immediately.

Sharing our Best / Bergen Lutheran Church

Rhubarb Dream

1 cup flour
5 tablespoons powdered
    sugar
1/2 cup butter or margarine
2 eggs

1 1/2 cups sugar
1/4 cup flour
3/4 teaspoon salt
2 cups rhubarb

Blend flour, powdered sugar, and butter. Press in ungreased 11 x 7 1/2-inch pan. Bake for 15 minutes at 350°. Beat eggs. Sift sugar, flour, and salt. Mix with eggs. Add to this mixture, rhubarb, finely cut. Pour over crust and bake for 35 minutes at 350°.

Recipes from St. Michael's

Mile-High Rhubarb Pie

Gives rise to lofty praise.

CRUST:
1 cup all-purpose flour
2 tablespoons powdered
    sugar

1/2 cup butter
Pinch of salt

FILLING:
2 1/2 cups cut-up rhubarb
1 1/3 cups sugar
3 egg yolks

2 tablespoons flour
1/3 cup milk

MERINGUE:
3 egg whites
1/4 teaspoon cream of tartar

6 tablespoons sugar
1/2 teaspoon vanilla

Heat oven to 350°. Mix crust ingredients together and press into 8-inch pie pan. Bake 20 minutes. Combine filling ingredients in saucepan, cook until thick; pour into baked crust. Heat oven to 400°. Beat egg whites and cream of tartar until foamy; gradually add sugar and beat until stiff but not dry. Fold in vanilla. Spread over filling; seal edges of meringue to crust. Bake about 10 minutes, until meringue is browned. Makes 1 (8-inch) pie.

From Minnesota: More Than A Cookbook

Raspberry Dessert

1½ cups crushed pretzels
½ cup sugar
½ cup melted butter
1 (8-ounce) package cream
cheese
1 (8-ounce) carton Cool
Whip

1 cup sugar
1 large package raspberry Jell-O
(or 2 small)
2 cups boiling water
2 (10-ounce) packages frozen
raspberries

Mix together first 3 ingredients. Pat in 9x13-inch pan. Bake 8 minutes at 325°. Cool. Mix well cream cheese, Cool whip and sugar. Spread over cooled crust for the filling. Combine Jell-O, water and raspberries. Pour over filling. (Does not need to cool before pouring over.) Cool until set and serve.

Our Heritage Cookbook

Four-Layer Delight

LAYER I:
1 cup flour   ½ cup butter
½ cup nuts

Mix all ingredients and press into a greased 9x13-inch pan. Bake at 350° for 15 minutes.

LAYER II:
1 cup Cool Whip, reserve
remainder
1 cup powdered sugar

1 (8-ounce) package cream
cheese, softened

Add Cool Whip and powdered sugar to cream cheese and spread on first layer.

LAYER III:
2 packages instant pudding   3 cups milk
mix (lemon or vanilla)

Mix pudding and milk with a fork until slightly thickened. (Do not cook.) Spread on second layer.

LAYER IV:
Cool Whip   Chopped nuts
Put remainder of Cool Whip on top of pudding and sprinkle with chopped nuts. Keeps several days in refrigerator.

Bethany Lutheran Church Celebrating 110 Years

Cream Puff Dessert

CRUST:

1 cup flour
1/2 cup margarine

1 cup boiling water
4 eggs, unbeaten

Boil margarine in water. Add flour into steadily boiling water. Cook and stir constantly until mixture leaves sides of pan and is in smooth compact mass. Remove from heat and add one egg at a time. Beat well after each egg added, by hand. Spread dough in jellyroll pan and bake in hot oven (400°) for 15 minutes. Reduce heat to 350° and bake for 10-15 minutes more.

FILLING:

1 (8-ounce) package cream
   cheese
2 (3-ounce) packages instant
   vanilla pudding

3 cups milk
1 large carton Cool Whip
Hershey's Chocolate Syrup

Beat cream cheese, pudding, and milk together and pour over crust. Spread Cool Whip over pudding. Drizzle syrup on Cool Whip and may add chopped peanuts. Refrigerate.

Kompelien Family Cookbook

Diane's Cream Puffs

1 cup water   1 cup flour
½ cup butter or margarine   4 eggs

Heat oven to 400°. Heat water and butter to rolling boil. Stir in flour. Stir vigorously over low heat about one minute or until mixture forms a ball. Remove from heat. Beat in eggs, all at one time; continue beating until smooth. Drop dough by slightly rounded teaspoonfuls onto ungreased baking sheet. Bake 35-40 minutes or until puffed and golden. Cool away from draft. Cut off tops and pull out any filaments of soft dough. Fill with filling.

FILLING:
1 (3½-ounce) package vanilla   1 cup milk
   instant pudding   1 cup chilled whipped cream

In small mixing bowl, blend one package vanilla instant pudding and one cup milk on low speed. Add chilled whipping cream; beat about 2 minutes on medium speed or until soft peaks form.

Old Westbrook Evangelical Lutheran Church Cookbook

Fruit Pizza

1 roll Pillsbury Refrigerator
  Sugar Cookies
1 (8-ounce) package cream
  cheese
1/2 cup powdered sugar
1 teaspoon vanilla
1 cup pineapple tidbits and
  juice
1 can mandarin orange slices
1 cup strawberries
1 1/2 tablespoons cornstarch
Banana slices
Blueberries

Spray a little Pam on a pizza pan. Spread cookie dough on pan and bake until light brown. Mix cream cheese, powdered sugar, and vanilla; spread on cooled crust. Arrange pineapple, orange slices, and strawberries on top of cream cheese layer. Heat pineapple and orange juice and thicken with 1 1/2 tablespoons cornstarch. Cool; pour over fruit. Banana slices, blueberries, and any other fresh fruit may be arranged on cream cheese layer as well.

Recipes and Memories

Fruit Pizza

CRUST:
2 sticks margarine
2 cups flour
1/2 cup powdered sugar

Mix and put in pizza pan. Bake 15 minutes at 300°. Cool.

1 (8-ounce) package cream
  cheese, softened
1/2 cup powdered sugar

Mix. Spread over cooled crust. Top with fresh fruit; strawberries, blueberries, kiwi, grapes, etc. Spread Glaze with pastry brush and refrigerate until ready to serve.

GLAZE:
2 tablespoons cornstarch
1/2 cup water
1/2 cup unsweetened fruit
  juice
1-2 teaspoons lemon juice

Clinton's 110th Cookbook

Wild Strawberry Dessert

One of the best of the fresh strawberry desserts in our collection.

CRUST:

1 cup flour
1/2 cup butter, melted
2 tablespoons powdered
  sugar

1/3 cup chopped pecans

Combine crust ingredients; pat in 9x13-inch pan and bake 20 minutes at 350°. Cool.

FIRST LAYER:

1 (8-ounce) Neufchatel cream
  cheese, softened

3/4 cup powdered sugar
1 cup Cool Whip

Mix and spread on chilled crust. Chill again.

SECOND LAYER:

1 cup sugar
3 tablespoons cornstarch
Pinch of salt
1 1/2 cups 7-Up
1/2 cup water
1 (3-ounce) package wild
  strawberry Jell-O

1 quart or more sliced fresh
  strawberries
Whipped cream
Jumbo strawberries for
  garnish

Combine in saucepan the sugar, cornstarch, salt, 7-Up and water. Cook until thickened. Remove from heat and add Jell-O. Cool. Then add strawberries. Put over first layer. Refrigerate. Cut in squares and top each with a dollop of whipped cream and a jumbo strawberry.

Dorthy Rickers Cookbook: Mixing & Musing

Mini Apple Pies

1 (12-ounce) package
  refrigerator biscuits
1 tart apple, peeled and
  chopped fine
1/4 cup raisins

3 tablespoons sugar
1 teaspoon cinnamon
2 tablespoons butter or
  margarine

Using a rolling pin, flatten each biscuit to a 3 to 4-inch circle.
Combine the apple, raisins, sugar, and cinnamon. Place a tablespoonful on each biscuit. Dot with butter. Bring up sides of
biscuits to enclose filling and pinch to seal. Place in ungreased
muffin cups. Bake at 375° for 11-13 minutes or until golden
brown. Serves 10.

A Taste of Kennedy Cook Book

Steffie's Apple Crisp

3/4 cup dark brown sugar,
  firmly packed
3/4 cup unbleached flour
1/2 cup uncooked regular
  oatmeal
1/2 teaspoon salt (optional)

1 teaspoon ground cinnamon
  (optional)
1/3 cup canola oil
4 large or 6 medium tart apples,
  washed, peeled, cored, and
  sliced

Preheat oven to 350°. In a large mixing bowl, using a large fork,
mix brown sugar, flour, oatmeal, salt, cinnamon, and oil. Stir
to combine into a crumbly mixture. Set aside. Spread sliced
apples in a 2-quart casserole dish or 9x9-inch baking dish sprayed
with nonstick spray. Sprinkle crumbly mixture evenly over
apples.

  Bake for 45 minutes, or until apples are soft and tender when
poked with fork. Serve warm. Store leftover apple crisp, covered, in refrigerator.

Bake Yourself Happy

Apple-Cranberry Crumble

A proven delight.

1 cup sugar
1 tablespoon all-purpose
  flour
1 teaspoon cinnamon

1/2 teaspoon nutmeg
6-8 apples, peeled and sliced
2 cups fresh or frozen
  cranberries

Combine and mix together. Pour apple mixture in a 9x13-inch Pyrex baking dish.

CRUMBLE TOPPING:
1 cup all-purpose flour
1 cup sugar
1/2 cup margarine

1 cup oatmeal
1/2 cup chopped nuts

Mix flour and sugar. Cut margarine in with pastry blender. Add remaining ingredients. Pour crumble topping over apple mixture and bake at 350° for 30-40 minutes. Yield: 8-10 servings.

Our Favorite Recipes

Apple Cuplets

1/4 cup sugar
1/2 teaspoon cinnamon
6 baking apples
2/3 cup flour
2/3 cup sugar
1/4 teaspoon baking powder

1/8 teaspoon salt
1 slightly beaten egg
3 tablespoons butter, melted
1 teaspoon vanilla
Cream

Combine the 1/4 cup sugar and cinnamon. Peel and core the apples. Roll in cinnamon-sugar mixture. Put apples in buttered custard cups, spooning the remaining cinnamon-sugar in centers of apples.

Combine flour, 2/3 cup sugar, baking powder, and salt. Combine beaten egg, melted butter, and vanilla. Add to the dry ingredients. Beat well. Place about 2 tablespoonsful of batter over each apple. Bake at 375° about 40 minutes. Serve warm (important) with lots of cream (doubly important).

Dorthy Rickers Cookbook: Mixing & Musing

Maultuschen

5 cups flour	8 baking apples, peeled, cored
1½ teaspoons salt	and thinly sliced
1½ cups shortening	4 tablespoons sugar
¾ cup ice cold water	Cinnamon

Sift flour and salt. Cut in shortening; add water, half at a time. Mix and press with a fork or fingers. Press together, making 4 balls. Chill. Roll out each pastry ball, one at a time, to a large thin round. Spread apples over pastry. Sprinkle one tablespoon sugar over apples and cinnamon to taste. Carefully roll and seal ends with cold water. Fit 4 rolls snuggly in a 9x13-inch pan. Bake at 375° for 30 minutes.

CUSTARD:

4 eggs, slightly beaten	3 cups milk, scalded
⅓ cup sugar	1 teaspoon vanilla
½ teaspoon salt	Dash of nutmeg

Beat eggs, sugar, and salt. Slowly add scalded milk and vanilla. Continue to beat. Add nutmeg. Pour over hot apple rolls, making certain tops are moist. Bake at 325° for 30 minutes. Cool 20 minutes before serving. Serve 1-inch slices with cheese for a meal. Keeps for several days in refrigerator. Also good cold. Serves 10.

Potluck Volume II

Romme Grot
(Scandinavian Cream Pudding)

1 quart whipping cream (at	1 teaspoon salt
least 24 hours old)	1 tablespoon sugar
1 cup flour	Butter
1 quart milk (boiled)	Sugar and cinnamon

Use heavy kettle, boil cream 10-15 minutes. Add flour slowly using a wire whip to keep mixture smooth, keep boiling on lower heat and stirring until butter appears. Add boiled milk and boil and stir to right consistency. Add sugar and salt. Put into bowl and pour butter over. Sprinkle with sugar and cinnamon. Serve lukewarm.

Bethany Lutheran Church Celebrating 110 Years

Bread Pudding

3 cups milk
1/3 cup butter
3 eggs
1 teaspoon vanilla
1/2 cup sugar

1/2 teaspoon salt
3 1/2 cups day old bread
  cubes
1 cup raisins
Dash of nutmeg

Scald milk, add butter and cool. Beat eggs, vanilla, sugar, and salt. Add to cooled milk mix. Place bread cubes into a 1 1/2 - 2-inch quart casserole. Pour egg mixture over the top. Fold in raisins. Sprinkle nutmeg on top. Bake at 350° for 40 minutes. Serve with cream.

Finn Creek Museum Cookbook

Mother's Bread Pudding

2 cups hot milk, skim or 2%
1 egg, beaten
1/2 cup sugar
1 tablespoon butter

1 teaspoon vanilla
Cinnamon
2 1/2 - 3 cups bread, broken
  into small pieces

Heat milk and mix eggs, sugar, butter, and vanilla together. Can also add a generous sprinkling of cinnamon. Mix altogether and pour buttered bread pieces in baking dish. Bake at 350° for 30 minutes. Serve hot with milk or cream. Also good cold.

Treasured Recipes of Chippewa County

Rice Pudding

1/2 cup rice (not Minute)	3 tablespoons water
1/2 teaspoon salt	1 cup whipping cream,
3 cups milk	whipped
1 package Knox gelatin	1 1/2 cups sugar

Cook rice, salt, and milk in a covered, double boiler until done, or about 1 1/2 - 2 hours. Stir occasionally. Soak gelatin in water and add to the cooked rice. Stir gently and chill. Add whipped cream and sugar to the cooked, cooled rice. Put the pudding in an oiled ring mold.

SAUCE:

2 packages of frozen	1/2 cup sugar
raspberries or strawberries	1 tablespoon lemon juice
2 1/2 tablespoons cornstarch	

Thaw berries (reserve 1 cup of juice). Add cornstarch and sugar to the juice and cook until thick. Add lemon juice after the mixture has cooked. Pour the mixture over the thawed fruit and cool.

Unmold the rice and serve the sauce in a dish placed in the middle of the rice ring.

Our Beloved Sweden: Food, Faith, Flowers & Festivals

Hanson's Favorite Rice Pudding

1 cup rice	2 cups milk
1/2 teaspoon salt	1/4 cup sugar
1 1/4 cups water	1 cup raisins

Place rice, salt, and water in saucepan. Cover, bring to boil. Reduce heat and cook for 15 minutes. Add milk and sugar and raisins. Bake in casserole in 350° oven about one hour. Add more milk, if needed, during baking. Serve with cinnamon, sugar, and milk.

One Hundred Years of Sharing

Swedish Smorgasbord Rice Pudding

1 cup rice in 2 cups water
6 eggs
5 cups milk
1 cup sugar
1 teaspoon vanilla

3/4 teaspoon almond
   flavoring
1 teaspoon ground nutmeg
1/4 teaspoon salt
1/2 cup raisins (optional)

Cook rice in water according to package directions, stirring 1 or 2 times over low heat until the water is absorbed. Beat eggs well. Add milk and beat. Add sugar and vanilla and continue beating. Add almond flavoring, nutmeg, and salt. Cook over boiling water until it slightly coats spoon. Add cooked rice and raisins, if desired, and mix well. Pour in baking dish and place in a pan of water. Bake at 350° for 1 - 1 1/2 hours (knife comes out clean). Can dot with butter and sprinkle top with cinnamon before baking, if desired. Serve with strawberries or raspberries.

Note: Some people separate (some or all) eggs and make a top layer of beaten whites (after cooking is done) over the top by adding 1/4 cup sugar and 1/4 teaspoon cream of tartar to beaten egg whites; continue baking until it starts to brown slightly.

Duluth Woman's Club 70th Anniversary Cookbook

Rice Porridge with Raspberry Sauce

This is a popular Norwegian dish of years ago.

PORRIDGE:

1 cup white rice, uncooked	2 heaping tablespoons
2 quarts milk	cornstarch
3 eggs	Pinch of salt
2/3 cup sugar	1-2 teaspoons vanilla

Place rice in double boiler with one quart of milk. Cook over low heat about one hour. Heat other quart of milk in larger kettle; add cooked rice and milk. Beat eggs, sugar, and cornstarch together. Add to hot milk and rice mixture, stirring as you add. Bring to boiling point and remove from heat. Add salt and vanilla. Serve warm or cold with cinnamon and sugar and/or cream, or top with Raspberry Sauce. Yields 20-25 (3-ounce) servings.

RASPBERRY SAUCE:

1/2 cup currant jelly	1 tablespoon lemon juice
1 pint or (10-ounce box frozen) raspberries	1 tablespoon cornstarch

Heat jelly in saucepan. Add raspberries. Stir in lemon juice. Remove from heat and put through a fine sieve or purée in blender to remove seeds. Reheat and add cornstarch dissolved in water. Bring to boil and boil 1-2 minutes. Cool and serve over rice porridge. Sauce can also be made with lingonberries.

Treasured Recipes of Chippewa County

Strawberry Applesauce Jell-O

2 (3-ounce) packages strawberry Jell-O	1 (10-ounce) package frozen strawberries, thawed
2 cups boiling water	1 1/2 cups applesauce

Stir together and put into mold. Top with whipping cream. Yield: 6-8 servings.

Salem Cook Book II

Double Decker Knox Blox

3 envelopes Knox unflavored
  gelatin
3 (3-ounce) packages flavored
  Jell-O (may use sugar free)

2½ cups boiling water
1 cup heavy cream
  (whipping)

In a large bowl combine Knox with flavored Jell-O. Add boiling water and stir until gelatin is completely dissolved. Stir in cream. Pour into shallow plastic 9x9-inch container with cover. Chill until firm. To serve cut in one-inch squares.

Note: Suggested combinations of flavored Jell-O are: 2 cherry with 1 black cherry or 3 watermelon.

A Taste of Kennedy Cook Book

Catalog
of
Contributing Cookbooks

Rushford. Southeast Minnesota.

CATALOG
of
CONTRITUTING COOKBOOKS

All recipes in this book have been selected from the Minnesota cookbooks shown on the following pages. Individuals who wish to obtain a copy of any particular book may do so by sending a check or money order to the address listed by each cookbook (not Quail Ridge Press). Please note the postage and handling charges that are required. State residents add tax only when requested. Prices and addresses are subject to change, and books may sell out and become unavailable. Retailers are invited to call or write to same address for discount information.

ANOKA COUNTY 4-H COOKBOOK

Anoka County 4-H Youth Development Program
550 Bunker Lake Boulevard NW
Anoka, MN 55304   612-755-1280

This is the third cookbook published by the Anoka County 4-H program. Approximately 600 4-H members, their parents, leaders, extension staff, and other friends have contributed their favorite recipes. 9 sections; 571 recipes; 397 pages. Included are some award-winning recipes used by 4-H members at the County Fair.

$ 9.00   Retail price
$ 3.00   Postage and handling
Make check payable to Anoka County 4-H Leaders' Council, Inc.

BAKE YOURSELF HAPPY

by Stephanie Kaye DeBenedet
808 Millwood Avenue
Roseville, MN 55113   612-483-1006

Eating quality baked goods makes me happy and healthy. This recipe book is written to encourage everyone to bake. Recipes are easy to prepare and bakers use lower fat ingredients and still enjoy great taste. Start baking; you'll feel great you baked it yourself!

$ 7.93   Retail price
$ .52   Tax for Minnesota residents
$ 1.50   Postage and handling
Make check payable to *Bake Yourself Happy*

BEARS IN MY KITCHEN: AN EXCLUSIVE COLLECTION OF BLACK BEAR RECIPES

Carol V. Suddendorf
173 County Road 8
Bovey, MN 55709   218-245-3608

A most unusual wild game cookbook, *Bears In My Kitchen* guides the outdoorsman's adventure into cooking with delectable black bear meat; and, substituting other meat; doubles as a classic cooking reference—soups, salads, entrees, desserts, even lard rendering and soap making. A must for every lover of great food!

$ 7.98   Retail price
$ .52   Tax for Minnesota residents
$ 1.50   Postage and handling
Make check payable to Carol V. Suddendorf
ISBN 0-9620852-0-0

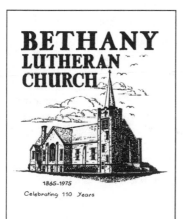

BETHANY LUTHERAN CHURCH CELEBRATING 110 YEARS

Lydia Circle/Bethany Lutheran Church
RR1 Box 241
Windom, MN 56101   507-847-5377

This cookbook was done in honor of our mothers and grandmothers for our churches 110th anniversary. There are 234 pages of recipes plus other helpful hints. The Norwegian recipes date back more than 100 years.

$ 7.00   Retail price
$ 2.50   Postage and handling
Make check payable to Lydia Circle

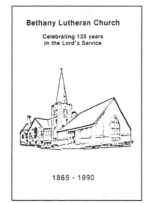

BETHANY LUTHERAN CHURCH CELEBRATING 125 YEARS

Bethany WELCA/VerJean Skrove
RR 1 Box 152
Jackson, MN 56143   507-847-5377

This cookbook was done for our church's 125th anniversary. There are 162 pages and 443 recipes. A section for special diet and microwave are included. There are time-saving and make-ahead and freeze recipes. Something for all.

$ 5.00   Retail price
$ 2.00   Postage and handling
Make check payable to Bethany WELCA

BRAHAM'S PIE COOKBOOK

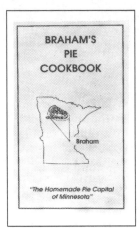

Pie Day Committee/Phyllis Londgren
1031 Legend Street
Braham, MN 55006   320-396-3063

Braham, Minnesota, is the official homemade pie capital of Minnesota. Annually the first Friday of August, Braham celebrates Pie Day by featuring delicious homemade pies. This recipe book contains 134 pie recipes and 8 pie crust recipes that have been perfected by those who specialize in pie baking.

$ 7.00   Retail price
$ 1.00   Postage and handling
Make check payable to *Braham Pie Cookbook*, Phyllis Londgren

CENTENNIAL COOKBOOK

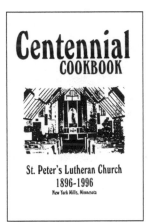

St. Peter's Lutheran Church
P. O. Box 7
New York Mills, MN 56567   218-385-2011 or 385-2633

Our centennial cookbook is a collection of tried and true recipes. It is full of time-honored favorites, as well as more updated low-fat, healthy recipes. There is something for everyone in this book! We use ingredients commonly found in a kitchen, so this is a practical, as well as economical, addition to any collection.

$ 6.00   Retail price
$ .39   Tax for Minnesota residents
$ 1.11   Postage and handling
Make check payable to St. Peter's Lutheran Church

THE CENTENNIAL SOCIETY COOKBOOK 1876-1996

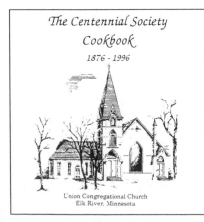

The Centennial Society Union Congregational Church
1118 Fourth Street
Elk River, MN 55330   612-441-1203

A delightful anniversary cookbook representing 120 years of great cooking from Elk River's finest cooks. 946 recipes to prepare simple or elegant dishes, snacks and crafts for kids, and a little This 'n That. Tastefully and efficiently arranged, and filled with good homey recipes. A true taste of Minnesota. 380 pages, 3-ring pocketed vinyl binder.

$14.95   Retail price
$ 3.00   Postage and handling
Make check payable to *The Centennial Society Cookbook*

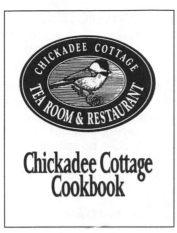

Chickadee Cottage Cookbook

CHICKADEE COTTAGE COOKBOOK

by Donna Hawkins
924 Pineridge Court
Mahtomedi, MN 55115   612-770-1576 or 345-5155

One hundred forty pages of Chickadee Cottage Tearoom favorites. Patterned after an English tearoom, Chickadee Cottage is a restored 1900's house on the Great River Road. Extensive flower and herb gardens provide a unique setting. Delicious recipes are presented in twelve sections including "Afternoon Tea and Herbs."

$ 9.95   Retail price
$ .65   Tax for Minnesota residents
$ 2.00   Postage and handling
Make check payable to *Chickadee Cottage Cookbook*.

Chickadee Cottage Cookbook II

CHICKADEE COTTAGE COOKBOOK II

by Donna Hawkins
924 Pineridge Court
Mahtomedi, MN 55115   612-770-1576 or 345-5155

The 275 recipes in *Chickadee Cottage Cookbook II* include more guest favorites as well as tested recipes from owner Donna Hawkins' files, family, and staff. The tearoom and restaurant bakes and cooks from scratch, using many locally produced products and produce. This is reflected in many of the recipes.

$10.95   Retail price
$ .71   Tax for Minnesota residents
$ 2.00   Postage and handling
Make check payable to *Chickadee Cottage Cookbook*.

**Clinton's
110th**

Clinton Ladies Civic Club
Clinton, Minnesota

CLINTON'S 110TH COOKBOOK

Clinton Ladies Civic Club
Box 368
Clinton, MN 56225   320-325-5280

A 214-page (plus index) collection of favorites from Clinton Community located in western Minnesota (population 540). Published to celebrate our 110th anniversary, the book contains short historic items and photos of the community. Minnesota cooks are noted for good recipes, and over 500 of them are listed in nine categories. Proceeds support community projects.

$ 6.00   Retail price
$ 2.00   Postage and handling
Make check payable to Clinton Women's Civic Club

THE CLOVIA RECIPE COLLECTION

Alumnae Association Beta of Clovia
Attention Margit Hauge
9757 Russell Avenue South
Bloomington, MN 55431   612-881-1871

This cookbook, 165 pages, features 250 recipes from members of the alumnae organization of Beta of Clovia Sorority, University of Minnesota. Many members are graduates of the University's home economics programs; their recipes reflect a love of food and family traditions. Proceeds support the collegiate chapter.

$10.95   Retail price
$ 4.00   Postage and handling
Make check payable to Alumnae Beta of Clovia

A DISH TO PASS

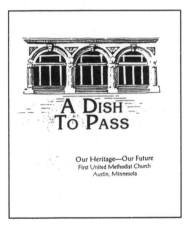

Our Heritage—Our Future
First United Methodist Church
Austin, Minnesota

First United Methodist Church
702 19th Avenue S.W.
Austin, MN 55912   507-437-4834

This cookbook is a "comfort" link from our heritage. Food has always been an important social part of religious events in First Church since its beginning in 1908. Good cooks have hosted receptions, bazaars, and congregational dinners and share here, 689 of their favorite Midwestern Recipes. 7¼ x 8¾, 328 pages, 689 recipes.

$ 9.00   Retail price
$ 2.00   Postage and handling
Make check payable to First United Methodist Church.

DORTHY RICKERS COOKBOOK: MIXING AND MUSING

by Dorthy Rickers
The Cows' Outside
326 10th Street
Worthington, MN 56187   507-372-7175

Dorthy's popular, long-time food column in the Worthington, Minnesota, *Daily Globe* yielded this fine collection of some 700 recipes in 430 pages, organized on a newspaper theme. The text is conversational and tempting, leading many to say they enjoy it for bedtime reading as well as good cooking.

$14.95   Retail price
$ .97   Tax for Minnesota residents
$ 4.00   Postage and handling
Make check payable to The Cows' Outside

DULUTH WOMAN'S CLUB
70TH ANNIVERSARY COOKBOOK

Duluth Woman's Club
2400 East Superior Street
Duluth, MN 55812   218-724-3168 or 724-5184

The Duluth Woman's Club 70th Anniversary Cookbook is particularly inviting not only for the unique recipes contained in its 315 pages, but carefully researched literature regarding food has been tucked into every page to make reading and eating a new adventure.

$15.00   Retail price
$ 2.50   Postage and handling
Make check payable to Duluth Woman's Club

FAVORITE RECIPES OF LESTER PARK
AND ROCKRIDGE SCHOOLS

Lester Park and Rockridge Schools PTAs
c/o Kathy Proctor
1120 N 54th Avenue E
Duluth, MN 55804   218-525-1445

This is a Northern Minnesota family cookbook. It is filled with a tempting variety of tried and true recipes. You don't have to be a gourmet cook to enjoy this book. This 170-page, 350-recipe cookbook was published as a fundraiser for two eastern Duluth elementary schools. Enjoy!

$ 8.00   Retail price
$ 2.25   Postage and handling
Make check payable to Lester Park/Rockridge PTA

FEEDING THE FLOCK

Maple Grove Evangelical Free Church
8588 Rice Lake Road
Maple Grove, MN 55311

Feeding the Flock is a Northwoods' favorite. This 128-page Minnesota collection cookbook includes Swedish Potatoes, Wild Rice Soup and Paul's Favorite Pheasant. Lots of hearty cabin fare and delectable desserts. Sit back, enjoy and listen for the sound of 10,000 lakes.

$ 7.00   Retail price
$ 3.50   Postage and handling
Make check payable to Maple Grove Evangelical Free Church

FINN CREEK
MUSEUM

COOKBOOK

OVER 1300 RECIPES

FINN CREEK MUSEUM COOKBOOK

Minnesota Finnish American Historical Society Chapter 13
Box 134
New York Mills, MN 56567   218-385-3962 or 385-2355

Finn Creek Museum Cookbook is a collection of favorite recipes handed down from generation to generation. The 600-page spiral cookbook includes recipes of various nationality groups, plus many good household hints. The profits are used to further the development of the museum near New York Mills, MN.

$12.50   Retail price
$ 3.00   Postage and handling
Make check payble to Finn Creek Museum

FIRST UNITED METHODIST CHURCH COOKBOOK

United Methodist Women
P. O. Box 668
Worthington, MN 56187-0668   507-372-2939

In the 228 pages of the *First United Methodist Church Cookbook,* you will find over 590 delicious, tried and true recipes. They have been gathered together in a handsome, hardcover 3-ring notebook with special divider pages listing prayers, helpful hints, and conversion charts. A cookbook sure to please everyone!

$12.50   Retail price
$ 3.00   Postage and handling
Make check payable to United Methodist Women

FROM MINNESOTA . . . MORE THAN A COOKBOOK

by Laurie and Debra Gluesing
4675 Hodgson Road
Shoreview, MN 55126   612-484-0267

A delightful 260-page cookbook with tried and true favorites. Most of the recipes use what you already have—no extra trips. Combine that with the folklore and humor of Minnesota, then blend together for sure success!

$11.95   Retail price
$ 2.50   Postage and handling
Make check payable to More than Souvenirs
ISBN 0-9631357-1-6

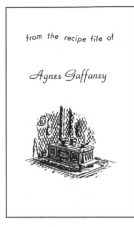

FROM THE RECIPE FILE OF AGNES GAFFANEY

by Cindy Stamness
721 Village Green Place
Mora, MN 55051   320-679-1058

Cindy Stamness' grandma, Agnes, was a Minnesota farm wife and mother, active in her church, family events, and clubs. With meat-and-potatoes meals, her recipes reflect the need for a variety of pies, cakes, bars, desserts, and cookies for morning and afternoon farm lunches, potluck suppers, and when company is coming.

$25.00   Retail price includes tax and postage
Make check payable to Cindy Stamness

GREAT COOKS OF ZION CHURCH

Zion United Church of Christ
240 South Elmwood Street
Le Sueur, MN 56058   507-665-6441

In observance of Zion Church's 125th Anniversary, the church's Historical Committee decided to publish a cookbook. A committee of seven women compiled this collection of favorite recipes. Zion has long had the reputation of having excellent cooks, as evidenced by its well attended Spring Luncheons and Roast Beef Dinners.

$ 7.00   Retail price
$ 2.00   Postage and handling
Make check payable to Zion United Church of Christ

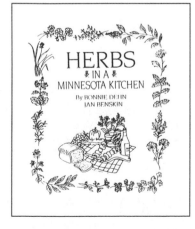

HERBS IN A MINNESOTA KITCHEN

by Jan Benskin and Bonnie Dehn
15701 Juniper Ridge Drive NW
Ramsey, MN 55303   612-422-1717

The 121-page *Herbs in a Minnesota Kitchen* will appeal to novice and experienced cooks who wish to expand their herbal repertoire. 113 excellent recipes, information on edible flowers and herbal teas, an herb chart as well as hand-lettered tips make this attractive cookbook a welcome addition to any kitchen.

$12.95   Retail price
$ 2.00   Postage and handling
Make check payable to Benskin, Inc.
ISBN 0-9637651-1-6

KITCHEN KEEPSAKES

The Houselog Family
c/o Linda Pommer
Rt. 1 Box 209
Ellsworth, MN 56129-9741   507-967-2241

First printed in 1988, *Kitchen Keepsakes* has remained a very popular book. People say, "This is the cookbook I go back to for good recipes." Submitted by family members known for their home-cooking the cookbook includes 382 recipes. Also a 5-page "Memories" section, which will bring warm memories to new readers.

$ 4.00   Retail price
$ 2.00   Postage and handling
Make check payable to Linda Pommer

KOMPELIEN FAMILY COOKBOOK

Janeen Kompelien
Rt. 1 Box 83
Cottonwood, MN 56229   507-423-6680

The *Kompelien Family Cookbook* was compiled from over 100 years of Norwegian cooking passed down through the generations; from great grandmother to great grandchildren. The cookbook has over 700 recipes in a wide variety of recipes from Lefsa to Elephant Stew.

$10.00   Retail price
$ 2.00   Postage and Handling
Make check payable to Janeen Kompelien

LICENSE TO COOK - MINNESOTA STYLE

by Gerry Kangas
Penfield Press
215 Brown Street
Iowa City, IA 52245   800-728-9998

Gerry Kangas and her husband owned and managed a board and lodging home in Minnesota for over 20 years; their reputation was built on "Good Home Cooking." This little 3½ x 5-inch 160-page cookbook is packed with great recipes.

$ 6.95   Retail price (Postage paid) 2/$12; 3/$18
Make check payable to Penfield Press
ISBN 1-57216-028-4

LUTHERAN CHURCH BASEMENT WOMEN: LUTEFISK, LEFSE, LUNCH AND JELL-O

by Janet Letnes Martin and Allen Todnem
Box 274
Hastings, MN 55033   800-950-6898

Nominated for Minnesota Book Award in 1993, this humorous cookbook offers hearty Midwest recipes by women of the Lutheran Church. Social commentaries, hilarious insights into the way things were cooked in the church basements. Over 100,000 copies in print.

$ 9.95   Retail price
$ .65   Tax for Minnesota residents
$ 3.00   Postage and handling ($6.00 max. any amount)
Make check payable to Martin House
ISBN 0-9613437-6-1

MAPLE HILL COOK BOOK 1992

Maple Hill Senior Citizens Club and Community Club
c/o Donna M. Lease
11553 Townline Road
Hibbing, MN 55746   218-262-3511

Maple Hill Cook Book 1992 is made up of 130 pages containing 385 tried and true recipes from our local Senior Citizens Club and Community Club. It has a great selection of recipes. It will be one of your favorite cookbooks to plan tasty meals for you and your family.

$ 5.00   Retail price
$ 2.00   Postage and handling
Make check payable to Maple Hill Hall Community Club

MARTHA CHAPTER 132 OES COOKBOOK

Order of Eastern Star
312 Harrison H106
Anoka, MN 55303   612-421-2864 or 755-6432

This is a book of favorite recipes from the members of the fraternal organization. Several are quantity recipes used for our money making projects. 130 pages.

$ 8.00   Retail price
$ 2.00   Postage and handling
Make check payable to Martha Chapter 132

MINNESOTA HERITAGE COOKBOOK VOL. I: HAND ME DOWN RECIPES

Edited by Sue Zelickson
American Cancer Society Minnesota Division
3316 West 66th Street
Minneapolis, MN 55435   612-925-6370 or 1-800-582-5152
(Minnesota Only)

These hand-me-down recipes from Minnesota cooks tell the ethnic heritage that is passed down from family kitchens throughout the state. The recipes were collected, tested, tasted, and made ready to be passed on to generations to come along and not be lost.

$15.95   Retail price
$ .96   Tax for Minnesota residents
$ 3.00   Postage and handling first book/$2.00 each addl.
Make check payable to American Cancer Society.
ISBN 0-87197-374-X

MINNESOTA HERITAGE COOKBOOK VOL. II: LOOK WHAT'S COOKING NOW!

Edited by Sue Zelickson
American Cancer Society Minnesota Division
3316 West 66th Street
Minneapolis, MN 55435   612-925-6370 or 1-800-582-5152
(Minnesota Only)

A new treasury of tested, tasted recipes for all occasions and the tastes and lifestyles of today's cooks. Over 300 light, fresh and natural recipes, delicous and easy to prepare. Ways to lower fat and add fiber and vitamins to lower the risk of certain cancers.

$15.95   Retail price
$ .96   Tax for Minnesota residents
$ 3.00   Postage and handling first book/$2.00 each addl.
Make check payable to American Cancer Society
ISBN 0-87197-375-8

THE OKE FAMILY COOKBOOK

by Barbara and Deborah Oke
Bethany House Publishers
11300 Hampshire Avenue South
Minneapolis, MN 55438   800-328-6109

Fascinating recipes in 220 pages, including holiday favorites, international foods, kid's stuff, unexpected guests, "wet your whistle" recipes and others for "zest and zip." Family anecdotes and photos give intriguing personal glimpses of well-loved author Janette Oke's family.

$ 9.99   Retail price
$ .65   Tax for Minnesota residents
$ 3.00   Postage and handling
Make check payable to Bethany House Publishers
ISBN 1-55661-529-9

OLD WESTBROOK EVANGELICAL LUTHERAN CHURCH: 125TH ANNIVERSARY

Old Westbrook WELCA
711 S. Fir Street
Lamberton, MN 56152   507-752-7470

The cookbook was compiled by Old Westbrook WELCA members as a fund-raiser for the 125th Anniversary of the oldest church in Cottonwood County. Norwegian and Finnish recipes along with "simple good-eatin'" recipes are featured. 134 pages, 316 recipes.

$ 6.00   Retail price
$ 2.00   Postage and handling
Make check payable to Old Westbrook WELCA

ONE HUNDRED YEARS OF SHARING

Calvary Covenant Women
Box 245
Evansville, MN 56326   218-948-2223

In 1987, we compiled this cookbook with the history of our church for our Centennial anniversary. It contains many Swedish heritage recipes that are used often in this area. The book contains about 800 recipes on 242 pages. We received recipes from past confirmands and members of the church.

$10.00   Retail price
$ 3.00   Postage and handling
Make check payable to Calvary Covenant Women

OUR BELOVED SWEDEN: FOOD, FAITH, FLOWERS & FESTIVALS

by Janet Letnes Martin and Ilene Letnes Lorenz
Box 274
Hastings, MN 55033   800-950-6898

This beautiful book divided by eight full-colored Swedish folk art paintings called Dala-paintings, is filled with wonderful Swedish recipes: Soup from the Meadow, Kristina's Torte, and the meatball recipe from the Swedish Royal Palace. Also contains a section on the world renouned Swedish smorgasbord.

$17.95   Retail price
$ 1.17   Tax for Minnesota residents
$ 3.00   Postage and handling ($6.00 max. any amount)
Make check payable to Martin House
ISBN 1-886627-02-9

OUR FAMILY'S FAVORITES

South Santiago Lutheran Church
Attention Rosalie Klinker
8575 175th Avenue
Becker, MN 55308

Our Family's Favorites is a collection of the favorite recipes from the membership of the
South Santiago Lutheran Church. This cookbook has 270 pages, is spiral bound and has a
laminated cover.

$ 8.50 Retail price
$ 2.00 Postage and handling
Make check payable to South Santiago WELCA

OUR FAVORITE RECIPES

Saint Marys Hospital Auxiliary
Saint Marys Gift Shop
1216 2nd Street Southwest
Rochester, MN 55902   507-255-5951

This collection was published to replace an
outdated former cookbook. We have included
historic information related to our Mayo heritage with each section divider. The outstanding collection contains over 500 recipes in 268
pages including a healthy, low-fat, low-sodium
section provided by our Dietetics Department.

$12.50 Retail price
$ .88 Tax for Minnesota residents
$ 3.00 Postage and handling
Make check payable to Saint Marys Auxiliary Gift Shop

OUR FAVORITE RECIPES

Aurdal Lutheran Church
Attention Doris Opsahl
Route 2, Box 866
Underwood, MN 56586   218-826-6972

A simple 160-page cookbook compiled by
women of one of the first country churches of
Scandinavian descent in our area. It includes
397 favorite recipes from over 80 contributors
and several pages of useful household hints and
information—the first cookbook of our 125-
year history.

$ 7.25 Retail price
$ 1.25 Postage and handling
Make check payable to Aurdal Cookbook Fund

OUR HERITAGE COOKBOOK

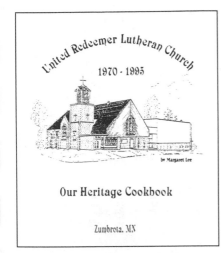

United Redeemer Lutheran Church
21302 450th Street
Zumbrota, MN 55992   507-732-5289

We know we have a good cookbook. We are
from a state that has a Scandinavian Heritage,
and we have a lot of excellent recipes from that
section. The Main Dish Section has excellent
recipes. Hard vinyl cover with fold back stand.
362 pages; over 900 recipes.

$15.00 Retail price
$ 4.00 Postage and handling
Make check payable to United Redeemer Heritage Fund

PEOPLE PLEASER

by Goldie Pope Lohse
2226 Albion Avenue
Fairmont, MN 56031   507-238-4998

"The everything cookbook," easy recipes, party
section, party games, quantity cooking (50-100
people), charts-tips-weights and measures, time
tables, spot removal, herb guide, treats and entertainment for kids. How to fold napkins, and
microwave cooking.

$15.95 Retail price
$ .48 Tax for Minnesota residents
$ 2.50 Postage and handling
Make check payable to Goldie Pope Lohse

POTLUCK VOLUME II

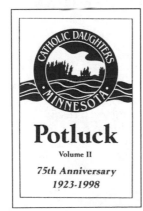

MN Catholic Daughters of the Americas
Box 161
Medford, MN 55049   507-455-1555

Potluck was compiled by CDA members across
Minnesota for our 75th anniversary as a state
court in 1998. There are 1,572 recipes the—
largest section "Main Dishes" includes 365 recipes! The 518 pages include an alphabetical
recipe index, and the divider pages cover all the
activities of our organization.

$15.00 Retail price
$ .97 Tax for Minnesota residents
$ 3.00 Postage and handling
Make check payable to MN CDA
ISBN 0-9653975-0-5

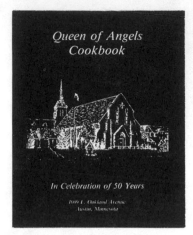

QUEEN OF ANGELS COOKBOOK

Queen of Angels Women's Council
c/o Sue Davison
811 14th Avenue SE
Austin, MN 55912   507-433-8025

Our 300-page Golden Anniversary cookbook contains over 800 family favorite recipes from the best cooks in our parish. You're sure to find a crowd pleasing casserole, salad or dessert for your next brunch, reunion, potluck or card party. Plastic cover, 3-ring binding, divided and easy to read.

$ 8.50   Retail price
$ 2.00   Postage and handling
Make check payable to *Queen of Angels Cookbook*

RECIPES AND MEMORIES

St. Peter Evangelical Lutheran Church
Attention Muriel Klenz
Route 1 Box 180
Fairmont, MN 56031

This book was published in celebration of our church's 100th anniversary. Recipes were collected from past and present members and from families of many deceased members. 245 pages; 760 recipes.

$ 8.00   Retail price
$ 2.00   Postage and handling
Make check payable to St. Peter's WELCA

RECIPES FROM MINNESOTA WITH LOVE

by Betty Malisow
Strawberry Point, Inc.
16163 Fillmore Avenue Southeast
Prior Lake, MN 55372   800-999-5858

Popular cooking instructor and cookbook author, Betty Malisow, shares the best of her recipe collection along with fascinating Minnesota history and folklore for a unique, memorable cooking and eating experience. Over 200 tantalizing recipes bound in a convenient lay-flat binding plus a comprehensive index.

$13.95   Retail price
$ .91   Tax for Minnesota residents
$ 1.50   Postage and handling
Make check payable to Strawberry Point, Inc.
ISBN 0-913703-00-1

RECIPES FROM THE FRIENDS AND FAMILY OF ST. MICHAEL'S LUTHERAN CHURCH AND PRESCHOOL

St. Michael's Cookbook Committee
9201 Normandale Boulevard
Bloomington, MN 55437   612-941-5372

"One of the best church cookbooks I have ever seen" is the comment we hear about our 900+ recipe cookbook with a wide variety of family favorite recipes. The drawings on the 15 colored divider pages are drawn by our preschool students. Spiral bound—412 pages.

$12.00   Retail price
$ 2.00   Postage and handling
Make check payable to St. Michael's Preschool

RECIPES FROM THE FLOCK

Tonseth Lutheran Church
RR 1
Erhard, MN 56534   218-736-7929

Recipes from the Flock is a collection of recipes submitted by the women of Tonseth Lutheran Church of rural Erhard. The book consists of 128 pages with over 450 tried and true recipes that have been passed down from generation to generation of church members. The book is a three-ring-binder with a laminated cover.

$ 8.50   Retail price
$ 4.00   Postage and handling
Make check payable to Tonseth Lutheran WELCA

RECIPES OF NOTE FOR ENTERTAINING

Rochester Civic Music Guild
P. O. Box 5802
Rochester, MN 55902

Looking to entertain; this cookbook has 328 pages filled with recipes to enjoy, from casual everyday recipes to elegant and easy. There are 15 complete menus to entertain with throughout the year, a very special Victorian Tea, and a Yulefest section to brighten your holidays. Music selections and wine suggestions complete each menu. Bon appetit!

$15.00   Retail price
$ 1.05   Tax for Minnesota residents
$ 3.00   Postage and handling
Make check payable to Rochester Music Guild
ISBN 0-9621066-1-5

RED OAK GROVE LUTHERAN CHURCH FAMILY COOKBOOK

Women of the Evangelical Lutheran Church of America
RR 1 Box 286
Austin, MN 55912   507-437-1483

The cookbook is loose-leaf with a variety of recipes identified by colored tabs for each group. Easy recipes from good cooks guarantee this book to be among your favorites.

$ 8.50   Retail price
Make check payable to WELCA

SALEM COOK BOOK II

Salem Lutheran Church Women
c/o Diane Schulte
4055 60th Street SW
Montevideo, MN 56265   320-269-6747

"Cookbooks represent history in the testing, the sharing of tradition and ourselves." This truly fits the Salem Lutheran Church cookbook. This 145-page book is a necessity in every kitchen. It is filled with delicious recipes ranging from modern delicacies to traditional Scandinavian favorites.

$10.00   Retail price (includes postage and handling)
Make check payable to Salem Lutheran Church Women

SEARS THROUGH THE YEARS

Stewartville Area Historical Society
Rt. 1 Box 35
Racine, MN 55967-0035   507-378-2384

Sears Through the Years; a collection of recipes by members of our society; of their family heritage; the dividers are actual pages from a 1918 Sears catalog of foods—a bit of history of the birthplace of Richard Sears, whose house is our restoration project. 200 tasty recipes and history of foods. 100 pages of joy to read and try.

$ 8.00   Retail price
$ .52   Tax for Minnesota residents
$ 1.93   Postage and handling
Make check payable to Stewartville Area Historical Society

SHARING OUR BEST TO HELP THE REST

Independent School District 196 and
United Way of the Saint Paul Area
166 Fourth Street East, Suite 100
St. Paul, MN 55101-1448   612-291-8329

Sharing Our Best to Help the Rest is a collection of 1000+ treasured recipes contributed by employees of Rosemount-Apple Valley-Eagan School District in Minnesota. All profits from the sale of this cookbook go to United Way of the Saint Paul Area to support the health and human service needs of area residents.

$10.00   Retail price
$ 3.00   Postage and handling
Make check payable to United Way of the Saint Paul Area

SHARING OUR BEST

Bergen Lutheran Church
c/o Carol Crosby
RR 4 Box 215
Montevideo, MN 56265   320-269-6685

Our book contains 239 pages with over 700 recipes and a number of pages with useful information and handy hints. The recipes are tried and true from some very good cooks.

$ 8.00   Retail price
$ 2.50   Postage and handling
Make check payable to Bergen Lutheran Church

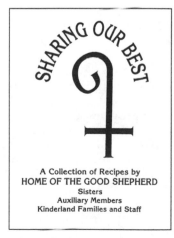

SHARING OUR BEST

Home of the Good Shepherd
5100 Hodgson Road
St. Paul, MN 55126-1297   612-484-0221

Over 400 delicious recipes obtained from Good Sheperd Sisters from all over the world and members of our local Good Shepherd Auxiliary all bound in a sturdy three-ring binder. Includes a special "Cooking with Kids" section.

$10.00   Retail price
$ .06   Tax for Minnesota residents
$ 1.25   Postage and handling
Make check payable to Good Shepherd Auxiliary Cookbook

A TASTE OF FAITH

Faith Lutheran Church
P. O. Box 71
Isle, MN 56342   320-676-3161

Our 150-page cookbook features recipes from wild game to traditional ethnic to heart smart. Recipes range, in preparation, from "fun for children" to "fun for the more seasoned cook." Our book is published in a three-ring, self-standing binder for convenience while using, and ability to add recipes and pages.

$10.00   Retail price
$ 3.00   Postage and handling
Make check payable to Faith Lutheran Church

A TASTE OF KENNEDY COOKBOOK

Kennedy Elementary PTSA
P. O. Box 374
Willmar, MN 56201   320-235-0757

This delightful book has over 300 pages containing 700 plus recipes from our elementary families. It has great illustrations by kids, a laminated cover for easy clean up, is spiral bound for ease in use, and has the added benefit of a variety of comments that the children included. Terrific book!

$10.00 Retail price (includes postage)
Make check payable to Kennedy PTSA Cookbook

THYME FOR ALL SEASONS

Junior League of Duluth
Duluth, MN

Northern Minnesota, known for its short growing season, still offers a potpourri of ingredients to tantalize the most creative cooks. *Thyme for All Seasons* provides a wide variety of recipes for year-round enjoyment in this 287-page soft-cover cookbook. It is no longer in print, but there may be a future cookbook from the Junior League of Duluth.

TREASURED RECIPES FROM TREASURED FRIENDS

by Colleen Beal
26628 Cabot Avenue
Faribault, MN 55021   507-332-2727

A collection of 691 favorites of the author. All tested, (some for years), tasted and easy recipes. Easy to follow instructions and nice bright crips print. A book enjoyed by both the novice and the experienced cook.

$ 9.00   Retail price
$ .59   Tax for Minnesota residents
$ 2.00   Postage and handling
Make check payable to Colleen Beal

TREASURED RECIPES OF CHIPPEWA COUNTY

Chippewa County Historical Society
P.O. Box 303
Montevideo, MN 56265   320-269-7637

Treasured Recipes of Chippewa County features 194 pages of taste-tingling sensations including many traditional Scandinavian favorites. Also packed not only with delicious recipes, but dozens of helpful cooking hints, home remedies and handy tips. We invite you to enjoy these time-tested ethnic delacacies.

$10.00   Retail price
$ 3.00   Postage and handling
Make check payable to Chippewa County Historical Society

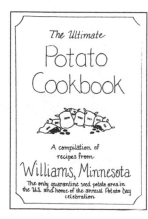

THE ULTIMATE POTATO COOKBOOK

Williams Community Commercial Association
c/o Nancy Jewell
HC 2 Box 122 B
Williams, MN 56686   218-783-2071

The Ultimate Potato Cookbook consists of 350+ potato recipes from appetizers to desserts. All are tried and tested; some of these recipes have won potato cookery contests at the annual Potato Day Celebrations. 106 pages.

$ 8.00   Retail price
$ 2.00   Postage and handling
Make check payable to Williams Community Commercial Assn.

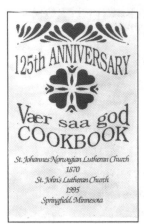

VAER SAA GOD COOKBOOK

WELCA St. John's Lutheran Church
P. O. Box 144
Springfield, MN 56087

This book has over 360 pages of favorite recipes contributed by church members, including a section of Scandinavian origin. It's one of those outstanding and interesting church cookbooks that people request and then have fun trying the variety of foods.

$10.00   Retail price
$ 2.50   Postage and handling
Make check payable to St. John's WELCA

WANNASKA CENTENNIAL

Riverside Lutheran Church
HCR #3 Box 38
Wannaska, MN 56761   218-425-7782 or 425-7523

The Wannaska Centennial Cookbook is a collection of 1240 favorite recipes contributed by the Riverside Lutheran Church Women, neighbors, friends and relatives. It includes the cookbook of 1951, and the favorites of our current Sunday school members. The divider pages have information concerning our community both past and present.

$13.00   Retail price
$ 3.00   Postage and handling
Make check payable to Riverside Church Women

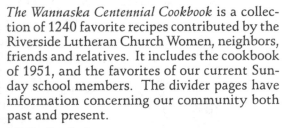

WHEN FRIENDS COOK

Friends of the Minneapolis Institute of Arts
The Friends Office MIA
2400 Third Avenue South
Minneapolis, MN 55404   612-870-3045

A collection of 300 tested recipes, from old family favorites to contemporary cuisine, including quick favorites for busy cooks, vegetarian entrées and splendid gourmet treats for special occasions. A collector's edition from its elegant cover to the 16 full-color reproductions of treasures from The Minneapolis Institute of Arts. Hardbound, 304 pages.

$18.00   Retail price
$ 2.00   Postage and handling
ISBN 0-9634248-0-7
Make check payable to The Friends of the Institute

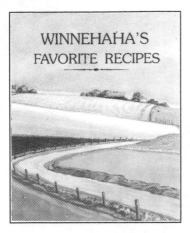

WINNEHAHA'S FAVORITE RECIPES

Winnehaha's of Minnesota
1030 Evergreen Trail
Circle Pines, MN 55014   612-785-0368

A collection of favorites from the Minnesota camper's club The Winnehaha's. Many recipes from potluck suppers, from some of Minnesota's great cooks!

$10.00   Retail price
$ 3.00   Postage and handling
Make check payable to Winnehaha's

WINNING RECIPES FROM MINNESOTA WITH LOVE

by The Cooks of Minnesota
Strawberry Point, Inc.
16163 Fillmore Avenue Southeast
Prior Lake, MN 55372   800-999-5858

These winning recipes were compiled in a statewide recipe contest and reflect the rich heritage and wide range of cultures that make up the people and cuisine of the heartland of America. So come on in and share some of the favorite recipes from the best cooks found throughout the state of Minnesota.

$13.95   Retail price
$ .91   Tax for Minnesota residents
$ 1.50   Postage and handling
Make check payable to Strawberry Point, Inc.
ISBN 0-913703-15-X

INDEX

Lake Scenic in Voyageurs National Park. Northern Minnesota.

THE QUAIL RIDGE PRESS
"BEST OF THE BEST" COOKBOOK SERIES

The cookbooks in the Quail Ridge Press "Best of the Best" series are considered the most complete survey available of a state's particular cooking style and flavor. They are compiled by searching out a comprehensive cross-section of the leading cookbooks written and published within the state, and then requesting the authors, editors, and publishers of these books to select their most popular recipes. A sampling of these recipes has been selected to create that state's "Best of the Best" edition. Each recipe included in the book is a proven favorite that conveys the state's unique cuisine.

A catalog section in each volume lists the contributing cookbooks with descriptive copy and ordering information on each book. This section is of particular interest and value to cookbook collectors. The volumes listed below have been completed as of January, 1998.

Best of the Best from Alabama
288 pages, (28-3) $14.95

Best of the Best from Arkansas
288 pages, (43-7) $14.95

Best of the Best from Florida
288 pages, (16-X) $14.95

Best of the Best from Georgia
336 pages, (30-5) $14.95

Best of the Best from Illinois
288 Pages, (58-5) $14.95

Best of the Best from Indiana
288 pages, (57-7) $14.95

Best of the Best from Iowa
288 pages, (82-8) $14.95

Best of the Best from Kentucky
288 pages, (27-5) $14.95

Best of the Best from Louisiana
288 pages, (13-5) $14.95

Best of the Best from Michigan
288 pages, (69-0) $14.95

Best of the Best from Minnesota
288 pages, (81-X) $14.95

Best of the Best from Mississippi
288 pages, (19-4) $14.95

Best of the Best from Missouri
304 pages, (44-5) $14.95

Best of the Best from New England
368 pages, (50-X) $16.95

Best of the Best from North Carolina
288 pages, (38-0) $14.95

Best of the Best from Ohio
352 pages, (68-2) $16.95

Best of the Best from Oklahoma
288 pages, (65-8) $14.95

Best of the Best from Pennsylvania
320 pages, (47-X) $14.95

Best of the Best from South Carolina
288 pages, (39-9) $14.95

Best of the Best from Tennessee
288 pages, (20-8) $14.95

Best of the Best from Texas I
352 pages, (14-3) $14.95

Best of the Best from Texas II
352 pages, (62-3) $16.95

Best of the Best from Virginia
320 pages, (41-0) $14.95

Best of the Best from Wisconsin
288 pages, (80-1) 4$14.95

All books comb bound.
ISBN Prefix: 0-937552-; suffix noted in parentheses under each title.
See next page for complete listing of Quail Ridge Press cookbooks.

QUAIL RIDGE PRESS • 1-800-343-1583

"Best of the Best" Cookbook Series:

Alabama	(28-3)	$14.95	*Missouri*	(44-5)	$14.95
Arkansas	(43-7)	$14.95	*New England*	(50-X)	$16.95
Florida	(16-X)	$14.95	*North Carolina*	(38-0)	$14.95
Georgia	(30-5)	$14.95	*Ohio*	(68-2)	$16.95
Illinois	(58-5)	$14.95	*Oklahoma*	(65-8)	$14.95
Indiana	(57-7)	$14.95	*Pennsylvania*	(47-X)	$14.95
Iowa	(82-8)	$14.95	*South Carolina*	(39-9)	$14.95
Kentucky	(27-5)	$14.95	*Tennessee*	(20-8)	$14.95
Louisiana	(13-5)	$14.95	*Texas I*	(14-3)	$14.95
Michigan	(69-0)	$14.95	*Texas II*	(62-3)	$16.95
Minnesota	(81-X)	$14.95	*Virginia*	(41-0)	$14.95
Mississippi	(19-4)	$14.95	*Wisconsin*	(80-1)	$14.95

Coming soon: **Colorado, Kansas, Louisiana II**

Individuals may purchase the full 24-volume set for a special "Best Club" price of $255.00 (a 30% discount off the regular price of $364.80) plus $5.00 shipping. Becoming a member of the "Best Club" will entitle you to a 25% discount on future volumes. Call for information on discounts for joining the "Best of the Month Club."

Other Quail Ridge Press Cookbooks

	ISBN SUFFIX
The Little New Orleans Cookbook (hardbound) $8.95	42-9
The Little New Orleans Cookbook (French Version) $10.95	60-7
The Little Gumbo Book (hardbound) $8.95	17-8
The Little Bean Book (hardbound) $9.95	32-1
Gourmet Camping $9.95	45-3
Lite Up Your Life $14.95	40-2
Hors D'Oeuvres Everybody Loves $5.95	11-9
The Seven Chocolate Sins $5.95	01-1
The Twelve Days of Christmas Cookbook $5.95	00-3
The Complete Venison Cookbook $19.95	70-4
Eat Your Way Thin $9.95	76-3
Kitchen Express $12.95	77-1
Best of Bayou Cuisine $14.95	78-X

ISBN Prefix: 0-937552-. All books are ringbound unless noted otherwise. Prices subject to change. To order, send check/money order to:

QUAIL RIDGE PRESS
P. O. Box 123 / Brandon, MS 39043

Or call toll-free to order by credit card:

1-800-343-1583

Please add $2.50 postage for any amount of books sent to one address. Gift wrap with enclosed card add $2.50. Mississippi residents add 7% sales tax. All orders ship within 24 hours. Write or call for free catalog of all QRP books and cookbooks.